**Regional
Network for
Equity in Health
in East and
Southern Africa**

RECLAIMING THE RESOURCES FOR HEALTH

A REGIONAL ANALYSIS OF EQUITY IN HEALTH IN EAST AND SOUTHERN AFRICA

**Fountain Publishers
Kampala – Uganda**

www.fountainpublishers.co.ug

WEAVER
PRESS

Acknowledgements

The report was produced under the overall direction of the EQUINET Steering Committee. It draws on the work of is the EQUINET Steering Committee and the many organisations and individuals working for health equity in east and southern Africa. The principal author was Rene Loewenson. Contribution across all sections was made by Lexi Bambas Nolen and Rebecca Pointer. The other main contributors to sections were: Section 1: Godfrey Woelk; Section 2: Percy Makombe, Riaz Tayob, Patrick Bond, Mickey Chopra, Mark Tomlinson, George Dor; Section 3: Lucy Gilson, Ireen Makwiza, Sally Theobald, Leslie London, Greg Ruiters, Nomafrench Mbombo, Gabriel Mwaluko; Section 4: Vimbayi Mutyambizi, Di McIntyre, Lucy Gilson; Section 5: Antoinette Ntuli, Scholastika Iipinge, Moses Kachima; Section 6: Itai Rusike, Aillet Mukono, TJ Ngulube, Martha Kwataine, Selemani Mbuyita, Hon Blessing Chebundo, Hon Austin Mtukula, Mwajuma Masaiganah, Fortunate Machingura.

Many individuals and organisations were consulted during the preparation of the report directly or through input at meetings. Not all are named and we thank all. Valuable input and advice was received from Helen Lugina, Firoze Manji, Barbara Kaim, Charles Mayombana, Ahmed Makemba, Kathe Hofnie Hoebes, Richard Jordi, Clara Mbwili-Muleya, Annie Holmes, Zvikie Mlambo, members of the secretariat of the East, Central and Southern African Health Community, members of the SADC directorate on Human Resources and Social Development, colleagues at the World Health Organisation at headquarters and AFRO, researchers in the network on participatory methods for people centred health systems in east and southern Africa, members of the Health Civil Society Network in East and Southern Africa, members of the Association of Parliamentary Committees in East and Southern Africa, members of the Community Working Group on Health, colleagues involved in the Commission on the Social Determinants of Health and from government, academic and civil society members involved in EQUINET work.

We gratefully acknowledge the peer review of the report by Chris Mwikisa, Eli Nangawi, Armando de Negri, Christina Zarowsky and the SIDA (Sweden) headquarters health team co-ordinated by Ulrike Hertel. We gratefully acknowledge the financial and institutional support of SIDA Sweden, IDRC Canada and of the institutions in the EQUINET steering committee.

Copyright © EQUINET 2007
Regional Network for Equity in Health in east and southern Africa (EQUINET)
c/o Training and Research Support Centre (TARSC), Box CY2720, Causeway, Harare, Zimbabwe

ISBN (Zimbabwe): 978-1-77922-066-0; ISBN(South Africa): 978-1-77009-409-3; ISBN (Uganda): 978-9970-02-754-5
Edit, design and layout: Margo Bedingfield
Illustrations: courtesy Mashet Ndhlovu, TARSC and Ifakara
Photography by: Brian Goddard, K Hofnie, Indymedia, Mwajuma Masaiganah, Itai Rusike, TAC and TARSC
Cover and section cover photographs by B Goddard, Indymedia, TAC, DfID, B Partridge and K Hofnie
Printed by: Précigraph Ltd Mauritius
Published by: EQUINET in association with Weaver Press, Zimbabwe (www.weaverpresszimbabwe.com), Fountain Publishers, Uganda (www.fountainpublishers.co.ug) and Jacana, South Africa (www.jacana.co.za)
For all queries on this publication or for orders please email admin@equinetafrica.org

Contents

LIST OF TABLES

LIST OF FIGURES

INTRODUCTION

The global attention to equity and to Africa has grown. The United Nations *Human development report, 2006* and *Report on the world social situation 2005* and the World Bank *World development review, 2006* focused on inequalities and equity, while in 2008 a World Health Organisation (WHO)Commission on the Social Determinants of Health reports on a global inquiry into options to improve health equity through action on the social determinants of health. Africa has been the focus of commissions and special programmes. In 2007, the WHO Director General stated that improved health in Africa was one of the organisations' top priorities.

Within Africa, millions of people experience deprivation of the most basic rights to water, shelter and food, millions of children have lost parents due to early adult death, most do not have secure incomes and many live in situations of conflict and social disruption. Also within the continent, health workers, teachers and others provide valuable services; state officials and university staff take on intense workloads with limited resources; and civil society and community organisations implement innovative local ways of improving life.

We present this analysis of equity in health in east and southern Africa cognisant of the enormous gap that continues to exist between global attention and local reality.

The Regional Network for Equity in Health in East and Southern Africa (EQUINET) was born out of the 1997 Kasane meeting that reported on equity to the newly formed health sector in the Southern Africa Development Community (SADC). We are a network of institutions within east and southern Africa – involving university, state, civil society, parliament and other institutions – that seek to support the regional community in its commitment to secure equity in health.

Ten years after Kasane we have brought together our collective experiences, knowledge, work and views from within the region, to explore the challenges we face in addressing inequalities in health and access to health care, and to support the development and implementation of policy choices that will strengthen health equity.

In late 2005, we reviewed EQUINET's work over the previous eight years to identify the major challenges to equity in health and focus on the opportunities for action. In early 2006, we reviewed a wider synthesis of evidence on these areas and drew up the framework for this book. The perspective that guides the book is thus based on shared values of equity and social justice in health and a spirit of self determination. We do not seek to simply describe our situation but to understand it in ways that generate and inform affirmative action from within the region.

Over the twelve months that followed this review, we presented the broad areas of the proposed framework in research, development programmes, civil society and parliamentarian meetings, at national and regional forums and more widely through our newsletter, and listened to the feedback. From this we finalised the focus on 'reclaiming the resources for health', for household wellbeing, for redistributive health systems and for east and southern African countries in the global economy.

We recognise that the resources for health include water, education, food, social networks and many other inputs from beyond the health sector, even while we give more focus to the role that health systems can play.

The book presents a synthesis of the evidence gathered from a range of sources. These include published literature on and from the region, reviews of current evidence, where available, and data drawn primarily from government, inter-governmental, particularly African Union and United Nations sources. We draw attention to the wider health reviews and policy documents on health in the region, keeping our focus on the issues specifically relevant to equity. We have also drawn on the less commonly documented and disseminated experience within the region, found in grey literature, interviews and testimonials, and gathered through participatory processes.

We acknowledge the limits to the evidence presented in the book, as well as its diversity. Dense tables and figures may be difficult to absorb but they feed the analysis. Case studies, quotes and images from different sources are an important source of evidence on the vision, views, experience and practices that stimulate and shape action. Despite limits and complexities, we contend that it is possible to learn from existing experience in order to act.

On some issues there is clear evidence of the kind conventionally accepted by public health practitioners as 'rigorous'. On others, action can be based on a combination of values and an assessment of how available evidence can be made useful in different contexts, understanding that action is imperative in the face of inequity.

The book is written for many audiences. For the diverse community involved in health equity within east and southern Africa, we hope it will provide a source of evidence and analysis to support and advance their work. We intend to 'repackage' the material into briefs, leaflets, presentations and other tools that will support its use, including at community level. We present it to those making decisions on policies and programmes within and beyond the health sector within our region, to inform, strengthen and, in some cases, to challenge the policies and programmes that impact on equity in health. The analysis shows that local and national realities are deeply influenced by the policies and actions of international global institutions and we address ourselves also to this level of international partners, particularly given the global commitments to equity raised at the beginning of this introduction.

It is our understanding that a book of this nature is a point in a process, within a rapidly changing world. It has drawn on many inputs, acknowledged in later pages. The book is also presented to encourage debate and dialogue, to draw out further experience and to stimulate research to gather new knowledge. We invite feedback, peer review and debate. As the book was being finalised, new policy commitments and strategies were being voiced by the African Union health ministers, new work was emerging on rights to health from civil society, new commitments were being made at the World Health Assembly and others will emerge that post-date the evidence we present.

Yet the determinants of unfair and avoidable inequalities in health that are presented appear to be persistent. They point to broad policy choices and specific options that fairly respond to these inequalities and more importantly to strategies to strengthen the autonomy and capability of disadvantaged communities to influence these choices. We are excited to be part of this process.

EQUINET steering committee
August 2007

EXECUTIVE SUMMARY

We have the knowledge, ability and experience to overcome persistent inequalities in health in east and southern Africa. This analysis provides an inspiring and empowering message, exploring several aspects of health and health systems and providing many examples of good practice in the region.

The evidence in this analysis points to three ways in which reclaiming the resources for health can improve health equity. These are:

- for poor people to claim a fairer share of national resources to improve their health;
- for a more just return for east and southern African countries from the global economy to increase the resources for health; and
- for a larger share of global and national resources to be invested in redistributive health systems to overcome the impoverishing effects of ill health.

Although the health picture for east and southern Africa is currently quite bleak, with high mortality rates, low life expectancy and high burdens of under-nutrition, HIV and AIDS, tuberculosis (TB) and malaria, the message that emerges from this book is one of hope and recognition of our strengths and possibilities for action.

The region has the economic and social potential to address its major health needs, yet improved growth has occurred with falling human development and increasing poverty. In many east and southern African countries, widening national inequalities in wealth block poor households from the benefits of growth, while substantial resources flow outwards from Africa, leaving most of its people in poverty and depleting the resources for health. The analysis adds evidence to the growing call for a fairer form of globalisation and a more just return to Africa from the global economy. The book maps the trade, investment and production policies and measures that have strong public health impact and offers options to address outflows and promote access to food, health care and medicines. National measures that redistribute these resources for wider economic and social gain provide clear pathways for equitable use of funds released from debt cancellation, improved terms of trade, increased external funding and other global measures.

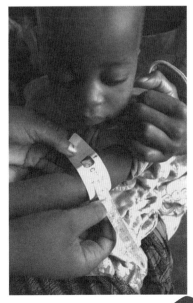

While many of these actions lie outside the health sector, the analysis argues that health systems can make a difference by providing leadership, shaping wider social norms and values, demonstrating health impacts and promoting work across sectors.

Drawing on a diversity of evidence and experience from the region, the analysis describes the comprehensive, primary health care oriented, people-centred and publicly-led health systems that have been found to improve health, particularly for the most disadvantaged people with greatest health needs. While resource scarcities and selective approaches weakened these universal systems in recent decades, the lessons presented from the roll out of prevention and treatment for HIV and AIDS continue to demonstrate their relevance, particularly at district level.

That those with highest health needs are being persistently disadvantaged in access to health care is thus of concern. The analysis explores the reasons for this – within the way health systems are funded and organised – and identifies the barriers that people encounter in using health services.

Addressing these problems demands a strengthened public sector in health. Current average spending on health systems in the region is below the minimum for a functional health system, or even for the most basic interventions for major public health burdens. Therefore one priority is for governments to meet the (largely unmet) commitment made in Abuja to 15 per cent of government spending on health, excluding external financing. We argue, however, for 'Abuja PLUS' – for international delivery on debt cancellation and for a significantly greater share of this government spending to be allocated to district health systems.

The analysis presents progressive options for mobilising these additional domestic resources for health systems without burdening poor households, and for increasing spending on district and primary health care systems. One focus area for increased spending is health workers. Without health workers there is no health system. In the face of massive shortfalls and significant outflows of health workers, the analysis explores what incentives countries in the region are using to train and retain health workers and to ensure they are effective and motivated. Recognising that many health workers prefer *not* to migrate, the report examines how bilateral agreements and compensatory investments can support these incentives to value and retain the health workforce.

These approaches are not without challenges, whether from local elites, competing approaches or global trade pressures. Yet health is a universal human right and international and regional conventions call for core rights and obligations to protect people's health. One basis for optimism is the significant social pressure for the goal of equity in health and the social resources, networks and capabilities available to achieve it. The analysis points to the many ways health systems can empower people, stimulate social action and create powerful constituencies to advance public interests in health. Tapping these potentials calls for a robust, systematic form of participatory democracy and a more collectively organised and informed society.

These measures are within our means to achieve in the region but demand concerted action.

To champion these values, policies and measures, to monitor progress and enhance accountability, the analysis proposes a set of targets and indicators that signal progress in key dimensions of health equity, and towards meeting regional and global commitments. EQUINET, as a network of institutions in the region, is committed to implementing and supporting the building of knowledge, skills and learning to meet these goals.

The analysis is a resource for the institutions and alliances working in and beyond the region towards goals of improved health and social justice. The evidence presented is diverse, some from the region and not commonly diseminated. Despite limits to the evidence and complexity in the context, we contend that it is possible to act, drawing on shared values and an assessment of how available evidence can be made useful in different contexts, recognising that action is imperative in the face of inequity

ACRONYMS

AIDS	acquired immune deficiency syndrome
ART	antiretroviral therapy
ARV	antiretroviral
AU	African Union
CAADP	Comprehensive Africa Agriculture Development Programme
CEDAW	Convention on the Elimination of All Forms of Discrimination against Women
CHP	Centre for Health Policy
CMH	Commission on Macroeconomics and Health
CMR	child mortality rate
CWGH	Community Working Group on Health
DAC	Development Assistance Committee
DHS	demographic health surveys
DOT	directly observed treatment
DRC	Democratic Republic of Congo
DSS	demographic surveillance system
ECA	Economic Commission for Africa
ECSA	East, Central, and Southern African Health Community
EPA	Economic Partnership Agreement
EQUINET	Regional Network for Equity in Health in east and southern Africa
ESA	east and southern Africa
EU	European Union
FAO	Food and Agriculture Organisation
FDI	foreign direct investment
FTA	free trade agreement
GATS	General Agreement on Trade in Services
GBS	general budget support
GDP	gross domestic product
GP	general practitioner
GST	general sales tax
HAI	Health Action International
HDI	Human Development Index
HIPC	Heavily Indebted Poor Countries
HIV	human immunodeficiency virus
HPI	Human Poverty Index
HRH	Human Resources for Health
IFAD	International Fund for Agricultural Development
IHRDC	Ifakara Health Research and Development Centre
IMF	International Monetary Fund
IMR	infant mortality rate
LDC	least developed country
MDGs	Millenium Development Goals
MMR	maternal mortality rate
MoH	Ministry of Health
MoHCW	Ministry of Health and Child Welfare
NEPAD	New Economic Partnership for African Development
NHA	national health accounts
ODA	overseas development aid
ODI	Overseas Development Institute
OECD	Organisation for Economic Co-operation and Development
OPM	Oxford Policy Management
PATAM	Pan African Treatment Access Movement
PPP	purchasing power parity
PRSP	poverty reduction strategy paper
SACU	Southern African Customs Union
SADC	Southern African Development Community
SAMWU	South African Municipal Workers Union
SASF	Southern Africa Social Forum
SATUCC	Southern African Trade Union Co-ordinating Council
SEATINI	Southern and Eastern African Trade Information and Negotiations Institute
SC	steering committee
STI	sexually transmitted infection
SURF	Sub-Regional Resource Facility for West and Central Africa
SWAp	sector wide approach
TAC	Treatment Action Campaign
TARSC	Training and Research Suppport Centre
TB	tuberculosis
TRIPS	Trade Related Intellectual Property Rights
UN	United Nations
UNDP	United Nations Development Programme
UN SCN	United Nations Standing Committee on Nutrition
USAID	United States Agency for International Development
VAT	value added tax
WCSDG	World Commission on the Social Dimension of Globalisation
WFP	World Food Programme
WHA	World Health Assembly
WHO	World Health Organisation
WONCA	World Organisation of Family Doctors
WTO	World Trade Organisation

Progress in
HEALTH
EQUITY

IN EAST AND SOUTHERN AFRICA

KEY ISSUES

Countries in east and southern Africa have the economic and social potential to address their major health needs. Their gross domestic products are, however, a poor reflection of their abundant natural wealth. Across the region, improved growth has occurred with falling human development and many countries have recorded increased poverty and widening national inequality in wealth. Globally, inequalities in wealth are also widening.

East and southern African countries have experienced persistent inequalities in health, both between the different countries in the region and within the countries themselves. Despite health services expanding in the past decades, inequalities in access to health care and other health inputs persist. Inevitably these gaps in access are widest in groups with the greatest health needs.

For decades, countries in the region have expressed their commitment to overcoming unfair differences in access to health and to allocating more resources to those with greater health needs. To do this in the current context, however, we need to reclaim the resources for health: Poor households need to access a fairer share of national resources. We need to invest a great deal more in the health services used by these communities and African countries need to have greater latitude in the global economy to effectively use their resources to improve the health of their citizens.

Waiting for antiretrovirals

Mr Banda, a 41 year old man, living in Sigolo district, had been ill for some time. When his illness began, he made visits to three different health facilities, including a district hospital, and underwent several tests for tuberculosis but was found negative. On several occasions he was admitted to hospital. His wife left him because he was sick and could no longer provide for the family. Finally, he was diagnosed with tuberculosis and started treatment, supported by a home-based care group operating in his village. But after finishing the tuberculosis treatment his health was still poor. Several years later, he tested HIV positive and was again diagnosed with tuberculosis. He restarted treatment but he was asked to bring a treatment supporter from his family so he could start on antiretrovirals. Mr Banda's response was simple:

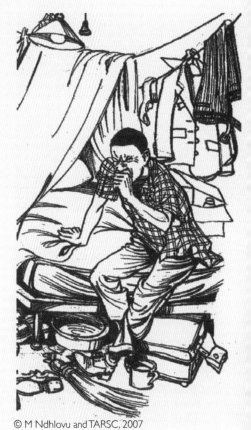

> 'I do not have a guardian, I come to the hospital alone. I cannot ask those who sometimes assist me because they are too poor to come to hospital.'

Mr Banda decided not to go back to the hospital.

> 'I actually have to walk to the hospital, I stop several times on the road to rest, sometimes it takes merciful people who pick me up on their bicycles, and when I come back from hospital, I don't feel well because of overworking my weak body.'

He is at home now wondering whether the health workers will find a way for him to start him on antiretrovirals. He can only wait and see.

Story, (names changed) REACH Trust Malawi, 2007

© M Ndhlovu and TARSC, 2007

Investing in health care

Several years ago in Uganda, a national quality assurance programme was invested in to strengthen district-level primary health care services. The programme found out about the needs of patients and their families, and used this information and local data to identify gaps in service quality. From this, standards and guidelines were developed for health care, with investments and support from the national level to meet them. The programme strengthened communication between health care providers and communities, and between national and district levels of the health system.

After 18 months, maternal mortality among pregnant women referred to the district hospital fell from 13.5 per cent to 2.9 per cent, the long waiting times to see medical staff were eliminated and patients were more satisfied with the services. Measles cases also dropped substantially. Morale grew amongst the district health team members, particularly as patients were much happier and their health had improved. Local government became more involved in the district health committee decision-making and in supporting plans for the district.

Omaswa et al., 1997

Mr Banda waits powerlessly for something to happen to take him out of ill health and poverty. Not far away, lives in a community are saved and transformed by investments and innovation in local health services. Both these stories are played out repeatedly across our region, within the same country and sometimes even in the same area.

Addressing the burden of ill health in east and southern Africa is central to improving the quality of life of the many people in the region. Opportunities exist for making significant improvements in health. This analysis explores these challenges and opportunities through the lens of equity in health. It presents a synthesis of work carried out by institutions working in and for the region, drawing on additional data and published reports, as a resource to support policies and programmes that advance equity in health.

There are limits to the evidence on differentials in wealth, human development and health. Many measurements of health inputs and outcomes do not measure differences across income, gender or other social factors, and there is limited evidence on the trends across time for such data where it does exist. The parameters used to measure health may be differently defined in different countries and at different points in time. National data sets are often more difficult to access than international ones and publicly available data is not always recent. Population data is often missing and progress and outcomes are usually measured by facility data reports which may be less accurate.

Data does not always capture the complexity of situations or interventions in the region. The health impacts of interventions may not be immediately apparent and, along with changes in the distribution and use of resources, may take time to emerge and have effect. To better understand our situation, throughout this report we complement data from formal data sets and survey reports with testimonials and experiences from communities, health workers, state and civil society sources, and present more focused local case studies from the region.

Equity in health implies addressing differences in health status that are unnecessary, avoidable and unfair. Equity motivated interventions seek to allocate resources preferentially to those with the lowest health status. This means understanding and influencing the redistribution of social and economic resources for equity oriented interventions, and understanding and informing the power and ability people (and social groups) have to make choices over health inputs and to use these choices towards better health.

EQUINET steering committee, 1998

Figure 1.1 The countries in the east and southern African region

Opportunities for health in east and southern Africa

East and southern Africa is a region of significant wealth. The sixteen countries covered in this analysis, shown in figure1.1, had a population of 304 million in 2005, and a combined gross domestic product of US$356 billion (World Bank, 2006). The region's major rivers, natural vegetation, abundant minerals and warm climate speak of promise. The size, population and resources of the region provide the economic and social potential to address the major health needs.

Yet the reality does not match this potential and varies widely across countries. The official per capita gross domestic product ranged in 2005 from US$121 in the Democratic Republic of Congo (DRC) to US$5314 in South Africa (see table 1.1 and figure 1.2).

As a sign of the paradox of poverty amidst wealth, the DRC, a global leader in strategic mineral reserves, with coltan, diamonds, copper, cobalt and gold, and with abundant hydroelectric power, timber, coffee and ivory, has one of the lowest official per capita levels of gross domestic product in the region. This raises the question – why this mismatch between national assets and overall national wealth?

Table 1.1 Economic indicators in east and southern Africa, 2000 and 2005

	Population (millions)		GDP (current US$million)		GDP per capita (US$)		GDP growth (annual %)	
	2000	2005	2000	2005	2000	2005	2000	2005
Angola	13.8	15.9	9,129	28,037	662	1,763	3.0	14.7
Botswana	1.8	1.8	5,250	9,350	2,917	5,194	7.6	3.8
DRC	50.1	57.5	4,305	6,973	86	121	-6.9	6.6
Kenya	30.7	34.3	12,705	17,977	414	524	0.6	2.8
Lesotho	1.8	1.8	859	1,452	477	807	1.3	1.2
Madagascar	16.2	18.6	3,877	5,039	239	271	4.8	4.6
Malawi	11.5	12.9	1,743	2,072	152	161	1.6	2.6
Mauritius	1.2	1.2	4,464	6,447	3,720	5,373	4.0	4.5
Mozambique	17.9	19.8	3,777	6,629	211	335	1.9	7.7
Namibia	1.9	2.0	3,413	6,126	1,796	3,063	3.5	3.5
South Africa	44.0	45.2	132,877	240,151	3,020	5,313	4.2	4.9
Swaziland	1.9	1.1	1,388	2,730	731	2,482	2.0	1.8
Tanzania	34.8	38.3	9,079	12,111	261	316	5.1	7.0
Uganda	24.3	28.8	5,926	8,711	244	302	5.6	5.6
Zambia	10.7	11.7	3,237	7,257	303	620	3.6	5.1
Zimbabwe	12.6	13.0	7,399	3,364	587	259	-7.9	-7.1

GDP = gross domestic product

Source: World Bank at http://devdata.worldbank.org/data-query/; World Bank, 2006

Figure 1.2 Per capita gross domestic product in east and southern Africa, 2005

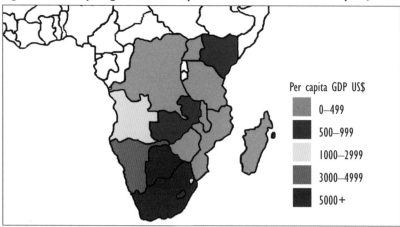

Source: World Bank, 2006

While more comprehensive economic and social analysis of the region can be found in other texts (AU, UN ECA, 2007; WHO Afro, 2006; UNDP SURF, 2000), the evidence provided in the tables and figures in this section explore further the relationship between the resources of the region and the health of its people.

Even with the gap described between national assets and national wealth, an average per capita gross domestic product of US$1171 in the

Table 1.2 Human development index trends in east and southern Africa, 1975–2003

HDI* rank 2004	1975	1980	1985	1990	1995	2000	2004
65 Mauritius	..	0.659	0.690	0.724	0.747	0.776	0.800
120 South Africa	0.655	0.674	0.702	0.735	0.742	0.696	0.653
125 Namibia	..	..	..	..	0.693	0.649	0.627
131 Botswana	0.503	0.577	0.638	0.681	0.659	0.596	0.570
144 Uganda	..	..	0.412	0.409	0.412	0.474	0.508
145 Zimbabwe	0.546	0.574	0.640	0.637	0.589	0.527	0.491
146 Madagascar	0.400	0.437	0.436	0.446	0.458	..	0.509
147 Swaziland	0.530	0.562	0.584	0.624	0.603	0.534	0.500
149 Lesotho	0.461	0.510	0.534	0.571	0.573	0.520	0.494
154 Kenya	0.461	0.509	0.530	0.546	0.524	0.499	0.491
160 Angola	..	..	..	..	..	..	0.439
164 Tanzania	..	..	..	0.435	0.422	0.416	0.430
165 Malawi	0.320	0.351	0.362	0.371	0.412	0.402	0.400
166 Zambia	0.468	0.475	0.484	0.462	0.424	0.409	0.407
167 DRC	0.414	0.423	0.431	0.422	0.393	..	0.391
168 Mozambique	..	0.299	0.287	0.311	0.328	0.360	0.390

* HDI values were calculated using a consistent methodology and data series. Range is 0 (lowest) to 1 (highest).
Source: UNDP, 2005

region suggests that households could be earning above poverty incomes and could be accessing essential health services.

How well are these resources benefiting the people? If the human development index is anything to go by, all countries of the region experienced an improvement in human development between 1975 and 1995, some faster than others. Between 1995 and 2004, however, only six of the sixteen countries showed an increase in their human development index (see table 1.2). As figure 1.3 shows, the slow improvements in human development stopped and even reversed in the late 1990s for most countries in the region. Given the nature of the index, the decline is a consequence of reduced survival, increased poverty or reduced education and literacy enrolments.

The fall in the human development index after 1995 puts people in the region at a significant disadvantage. For example, as shown in figure 1.3, although China, Malaysia and Thailand may have been at similar levels to east and southern African countries in the 1970s, their sustained increases in human development over the same period have now given their people a definite advantage.

This fall in human development cannot simply be attributed to falling gross domestic product, nor was it buffered by improved gross domestic product. From the late 1990s, improved gross domestic product did not automatically translate into improved human development.

> The **human development index (HDI)** is a summary measure of human development. It measures the average achievements in a country in three dimensions:
>
> 1 a long and healthy life, as measured by life expectancy at birth;
>
> 2 knowledge, as measured by adult literacy (with two-thirds weight) and the combined primary, secondary and tertiary gross enrolment ratio (with one-third weight); and
>
> 3 a decent standard of living, as measured by per capita gross domestic product (purchasing power parity – PPP in US$).

Figure 1.3 Human development index trends in east and southern Africa, 1975-2004

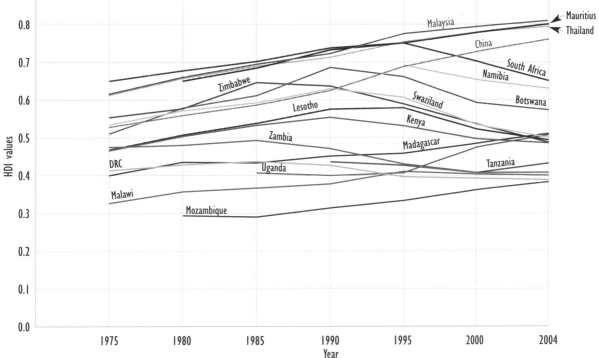

Data for Angola only available for 2004 = 0.439

Source: UNDP, 2005

Figure 1.4 Gross domestic product rank minus human development index rank for east and southern Africa,* 2004

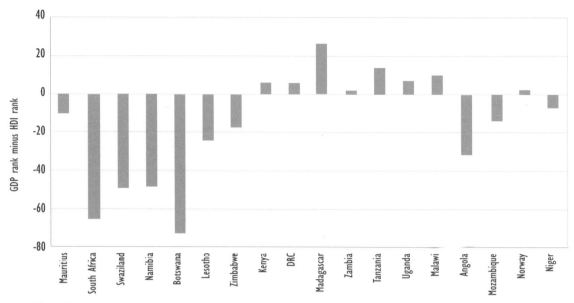

*Comparison is given with the countries rated highest (Norway) and lowest (Niger) on human development index.

Source: UNDP, 2006

Figure 1.4 shows the gap between gross domestic product and human development. A negative difference between gross domestic product rank and the human development index rank suggests a faster improvement in gross domestic product than in human development index (or a smaller decline in gross domestic product than in the human development index). The difference between countries' global rankings on gross domestic product and their human development index rank was negative for nine of the sixteen countries in the region, suggesting poorer relative performance on human development than on economic growth. Ironically, this negative relationship between gross domestic product and human development index was more common for countries with higher levels of gross domestic product.

This gap between human development needs and economic resources is felt most at household level.

'*The health workers at our facility go out for outreach programmes in turns. One day when it was my turn, I visited a village that is about 10 km from here. In one of the households I saw a patient who had had diarrhoea for more than four days. She was a mother of a one-year-old baby boy. She was fast asleep and very weak.*

'*I asked them why they had not brought her to the dispensary and the aunt replied, "Nurse, you know when people have money and when they don't. This is a hard time and we don't have money to bring her to the clinic. Had it been the harvesting season we could have brought her from the first day. We know that her diarrhoea is very bad."*'

Narration from a rural nurse, story from Ifakara Health Research Development Centre, Tanzania

The human poverty index increased in the region between 1997 and 2004 for all but three countries. The increase in the human poverty index seems to have been higher in countries of medium human development and in many with higher gross domestic products (see table 1.3).

This raises concern as to why poverty appears to have grown faster in countries with higher overall national production and development.

For households living below US$2 or even US$1 a day, the mismatch between human development needs and access to the resources to meet these needs is most profound. This is the case for over half the households in the region. For five countries in the region, more than 70 per cent of households in the country fall below income poverty levels of US$2 per day (see figure 1.5). Poverty is a central determinant of health in the region.

The **human poverty index** (HPI) is a measure of survival, income, employment and literacy within households. Its range is 0–100.

The **gender-related development index** (GDI) measures the same variables as the human development index except that it adjusts the average achievement of each country in life expectancy, literacy, gross enrolment and income in accordance with the difference in achievement between men and women.

Table 1.3 Indicators of human development, gender development and poverty in east and southern Africa*

	Human development index (HDI)**			GDP rank minus HDI rank		Gender-related development index (GDI)		Human poverty index (HPI)	
Year	1975	1997	2004	1997	2004	1997	2004	1997	2004
Medium human development									
Mauritius	n.a.	0.76	0.8	-15	-10	0.75	0.792	12.1	11.3
South Africa	0.64	0.70	0.653	-47	-66	0.69	0.646	19.1	30.9
Swaziland	0.50	0.64	0.5	-15	-50	0.64	0.479	27.6	52.5
Namibia	0.60	0.64	0.627	-44	-50	0.63	0.622	25.0	32.5
Botswana	0.50	0.61	0.57	-70	-73	0.61	0.555	27.5	48.3
Lesotho	0.47	0.58	0.494	-2	-26	0.57	0.486	23.0	47.5
Zimbabwe	0.54	0.56	0.491	-16	-18	0.55	0.483	29.2	46.0
Kenya	0.46	0.52	0.491	16	7	0.52	0.487	28.2	35.5
Low human development									
DRC	0.41	0.48	0.391	21	6	n.a.	0.378	n.a.	40.9
Madagascar	0.40	0.45	0.509	13	26	n.a.	0.507	n.a.	36.3
Zambia	0.45	0.43	0.407	8	2	0.43	0.396	38.4	45.6
Tanzania	n.a.	0.42	0.43	16	13	0.42	0.426	29.8	36.3
Uganda	n.a.	0.40	0.508	-5	7	0.40	0.498	40.6	36.0
Malawi	0.33	0.40	0.4	10	10	0.39	0.394	42.2	43.0
Angola	n.a.	0.40	0.439	-17	-32	n.a.	0.431	n.a.	40.9
Mozambique	0.30	0.34	0.39	-2	-14	0.33	0.387	49.5	48.9
Global range of human development									
Norway (highest HDI)	0.868	0.927	0.965	2	3	0.927	0.962	11.3	7.0
Niger (lowest HDI)	0.236	0.298	0.311	-8	-7	0.286	0.292	65.5	56.4

* Listed from highest to lowest HDI in 1997 ** Data for 1975, except for Namibia and Mozambique where data are for 1980.

Source: EQUINET SC, 2000; UNDP, 1999, 2002, 2005, 2006

The **Gini coefficient** is the distribution of income (or consumption) among individuals or households in a country.

A value of 0 represents perfect equality, a value of 1 represents perfect inequality.

©M Ndhlovu and TARSC

The presence of high and growing levels of poverty in countries that are also experiencing higher and growing gross domestic products suggests that there may be significant inequalities in the distribution of incomes. The Gini coefficient is one measure of this income inequality. Eight of fourteen countries in the region for which data is available had 2003 Gini coefficients in 2003 in excess of 0.50 (see table 1.4).

The level of poverty in a country is determined by many factors and this analysis recognises the ongoing debates on the poverty–inequality trade-off (Ravallion, 2005). The relationship between poverty and inequality is not simple. Table 1.4 shows that income poverty is high across most of the region. The evidence suggests, however, that while countries with high Gini coefficients, such as Botswana, Lesotho, Namibia, South Africa and Zimbabwe, have somewhat higher gross domestic products and lower overall levels of poverty (see figure 1.6), they have had higher levels of growth in poverty since 1995 (as shown in table 1.3).

It seems that inequality, as measured by the Gini coefficient, is a more critical factor in higher income rather than lower income countries in the region in limiting the access households have to resources for human development, and that this has been intensifying since 1995. For lower income countries in the region, a wider overall scarcity of resources undermines household resources for health.

We are aware that this contradicts Kuznets' hypothesis that poverty reduction is linked to inequality in the early stages of growth (Kuznets, 1955). There is, however, debate around this hypothesis. A recent World Bank paper analysing 70 developing and transition country economies in the 1990s found reduced poverty with lower relative inequality, noting that rising relative inequality 'appears more likely to be putting a brake on poverty reduction than to be facilitating it' (Ravallion, 2005: 1). Addressing inequality does appear to be important in reducing poverty in the region.

Figure 1.5 Population living below US$1 and US$2 per day (1993 purchasing power parity in US$), 1990–2003*

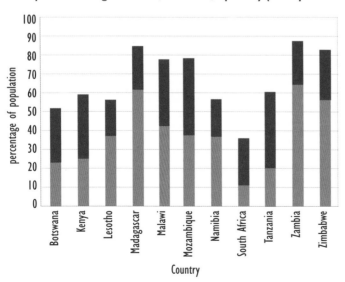

Source: UNDP, 2005

Table 1.4 Poverty and inequality in east and southern Africa

	GDP/ capita US$ 2003	% population living on <$1 /day 1990-2003	% population living on <$2 /day 1990-2003	GINI co-efficient 2003*
Angola	919	n.a.	n.a.	0.38
Botswana	4366	23.5	50.1	0.63
DRC	105	n.a.	n.a.	n.a.
Kenya	459	22.8	58.3	0.43
Lesotho	592	36.4	56.1	0.63
Madagascar	311	61.0	85.1	0.48
Malawi	143	41.7	76.1	0.50
Mauritius	4288	n.a.	n.a.	0.48
Mozambique	251	37.9	78.4	0.40
Namibia	2252	34.9	55.8	0.71
South Africa	3626	10.7	34.1	0.58
Swaziland	1722	n.a.	n.a.	0.61
Tanzania	279	19.9	59.7	0.38
Uganda	233	n.a.	n.a.	0.43
Zambia	384	63.7	87.4	0.53
Zimbabwe	615	56.1	83	0.57

*Latest year available. GDP = gross domestic product n.a. = data not available
Correlation coefficient poverty (<$1/day) and Gini coefficient R= 0.0102
Source: UNDP, 2005

Figure 1.6 Gini coefficients in east and southern Africa

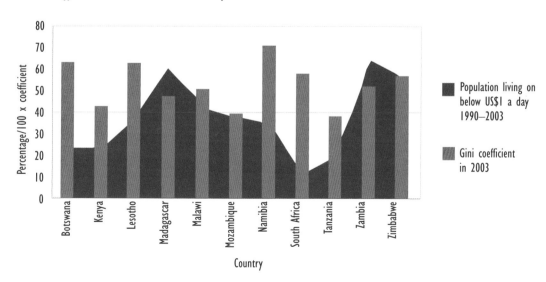

Source: UNDP, 2005

A recent analysis of inequality in seven African countries found that inequality in assets between households was wider in rural than in urban areas, although rural inequality was decreasing and urban inequality increasing. The share of wages to profits was found to be one key determinant of income inequality. Studies in Uganda, South Africa, Namibia, Mozambique and Ethiopia all found that current rates of growth would not produce a sufficient rate of reduction in poverty to meet the United Nations' Millennium Development Goals unless there was also a reduction in income or asset inequality (Okojie and Shimeles, 2006).

In all east and southern African countries the possibilities for human development are weak in many households. In all these countries there are warning signs that growth is occurring with increasing poverty and that increased poverty is one important determinant of poor outcomes in human development. For many of these countries, reducing inequality appears to be important for growth to translate into meaningful levels of poverty reduction.

> In all east and southern African countries the possibilities for human development are weak in many households. In all these countries there are warning signs that growth is occurring with increasing poverty and that increased poverty is one important determinant of poor outcomes in human development. For many of these countries, reducing inequality appears to be important for growth to translate into meaningful levels of poverty reduction.

Widening inequality in wealth is most deeply obvious at global level. While Namibia had the highest Gini coefficient in the region with 0.71 (table 1.4) the global wealth Gini (measuring inequality across countries) is higher still at 0.892. 'This roughly corresponds to the Gini value that would be recorded in a 10-person population if one person had $1000 and the remaining nine people each had $1' (Davies *et al.*, 2006: 26).

Globally, the richest 2 per cent of adults own more than half of household wealth. In contrast, the bottom half of the world adult population owns barely 1 per cent of global wealth. Wealth is heavily concentrated in North America, Europe and high-income Asia-Pacific countries. People in these countries collectively hold almost 90 per cent of total world wealth. High-income countries tend to have a bigger share of world wealth than of world gross domestic product (Davies *et al.*, 2006).

These gaps are widening (UNDP, 2005). In the four decades between 1960 and 1997 the income gap between the fifth of the world's people living in the richest countries and the fifth in the poorest rose from 30:1 to 74:1 (UNDP, 1999). By 2005, UNDP (2005) reported that 40 per cent of the world's population accounted for 55 per cent of global income, while the richest 10 per cent accounted for 54 per cent. Even for wealthier countries in the region, integrating into this highly unequal global economy appears to intensify internal inequalities, undermining household access to the resources for health.

Figure 1.7 Regional shares of world wealth

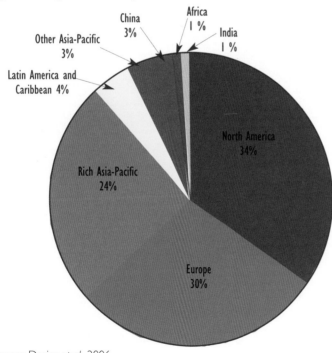

Source: Davies *et al.*, 2006

Health status in east and southern Africa

Health status indicators reflect the wider economic and human development outcomes, and contribute to them.

Certainly, human development in the region has been strongly influenced by a fall in life expectancy over the late 1990s and 2000s, driven primarily by HIV and AIDS (see table 1.5). The fall in life expectancy due to AIDS is a contributor, with poverty, to the post-1995 declines in the human development index.

There are significant differences in health within and across countries of the region. For example, life expectancy at birth in 2003 ranged from 32.5 years in Swaziland to 72.2 years in Mauritius, a range of 40 years in the same geographical region. A child born in Mozambique has a

©M Ndhlovu and TARSC

Table 1.5 Overview of demographic indicators in east and southern African countries*

Year	Life expectancy at birth		Adult literacy		HDI	% < fives underweight	Under five CMR/1,000	IMR /1,000	MMR /100,000
	1997	2004	1997	2004	2004	1995-2003	2004	2004	1990-2004
Medium human development									
Mauritius	71.4	72.4	83.0	84.4	0.80	15	15	14	22
South Africa	54.7	47.0	84.0	82.4	0.65	12	67	54	150
Swaziland	60.2	31.3	77.5	79.6	0.50	10	156	108	230
Namibia	52.4	47.2	79.8	85.0	0.63	24	63	47	270
Botswana	47.4	34.9	74.4	81.2	0.57	13	116	84	330
Lesotho	56.0	35.2	82.3	82.2	0.49	18	82	61	n.a
Zimbabwe	44.1	36.6	90.9	n.a.	0.49	13	129	79	700
Kenya	52.0	47.5	79.3	73.6	0.49	20	120	79	410
Low human development									
DRC	50.8	43.5	77.0	67.2	0.39	31	205	129	1300
Madagascar	57.5	55.6	47.0	70.7	0.51	33	123	76	470
Zambia	40.1	37.7	75.1	68.0	0.41	28	182	102	730
Tanzania	47.9	45.9	71.6	69.4	0.43	29	126	78	580
Uganda	39.6	46.4	64.0	66.8	0.51	23	138	80	510
Malawi	39.3	39.8	57.7	64.1	0.40	22	175	110	1100
Angola	46.5	41.0	45.0	67.4	0.44	31	260	154	n.a
Mozambique	45.2	41.6	40.5	n.a.	0.39	24	152	104	410

*Listed from highest to lowest HDI in 1997.

HDI = human development index   CMR = under five year old child mortality rate   n.a. = data not available

IMR = infant mlortalityr rate   MMR = maternal mortality rate

Sources: EQUINET SC, 2000; UNDP, 1999; 2002; 2006; WHO, 2006

Life expectancy at birth in 2003 ranged from 32.5 years in Swaziland to 72.2 years in Mauritius, a range of 40 years in the same geographical region.

A child born in Mozambique has a projected life 16 years shorter than one born in neighbouring South Africa.

A child born in Angola has three times more chance of dying before their first birthday than one born in neighbouring Namibia.

projected life 16 years shorter than one born in neighbouring South Africa. A child born in Angola has three times more chance of dying before his or her first birthday than one born in neighbouring Namibia.

The differences are even more profound globally. Africa has 10 per cent of the world's population, 25 per cent of the global disease burden, 60 per cent of the people living with HIV and AIDS, and the highest disease burden for tuberculosis and malaria in the world. Yet Africa accounts for less than 1 per cent of the global health spending and contains only 2 per cent of the global health workforce (Atim, 2006).

In six of the sixteen countries life expectancy at birth in 2003 was below 40 years, and below 50 years in fourteen countries (see table 1.5). Thirteen countries experienced falling life expectancy between 1997 and 2003, the exceptions being Uganda, Malawi and Mauritius. In Uganda this may have been due to falling HIV incidence and prevalence, in Mauritius due to the low HIV prevalence and in Malawi due to an already extremely high level of mortality. The decline has been profound in some countries, with reductions of 28 years in Swaziland and 11 years in Botswana between 1997 and 2003, and a loss in the period of over 5 years in seven countries. This fall in life expectancy has been higher in countries with medium human development indexes compared to those with low human development indexes.

Table 1.6 Infant and child mortality in east and southern African countries

Country	under 5 years mortality rate				under 1 year mortality rate			
	1970	1990	1996	2004	1970	1990	1996	2004
DRC	245	205	207	205	148	129	128	129
Lesotho	190	120	139	82	128	84	96	61
Malawi	330	241	217	175	189	146	137	110
Mozambique	278	235	214	152	163	158	133	104
South Africa	n.a.	60	66	67	n.a.	45	50	54
Zambia	181	180	202	182	109	101	112	102
Zimbabwe	138	80	73	129	86	53	49	79
Tanzania	218	161	144	126	129	102	93	78
Angola	300	260	292	260	180	154	170	154
Namibia	135	86	77	63	104	60	60	47
Mauritius	n.a.	n.a.	23	15	64	n.a.	20	14
Uganda	170	160	141	138	100	93	88	80
Madagascar	180	168	164	123	109	103	100	76
Kenya	156	97	90	120	96	64	61	79
Swaziland	196	110	97	156	132	78	68	108
Botswana	142	58	50	116	99	45	40	84

n.a. = data not available

Sources: Woelk, 2000; UNDP, 2005; UNICEF database, www.unicef.org/statistics

This evidence suggests that where there were greater improvements in social gains before the AIDS epidemic, particularly in health and education, there have been greater losses after.

The differences found in life expectancy are also found in relation to infant, child and maternal mortality (see tables 1.5 and 1.6). Within the region:

- The chances of dying in the first year of life range from 14/1,000 to 154/1,000 (in 2004). The country with the highest infant mortality rate has an infant death rate nearly 11 times higher than the country with the lowest infant mortality rate.

- The chances of dying in the first five years of life range from 15/1,000 to 260/1,000 (in 2004). The country with the highest child mortality rate has a child death rate 17 times higher than the country with the lowest child mortality rate.

- The rate of mothers dying due to pregnancy or childbirth ranges from 22/100,000 to 1,300/100,000 (in 2004). The country with the highest maternal mortality rate has a maternal death rate 59 times higher than the country with the lowest maternal mortality rate.

As shown in table 1.6, while child mortality is high, there has been a slow improvement in infant and child mortality rates in 11 east and southern African countries since 1996. The most recent available demographic and health surveys also report some improvements and further falls in infant and child mortality. The estimates from these surveys for Tanzania, Madagascar and Malawi are as follows:

- Tanzania: infant mortality rate – 68/1,000 and child mortality rate – 112/1,000

- Madagascar: infant mortality rate – 58/1,000 and child mortality rate – 94/1,000

- Malawi: infant mortality rate – 76/1,000 and child mortality rate – 133/1,000

(OCR Macro, 2007).

While there are wide differences in mortality rates across countries, there are also differences *within* countries. Poverty is one determinant of these differences. Data from various surveys indicate that children in the poorest income quintile had a median of 1.5 times the rate of chronic under-nutrition and double the infant and child mortality, rising to up to four times the rate in the richest country in the region, South Africa (see table 1.7 on page 16). Once again, higher overall gross domestic product is associated with higher and not lower inequality.

> This evidence suggests that where there were greater improvements in social gains before the AIDS epidemic, particularly in health and education, there have been greater losses after.

Mother and son, Malawi
Source: B Goddard

Table 1.7 Inequalities in nutrition and mortality across income groups

	Survey year	Ratio bottom quintile to top quintile		
		< 5 stunting (using height for age)	Infant mortality rate	< 5 mortality rate
Kenya	1998	2.6	2.4	2.2
Madagascar	1997	1.0	2.1	1.9
Malawi	2000	1.1	1.5	1.5
Mozambique	1997	1.6	2.0	1.9
Namibia	2000	2.0	1.6	1.8
South Africa	1998	n.a.	3.6	4.0
Tanzania	1999	1.8	1.3	1.2
Uganda	2000	1.4	1.8	1.8
Zimbabwe	1999	1.5	1.3	1.6
Zambia	2001	1.4	2.0	2.1

<5 = children under 5 years old
Data not available for Angola, Botswana, DRC, Lesotho, Mauritius and Swaziland
Source: UNDP, 2005

Figure 1.8 Inequalities in under-five mortality by wealth, maternal education and rural/urban divides, east and southern African countries, 1998–2004

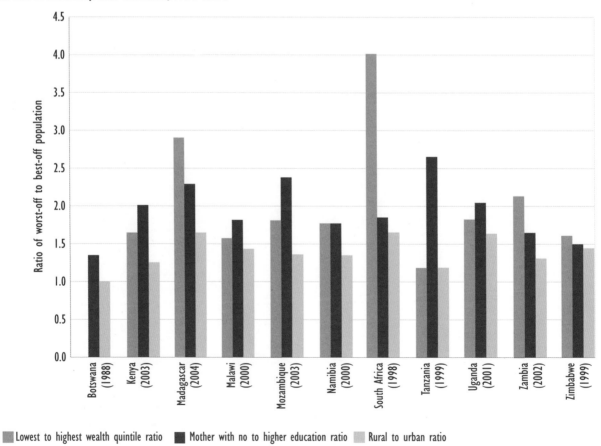

Source: WHO, 2006

Figure 1.8 highlights some dimensions of this inequality. Differences in child mortality appear to be greatly affected by wealth and mother's education. These two factors have more impact on differentials than rural–urban residence in most countries in the region.

Poor opportunities for health are being passed across generations through the social and economic development conditions of parents. If, as indicated earlier, poverty and inequality are intensifying, these long-standing social differentials may make households even more susceptible to more recent drivers of poverty and inequality. Poor health outcomes are not simply a matter of old legacies or new policies – they arise from both.

Figure 1.9 suggests that while place of residence influences access to resources for health, so too do other factors like mother's education. The evidence points to the public health importance of allocating resources and making real improvements in:

- **literacy levels**, particularly in Angola, DRC, Kenya, Madagascar, Malawi, Tanzania, Uganda and Zambia (see figure 1.9);

- **primary school enrolments**, particularly in Mozambique, Angola, Kenya and Zambia (see figure 1.10); and

- **student retention** from primary to secondary school in all countries in the region, except Botswana, Mauritius and South Africa (see figure 1.10).

> Poor opportunities for health are being passed across generations through the social and economic development conditions of parents. If, as indicated earlier, poverty and inequality are intensifying, these long-standing social differentials may make households even more susceptible to more recent drivers of poverty and inequality. Poor health outcomes are not simply a matter of old legacies or new policies – they arise from both.

Figure 1.9 Adult literacy and female literacy in east and southern Africa, 2004

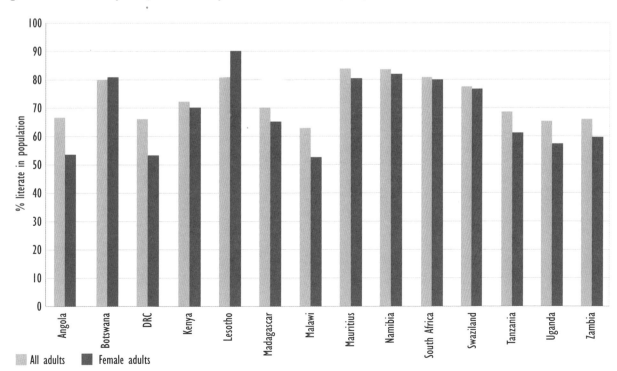

Source: World Bank, 2005

Figure 1.10 School enrolment in east and southern Africa, 2002–2003

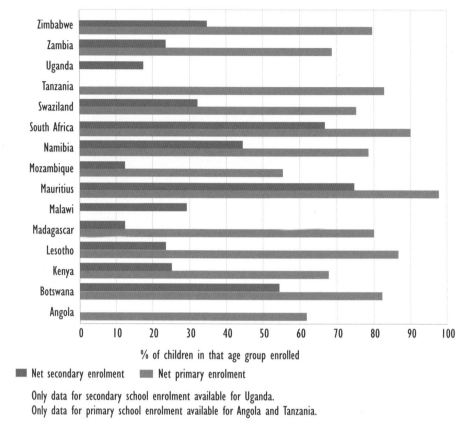

% of children in that age group enrolled

■ Net secondary enrolment   ■ Net primary enrolment

Only data for secondary school enrolment available for Uganda.
Only data for primary school enrolment available for Angola and Tanzania.

Source: UNDP, 2005

Figure 1.11 Adult prevalence of HIV infection: east and southern African countries, 2005

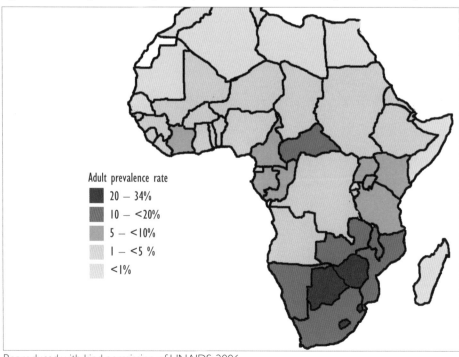

Reproduced with kind permission of UNAIDS, 2006

An analysis of inequality in access to public services in African countries found that while overall access had improved in the past two decades, the relative disadvantage in access in rural areas persisted (Okojie and Shimeles, 2006).

Analyses from within the region have attributed increases in mortality in the past decade to: food insecurity; poor access to safe water, sanitation, energy, transport and shelter; high prevalence levels of HIV and AIDS, tuberculosis, malaria and other communicable and non-communicable diseases; and illness and mortality related to reproductive roles (SADC, 2003; WHO Afro, 2006). These reports provide comprehensive reviews of the overall health status in the region (WHO Afro, 2006). They indicate that AIDS has had the greatest impact on mortality across almost all of the countries of the region.

> *'The HIV and AIDS pandemic is reversing the developmental gains made in the past decades and is posing the greatest threat to sustainable development of the region..'*
> SADC Heads of State, 2003

The HIV and AIDS statistics for east and southern Africa are staggering (see also figures 1.11 and 1.12):

- 16 million adults and children are currently infected with HIV.
- Almost 1.4 million people died of AIDS-related diseases in 2005.
- Globally, 75 per cent of women and 90 per cent of children living with HIV are found in sub-Saharan Africa.
- 1.35 million children under 15 years of age are HIV positive in east and southern Africa.
- 7.5 million children aged 0–14 years are orphaned due to AIDS in east and southern Africa (UNAIDS, 2006).

There is variation in the epidemic across countries in the region – from low rates of 0.6 per cent in Mauritius to 33.4 per cent in Swaziland (see table 1.8). By 2005, four countries in the region had HIV seroprevalence rates of over 20 per cent. While high, there is some evidence of a decline with two countries, Zimbabwe and Uganda, recording a fall in HIV prevalence in this decade, particularly in younger age groups. The reasons for these declines are more fully explained in other reports and are linked to 'increased condom use, fewer partners and delayed sexual activity' (UNAIDS, 2006:9).

Even while AIDS has dominated the health profile of the region overall, it has also had differential effects on the various socio-economic groups. Urban dwellers have generally been more affected than rural dwellers, although this gap is closing. The HIV prevalence in young women aged 15–24 years is more than twice that of their male counterparts throughout the region (SADC, 2003b). HIV initially moved through skilled, mobile, educated and urban groups in the region but has rapidly spread to rural, lower-income groups, and from adults to adolescents (Forsythe, 1992). Areas of migrant employment, transport

Figure 1.12 Regional comparison of number of people living with HIV or AIDS, 2005

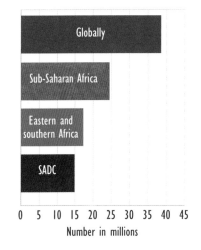

Reproduced with kind permission of UNAIDS, 2005

Table 1.8 HIV and AIDS data in east and southern African countries, 2005

Country	Adult HIV prevalence rate (aged 15-49) 2005	Estimated no. of people living with HIV/AIDS 0-49 years 2005	Estimated no. of people in need of ARV treatment 2005	AIDS deaths in 2005	Estimated no. of children orphaned by AIDS, 2005
Angola	3.7	320,000	52,000	30,000	160,000
Botswana	24.1	270,000	84,000	18,000	120,000
DRC	3.2	1,000,000	209,000	90,000	680,000
Kenya	6.1	1,300,000	273,000	140,000	1,100,000
Lesotho	23.2	270,000	58,000	23,000	97,000
Madagascar	0.5	49,000	20,000	2,900	13,000
Malawi	14.1	940,000	169,000	78,000	550,000
Mauritius	0.6	4,100	n.a.	<100	n.a.
Mozambique	16.1	1,800,000	216,000	140,000	510,000
Namibia	19.6	230,000	41,000	17,000	85,000
South Africa	18.8	5,500,000	983,000	320,000	1,200,000
Swaziland	33.4	220,000	42,000	16,000	63,000
Tanzania	6.5	1,400,000	315,000	140,000	1,100,000
Uganda	6.7	100,000	148,000	91,000	100,000
Zambia	17.0	1,100,000	183,000	98,000	710,000
Zimbabwe	20.1	1,700,000	321,000	180,000	1,100,000

n.a. = data not available; ARV = antiretrovirals
Source: UNAIDS, 2006

routes and urban and peri-urban areas have, for example, been identified as high-risk environments for HIV transmission. The epidemic pattern suggests that HIV has spread from more socially and economically powerful adult males to poor and economically insecure females, particularly female adolescents (ILO, 1995; ILO, 1995b; ILO, 1995c; Gillies *et al.*, 1996; Forsythe, 1992).

The coincidence of wealth and poverty and the high inequality found in a number of countries in the region, as reported earlier, thus presents an extremely high-risk environment for HIV.

> The coincidence of wealth and poverty and the high inequality found in a number of countries in the region … thus presents an extremely high-risk environment for HIV.

Where the AIDS epidemic exacerbates this inequality, such as through loss of labour or the impoverishing effects of household spending on care, it worsens these risk environments. This provides strong public health motivation for intervening in areas of inequality that increase risk of HIV, such as economic inequality across gender and inequalities in reproductive choice across age groups. It also provides public health motivation for preventing the consequences of AIDS, such as food insecurity due to lost labour and earnings, that further intensify risk and vulnerability.

Access to health care
in east and southern Africa

If inequalities in wealth and social conditions underlie inequalities in health, with significant effects on the quality and duration of life across communities in the region, then the availability, accessibilty and use of health care should reflect the opposite and therefore improve health.

After independence, for many countries in the region, the critical task was to increase the availability of health care, given the large proportion of people unable to access relevant health services at that time. Across east and southern African countries, the demand that no-one be deprived of access to health care and the focus on primary health care motivated a rapid expansion of health-related infrastructure, including primary care clinics, water supplies and sanitation, particularly in rural areas. As we discuss in more detail in Section 3, where it happened, this expansion in accessible health services and primary health care outreach had a positive impact on health.

Even while availability of services was improved, the experience of the past decade in the region suggests that access and use have had a more mixed performance, with more recent challenges to sustaining availability.

Even while availability of services was improved, the experience of the past decade in the region suggests that access and use have had a more mixed performance, with more recent challenges to sustaining availability.

Growth monitoring at a primary health care clinic in Malawi
Source: B Goddard

Figures 1.13 to 1.16 show the distribution of key areas of primary health care access in the region.

Safe water supplies and sanitation coverage is lower for rural than urban populations, with less than 50 per cent of rural households accessing safe water in seven countries in the region. These inequalities are wider in lower-income countries (figures 1.13 and 1.14). While access to immunisation improved over the decade in three countries, progress has faltered somewhat, particularly in six countries where coverage is still below 75 per cent (figure 1.15). Contraceptive prevalence is below 20 per cent in six countries. Generally, rural water and sanitation coverage is also poorer in countries with lower immunisation and contraceptive prevalence.

Figure 1.13 Rural and urban access to sanitation, east and southern African countries, 2002

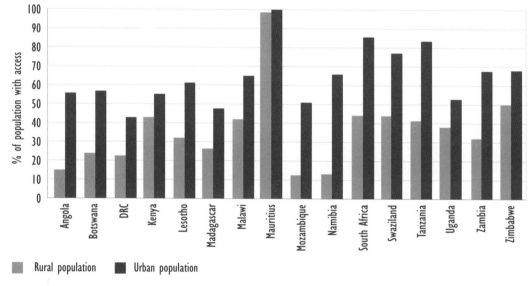

Source: World Bank, 2004

Figure 1.14 Rural and urban access to safe water, 2002

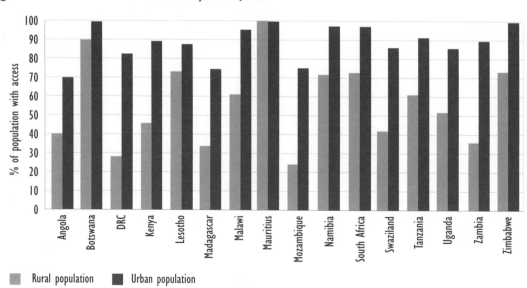

Source: World Bank, 2004

Figure 1.15 Measles immunisation, children 12–23 months in east and southern Africa, 1997–2004

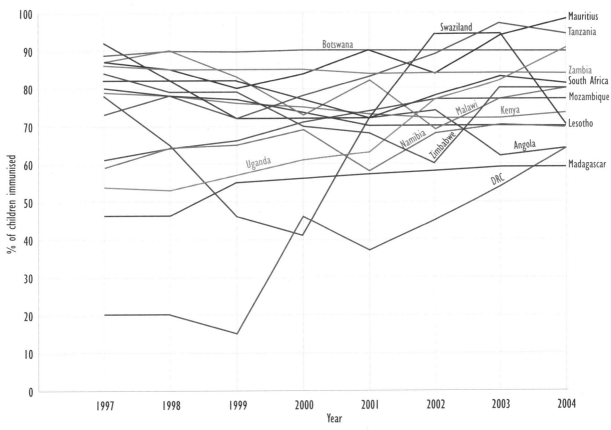

Source: World Bank, 2005

Figure 1.16 Contraceptive prevalence rate in east and southern African countries, women 15–49 years

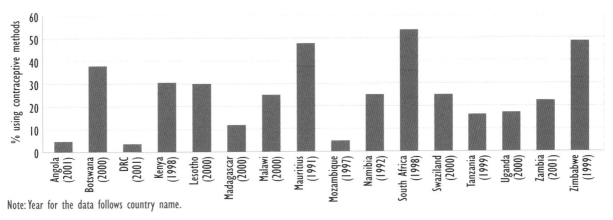

Note: Year for the data follows country name.

Source: WHO, 2005

Almost all east and southern African countries thus face a challenge to expand these basic primary health care inputs. For the lowest income countries there is an additional demand to allocate scarce resources to close the wide gaps in access between rural and urban areas. Even in higher income countries in the region, while geographic inequalities may be lower, income-related differentials can be wide in access to basic facilities (see figure 1.17 overleaf).

Figure 1.17 Access to basic facilities according to income in South Africa, 2000

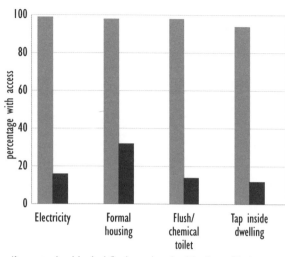

(Access to electricity is defined as using electricity for cooking.)

■ Richest   ■ Poorest

Source: Statistics SA, 2001 in Ntuli, et al. 2003

Income differentials appear to be associated with differential access to a range of health care inputs. Using data from the Tanzanian demographic and health survey, for example, Smithson (2006) found large differences between women from richer households and the poorest women in contraceptive use, skilled assistance at delivery, caesarean section, post-natal care and use of treated bed nets. Even services believed to be nearly universal, like measles immunisation, showed such differences between wealth groups. Women from richer households were:

- **3.4 times** more likely to use modern contraception than the poorest;
- **2.8 times** more likely to receive skilled assistance at delivery than the poorest; and
- **8.7 times** more likely to give birth by caesarean section than the poorest.

The poorest women are more than 7 times more likely to give birth at home and receive no post-natal check-up for their infants.

Compared to their poorer counterparts, the children of richer women are:

- **40 per cent** more likely to receive measles vaccination;
- **40 per cent** more likely to receive treatment for fever at a health facility;
- **20 per cent** more likely to receive any oral rehydration solution for diarrhoea; and
- **14 times** more likely than the poorest to have slept under a treated bed net the previous night (Smithson, 2006).

Figure 1.18 Births attended by skilled personnel for east and southern African countries, 1998–2004

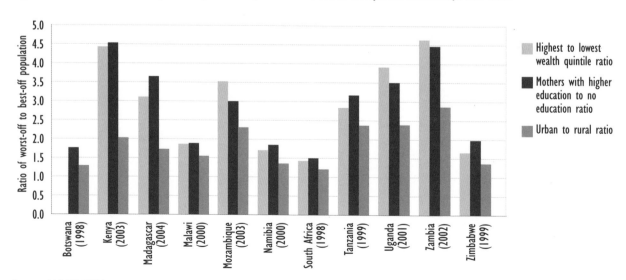

Source: WHO, 2006

Table 1.9 Trends in health inequalities in selected east and southern African countries, 1990-2002

Country	Year	Poor-rich ratio		Rich-poor ratio	
		Under 5 mortality	Malnutrition among women	Children ages 12-23 mths who were vaccinated	Women delivering assisted by doctor/nurse/midwife
Malawi	1992	1.5	2.4	1.2	1.7
	2000	1.5	1.7	1.2	1.9
Namibia	1992	1.5	3.6	1.2	1.8
	2000	1.8	n.a.	1.1	1.8
Tanzania	1996	1.4	1.7	1.4	3.0
	1999	1.2	n.a.	1.5	2.9
Uganda	1995	1.7	2.2	1.8	3.1
	2000/1	1.8	3.1	1.6	3.9
Zambia	1996	1.6	1.3	1.2	4.7
	2001/2	2.1	2.0	1.3	4.6
Zimbabwe	1994	1.5	4.8	1.2	1.7
	1999	1.6	2.1	1.0	1.6

Adapted from: Carr, 2004; Source: WHO, 2006

Access to services was also affected by mother's education, place of residence (rural or urban) and physical distance to services, with women citing cost as the biggest barrier to access (Smithson, 2006).

Such inequalities are found across the region. Household wealth and mother's education have greater impact on access to support in birth attendance than rural/urban residence (see figure 1.18), indicating that economic and social differentials may have a greater influence on health care outcomes than differences in service availability by geographical area. While expanding the provision of services has improved availability, these socio-economic differences affecting access and use are more difficult to resolve, as suggested by the persistent income differentials in access to basic health services in the region, even for the most essential primary health care interventions (see table 1.9).

One factor influencing differences in health care outcomes is the mismatch between health needs and resources. In seven African countries Castro-Leal *et al.* (2000) found the share of spending that went to the poorest quintile of households was significantly less than the share going to the richest 20 per cent. This is further confirmed by other studies (Gwatkin *et al.*, 2004) and even in low-income rural communities of Tanzania where one would expect households to be more similar (Schellenberg *et al.*, 2003).

However the reasons for differences in health care outcomes go beyond supply side factors. In understanding the reasons why health care coverage seems to be inverse to need, Smithson (2006) identified a chain of disadvantage that applies at different stages in people's efforts to use health services, shown in figure 1.19 on page 26.

While expanding the provision of services has improved availability, these socio-economic differences affecting access and use are more difficult to resolve…

Figure 1.19 Chain of disadvantage from morbidity to treatment outcomes

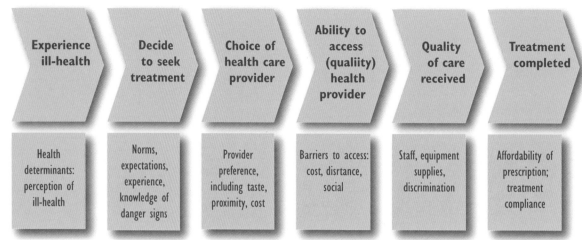

Source: Smithson, 2006

This points to areas for further exploration to understand why, when care is provided, differentials in access and uptake occur, particularly if health systems are to overcome inequalities in health care access under conditions of the growing economic inequalities and poverty described earlier:

> 'There is a new practice in our community nowadays. A woman in labour, who has been instructed early enough to go and have her delivery in a district hospital, will be accompanied by her husband and other relatives until a few metres away from our health centre. Then they will ask an old man to get her to us. When he presents her to us, he will say that he helped the woman, but he doesn't know her. The woman will say there was nobody to help her at home. It will then be up to us to make sure that this woman gets to the hospital. Since our ambulance services are not reliable, a nurse on duty will have to accompany the woman using any public transport available. Usually, we have to pay for our own fare and our patient's fare from our own pockets. We could also assist the woman to deliver here at the health centre but this is very risky. People are doing this because they can't afford the transport to the district hospital and they say it is the responsibility of the health system to provide transport to patients wherever treatment is available.'

Narration from a midwifery nurse at a rural clinic, story from IHRDC Tanzania, 2007

There is evidence that poor households lack the information and power to demand effective services from the health system (Bernal and Meleis, 1995; Jayawardene, 1993). When poor households and individuals use scarce resources to travel to health services, and these services lack drugs or personnel, they suffer a more significant loss to income and health than those better off. They have fewer resources to pursue alternatives and may delay seeking further treatment with costs to their health (Bloom *et al.*, 2000; Jayawardene, 1993). Poor households may have to dispose of assets and become indebted to meet health needs (Goudge and Govender, 2000).

'*The women said they find it difficult to negotiate safe sex and have inadequate income to buy drugs to treat sexually transmitted infections. They observed that culture is forcing HIV positive women to keep on giving birth despite the deterioration in their health and the opportunistic diseases they experience. Women saw that reproductive health problems were a major issue and noted the unavailability of antiretroviral drugs at district hospitals. While it was noted that one clinic in the area had a programme for prevention of mother to child transmission, some participants raised concerns that they were not comfortable with the compulsory HIV test.*'

Facilitators feedback from participatory discussions on health in rural Zimbabwe, 2006

Expanding the supply of services is necessary but not sufficient to address access. The region is experiencing a high proportion and rate of increase of poverty and widening inequalities in wealth. This is associated with significant differentials in access to even basic health inputs. If most poor households are to get the health inputs they need to address their higher levels of ill health, then east and southern African countries are challenged to increase service availability and to overcome differentials in how poor households obtain and access the resources for health.

New demands on health care services can overshadow this deeper trend in inequality. The AIDS epidemic, losses in health workers and rising costs of medical care have increased demands on services. Expanding the currently low levels of coverage of antiretrovirals (shown in table 1.10) to universal coverage, or providing universal access to prevention of mother to child transmission of HIV for pregnant women is no small challenge.

The discussion of the roll out of antiretrovirals in Section 3 explores how this can and is being done so that the possibilities for children accessing safe water or women preventing unwanted pregnancy are not traded off against the possibilities of accessing antiretrovirals.

The region thus faces the twin demands of expanding new health interventions and sustaining provision of priority health care services, while overcoming differentials in access and use of services, including basic primary health care services.

Table 1.10 Provision of antiretrovirals in east and southern African countries

Indicator	No. in need of ART (2005)	No. receiving ART (2005)	% total in need receiving ART
Angola	52,000	3,000	6
Botswana	84,000	72,000	85
DRC	209,000	7,750	4
Kenya	273,000	66,000	24
Lesotho	58,000	8,250	14
Madagascar	20,000	<200	0
Malawi	169,000	33,000	20
Mauritius	n.a.	<200	n.a.
Mozambique	216,000	20,000	9
Namibia	41,000	29,000	71
South Africa	983,000	206,500	21
Swaziland	42,000	13,000	31
Tanzania	315,000	21,500	7
Uganda	148,000	75,000	51
Zambia	183,000	48,500	27
Zimbabwe	321,000	24,500	8

ART = antiretroviral treatment; n.a. = data not available

Source: WHO, 2006a

Equity through reclaiming the resources for health

'Inequity is increasing between and within countries, widening the health gap and sub-Saharan Africa carries the greatest burden of disease and underdevelopment.

The summit should agree on steps to reduce inequity in society, to narrow the gap between rich and poor, and within and between countries and, to this end, to focus measures on those most vulnerable.'

Johannesburg Declaration on Health and Sustainable Development, SADC Ministers of Health, Summit on Sustainable Development, 19-22 January 2002

Drawing on evidence from east and southern Africa, this section identifies that gross domestic product is often a poor reflection of the natural assets and wealth of those countries. There is wide variability in aggregate gross domestic product across the region and, while there has been economic growth, this has often not translated into human development improvements. The evidence presented suggests that the benefits of growth are not reaching households, particularly where there is a rise in household poverty and widening inequality in access to wealth. That this is happening at a higher rate in the countries with higher overall gross domestic product reflects possible problems in the paths to growth. The evidence suggests that relative inequality in incomes and wealth may be acting as a brake to poverty reduction, even where growth occurs. The burden of AIDS mortality on human development adds further imperative to addressing this.

The Millennium Development Goals set by the United Nations seek to free men, women, and children from the dehumanising conditions of extreme poverty. The targets for these goals are used as a framework to measure development progress. The eight goals are to:

1. eradicate extreme poverty and hunger;
2. achieve universal primary education;
3. promote gender equality and empower women;
4. reduce child mortality;
5. improve maternal health;
6. combat HIV and AIDS, malaria and other diseases;
7. ensure environmental sustainability; and
8. develop a global partnership for development.

This analysis does not repeat the well-documented performance of east and southern African countries against the goals, found, for example, at the following website:

http://web.worldbank.org/WBSITE/EXTERNAL/COUNTRIES/AF RICAEXT/0,,contentMDK:20234497~menuPK:485868~pagePK:14673 6~piPK:226340~theSitePK:258644,00.html (World Bank, 2000).

The evidence in this section suggests, however, that the limited returns from growth to households challenges delivery on these commitments to development. This echoes similar warnings made in other global reviews (UNDP, 2005).

Poverty and inequality in wealth are associated with inequalities in health, while improvements in health can contribute to reducing poverty. In addition to the significant reversals in life expectancy at birth that resulted from the AIDS epidemic, households with lower levels of income, poor education or living in under resourced rural communities experience both higher levels of ill health and have less access to the inputs for health.

The effect of economic policy choices on these health outcomes is significant and potentially long term. Zimbabwe's experience described on page 30 shows that economic policies can differently affect groups across the wealth spectrum, fragmenting their relationship with health services and setting the basis for their subsequent health experience.

While health systems can make a difference to health outcomes., a recent analysis of inequality in Africa highlights the role of public expenditure, particularly on primary health care services, in redistributing resources and addressing inequalities in assets and income (Okojie and Shimeles, 2006). So the expansion of health services in east and southern Africa in the past decades is likely to have played an important role in reducing both poverty and inequality. Health services now appear to face new challenges, however, with the following demands to:

- develop new interventions due to AIDS and other chronic diseases;
- maintain service provisioning, sometimes in the face of rising costs (discussed further in the next section); and
- address the continuing gaps in access to and use of these services among those groups with greatest health needs.

There is a long-standing commitment in this region to close up these gaps. Challenges to unfair and avoidable inequalities in health were an inherent part of most liberation movement policies, incorporated into founding health policies and programmes of independent governments in the region. When the Southern African Development Community (SADC) health sector was formed in the late 1990s, it included a focus on addressing these unfair inequalities in health, building on a report tabled by the Ministry of Health (Botswana) from the regional meeting held in Kasane, Botswana. Commitments to equity have since been expressed by SADC and by the health ministers in east, central and southern Africa.

The current health conditions in the region described in this section indicate that this commitment to equity remains relevant. According to the definition of equity given at the beginning of the section, equity-oriented policies seek to overcome avoidable and unfair differences in health, such as those along dimensions of wealth, gender, place or education, that have been outlined in this section.

Poverty and inequality in wealth are associated with inequalities in health, while improvements in health can contribute to reducing poverty.

What happened to health differentials in Zimbabwe, 1988–1994?

In Zimbabwe between 1988 and 1994, the major determinants of health – education, water and sanitation – registered marginal improvements. Declines emerged, however, in health status and access to health services in the lowest and highest income quintiles. As shown for immunisation below, the two lowest income quintiles and the highest income quintiles experienced a fall in immunisation, while those in the middle did not. Higher income groups still had higher rates of immunisation, and any decrease in the gaps between the rich and poor was due to a decline in the situation of the better-off respondents rather than an improvement among the poor.

Percentage of children fully immunised by quintile 1994 and 1988

Socio-economic quintile	Children immunised 1994	% total immunised in quintile 1994	Children immunised 1998	% total immunised in quintile 1998
1	348	20.7	378	19.7
2	366	21.8	384	20.0
3	283	16.8	371	19.3
4	344	20.5	453	23.6
5	341	20.3	332	17.3
Total	1682	100.0	1918	100.0
Poor/rich ratio	1.02		1.14	
Relative risk	0.56		0.22	

Number of children in 1994 = 2116 Number of children in 1988 = 2299
Table shows the percentage of all children immunised in the different quintiles.

The evidence suggests that the market reforms introduced in the structural adjustment programme in the early 1990s affected the income groups differently. For the poorest households, falling provision of care, especially outreach to marginal areas, and reduced resources to pay for costs of using services were likely factors in the reduced access to services. For higher income groups, increased privatisation of care and a shift in use from public to private services may have led to reduced cover with primary health care services not as well covered in the private sector.

Woelk and Chikuse, 2001

Kasane 1997: An agenda for action on equity in health

The regional meeting on 'Equity in Health – Policies for Survival in Southern Africa' (March 1997, Kasane, Botswana) discussed issues of equity in health in southern Africa and explored possible joint solutions and actions. 'Equity in health' was understood to involve addressing inequalities in opportunities within and beyond the health sector for achieving health, and inequalities in the provision of and access to health care. The meeting observed that while equity in health should be central to health and development efforts, disparities in health status persist and equity concerns have lost prominence to issues of macro-economic stability, fiscal policy and efficiency, often under the influence of external actors. The AIDS epidemic has further threatened health and has placed its heaviest burdens on the poorest households. Among the resolutions the meeting made, there were thus calls for SADC communities to:

- make the concept of equity clear, prioritising vertical equity;
- provide for the constitutional right to equitable access and provision of health care and health promoting services;
- promote people-centred development paths that prioritise the determinants of health, such as education, employment, clean water, sanitation, food security and clean environments, and provide inter-sectoral mechanisms for delivery of these priority inputs;
- develop resource allocation planning tools that locate equity as a desirable goal;
- shift the allocation of resources towards preventive and promotive health services;
- establish research on equity issues, train to build public health and health management capacity, particularly at district level, and set up equity monitoring; and
- develop measures and incentives to curb regional brain-drain of public health trained personnel.

The Kasane meeting endorsed continuing regional networking on equity in health and input to SADC on equity policies.

Ministry of Health (Botswana), 2001

Source: B Goddard

Equity-oriented policies would thus seek to overcome care inverse to need and to allocate more resources to those with greater health needs.

The next sections explore how we can operationalise our commitment to equity and, in so doing, respond to the health and human development challenges in the region. The evidence in this section suggests one dimension of this – for poor households to access a fairer share of growing national resources for their health and health care.

Health systems can play an important role in redistributing resources to poor households and we explore this further in later sections. This is not simply a technical question. Our definition of equity suggests that it is a matter of political choice, arising from the social norms and values held within the region.

These challenges are being addressed in the context of global commitments to human development but also of significant global inequalities in incomes and wealth. In the next section we explore the implications of this context for east and southern African countries, particularly if national assets and production are to yield the returns needed to meet these obligations to health and human development.

World Social Forum, Kenya 2007
Source : I Rusike

REFERENCES

Atim C (2006) *Financial factors affecting slow progress in reaching agreed targets on HIV/AIDS, TB and malaria in Africa*, DFID Health Resource Centre, prepared for the AU, Addis Ababa, downloaded 7 March 2007 at www.africa-union.org

African Union (AU), United Nations Economic Commission for Africa (UNECA) (2007) *Accelerating Africa's development through diversification*, AU/UNECA, Ethiopia.

Bernal P and Meleis A (1995) 'Self care actions of Colombian Por Dia domestic workers: On prevention and care', *Women and Health* 22 (4): 77-95.

Bloom G, Lucas H, Edun A, Lenneiye M and Milimo J (2000) *Working paper 103: Health and poverty in sub-Saharan Africa*, Institute of Development Studies, Brighton.

Carr D (2004) 'Improving the health of the world's poorest people', *Health Bulletin 1*, Population Reference Bureau, Washington DC, accessed 6 Dec 2006 at http://www.prb.org/pdf/Improvingthe HealthWorld_Eng.pdf

Castro-Leal F, Dayton J, Demery L, Mehra K (2000) 'Public spending on health care in Africa: Do the poor benefit?', *Bulletin of the World Health Organisation* 78(1).

Davies JB, Sandstrom S, Shorrocks A, Wolff EN (2006) 'The world distribution of household wealth,' UN Univ., *World Institute for Development Economics research paper*, WIDER, Helsinki, Finland.

EQUINET Steering Committee (1998) 'Equity in health southern Africa: Overview and issues from an annotated bibliography', *EQUINET policy paper* 2, EQUINET, Harare.
– (2000) 'Turning values into practice: Equity in health in southern Africa', *EQUINET policy paper* 7, EQUINET, Harare.

Forsythe S (1992) 'The economic impact of HIV and AIDS in Malawi', *Report for the National AIDS Control Programme* (confidential mimeo), Government of Malawi, Lilongwe.

Gillies P, Tolley K and Wolstenholme J (1996) 'Is AIDS a disease of poverty?', *AIDS Care* (8)3: 351-364.

Goudge J and Govender V (2000) 'A review of experience concerning household ability to cope with the resource demands of ill health and health care utlisation', *EQUINET policy paper* 3, EQUINET, Harare.

Gwatkin DR, Bhuiya A, Victora CG (2004) 'Making health systems more equitable', *The Lancet* 364: 1273-1280.

International Labour Organisation (ILO) (1995) 'The impact of HIV/AIDS on the productive labour force in Africa', *EAMAT working paper* 1, ILO, Addis Ababa.
– (1995b) 'The Impact of HIV/AIDS on the productive labour force in Zambia,' *EAMAT working paper* 5, ILO, Addis Ababa.
– (1995c) 'The Impact of HIV/AIDS on the productive labour force in Tanzania,' *EAMAT working pape*r 3, ILO, Addis Ababa.

Jayawardene R (1993) 'Illness perception: Social cost and coping strategies of malaria cases', *Social Science and Medicine* 37 (9):1169-1176.

Kuznets S (1955) 'Toward a theory of economic growth', in Lekachman R, *National policy for economic welfare at home and abroad*, Doubleday, Garden City, New York.

Ministry of Health (Botswana) (2001) 'Equity in health: Kasane report', memo, feedback to the SADC health sector, Govt of Botswana, Gaborone.

OCR Macro (2007) 'MEASURE DHS STAT compiler', accessed 8 June 2007 at www.measuremenths.com

Okojie C, Shimeles A (2006) *Inequality in sub-Saharan Africa: A synthesis of recent research on the levels, trends, effects and determinants of inequality in its different dimensions*, The Inter-Regional Inequality Facility, ODI, UK.

Omaswa F, Burnham G, Baingana G, Mwebesa H and Morrow R (1997) 'Introducing quality management into primary health care services in Uganda', *Bulletin of the World Health Organisation* 75(2): 155-161.

Ravallion M (2005) 'A poverty–inequality trade off?', *World Bank policy research paper* 3579, April 2005, accessed 4 June 2007 at http://econ.worldbank.org/external/default/main?Img PagePK=64202990&entity ID=000012009_20050505134719&menuPK=64168175&pagePK=64210502&theSitePK=477894&piPK=64210520

Schellenberg JA, Victora CG, Mushi A, de Savigny D, Schellenberg D, Mshinda H and Bryce J (2003) 'Inequities among the very poor: Health care for children in rural southern Tanzania', *The Lancet online* 4 February 2003, at http://image.thelancet.com/extras/02Art2280web.pdf

Smithson P (2006) *Fairs fair: Health inequalities and equity in Tanzania*, Womens Dignity Project, Ifakara Health Research Development Centre, Dar es Salaam.

Southern African Development Community (SADC) (4 July 2003) *Maseru declaration on HIV/AIDS*, Maseru, Lesotho, SADC, Gaborone.
– (2003b) *SADC HIV/AIDS framework and strategic programme of action 2003–2007*, SADC, Gaborone.

Statistics South Africa (2001) 'Census in brief 2001', Pretoria, 2003 cited in Ntuli A, Ijumba P, McCoy D, Padarath A and Berthiaume L (2003) 'HIV/AIDS and health sector responses in South Africa: Treatment access and equity: Balancing the act', *EQUINET discussion paper* 7, EQUINET and OXFAM GB, Hararc.

UNAIDS (2005) *Regional comparison in people living with HIV and AIDS*, 2005, UNAIDS, Geneva.
– (2006) *Report on the global AIDS epidemic*, May 2006, UNAIDS, Geneva accessed 2 June 2007at http://www.unaids.org/en/HIV_data/2006GlobalReport/default.asp

United Nations Development Programme (UNDP) (1999) *Human development report 1999*, OUP: New York, accessed 2 June 2007 at http://hdr.undp.org/reports /view_reports.cfm?type=
–(2002) *Human development report 2002*, OUP, New York, accessed at http://hdr.undp.org/reports/ view_reports.cfm?type=1 June 2 2007

–(2005) *Human development report 2005– International co-operation at a crossroads:Aid, trade and security in an unequal world*, OUP , New York, accessed 1 June 2 2007 at http://hdr.undp.org/reports/view_reports.cfm?type=

– (2006) *Human development report 2006*, OUP, New York, accessed 2 June 2007 at http://hdr.undp.org/hdr2006/

UNDP Sub-regional Resource Facility (SURF) for Southern Africa (2000) *United Nations southern Africa regional human development report 2000*, UNDP, Pretoria.

United Nations Children's Fund (UNICEF)(2007) *Monitoring and statistics web databases* accessed 2 June 2007 at www.unicef.org/statistics

Woelk G (2000) 'Analysing inequities in health status and in health care using demographic and health survey data: Zimbabwe', paper presented at the *EQUINET conference, Midrand South Africa, September 2000*, EQUINET, Harare.

Woelk G and Chikuse P (2001) 'Using demographic and health survey data to describe intra-country incqualities in health status: Zimbabwe', *EQUINET policy paper 9*, EQUINET, Harare.

World Bank (2000) *Millenium Development Goal indicators: Africa*, World Bank, New York available at http://web.worldbank.org/WBSITE/EXTERNAL/COUNTRIES/AFRICAEXT/0,,contentMDK:20234497~menuPK:485868~pagePK:146736~piPK:226340~theSitePK:258644,00.html

– (2004) *World development indicators database 2004*, World Bank, Washington, accessed 2 June 2007 at http://devdata.worldbank.org/wdi2004/index2.htm

– (2005) *World development indicators database 2005*, World Bank, Washington, accessed 2 June 2007 at http://devdata.worldbank.org/wdi2005/index2.htm

– (2006) *World development indicators database 2006*, World Bank, Washington, accessed 2 June 2007 at http://devdata.worldbank.org/wdi2006/contents/Section4.htm

World Health Organisation (WHO) (2005) *WHO global health atlas*, WHO, Geneva, accessed March 2006 at http://globalatlas.who.int.

– (2006) *Core health indicators database 2006*, WHO, Geneva, accessed Nov 2006 at: http://www.who.int/whosis /en/

– (2006a) *Progress on global access to antiretroviral therapy: A report on '3 by 5' and beyond*, WHO, Geneva, available at: http://www.who.int/hiv/mediacentre/news57/en/index.htl

WHO Afro (2006) *The African regional health report 2006*, WHO-Afro Region, Brazzaville, accessed 2 June 2007 at http://www.afro.who.int/regionaldirector/african_regional_health_report2006.pdf

WHO, Dept of Health (SA) and SADC (2002) 'Johannesburg declaration on health and sustainable development: Meeting of senior officials and ministers of health', *World Summit on Sustainable Development, Johannesburg, 19–22 January*, WHO, Geneva, available at: http://www.who.int/mediacentre/events/HSD_Plaq_02.8_def1.pdf

Reclaiming
THE ECONOMIC RESOURCES FOR
HEALTH

KEY ISSUES

Is Africa a 'poor continent'? We don't believe so – but Africa's substantial resources tend to flow outwards. This resource drain, and the inequality in wealth described in Section 1, leaves most of Africa's people in poverty and depletes the resources for health. It takes place in many different ways – through debt; falling terms of trade; capital and financial market outflows; reduced foreign direct investment and domestic savings; as well as through the outflow of human and natural resources. Private finance in Africa has shifted from recording net inflows in the 1970s to gradual outflows during the 1980s and finally to substantial outflows after the 1990s.

These outflows deplete the national and household resources for health. To reclaim these resources, policies and measures outside the health sector must become matters for public health concern.

For example, the rising levels of under-nutrition in parts of the region have drawn attention to food and agriculture policies. Trade liberalisation, unfair trade barriers and monopoly control over food production have not only weakened household and smallholder production, they have also undermined the basis for improved nutrition. An alternative route lies in promoting food sovereignty – increasing investments in smallholder farmers, especially women, and enhancing their control over land, seed and other production inputs.

Trade agreements are increasingly influencing health and health care, particularly in relation to people's access to medicines and the financing and provision of health care. Dialogue across trade and health ministries enables us to audit the impact these agreements may have on health, to fully use the flexibilities they provide and to negotiate the policy space and government authority needed to protect public health.

Health systems can make a difference to these wider influences on health and provide leadership – shaping wider social norms and values, motivating public health awareness and working across sectors in a common approach. What kind of health system plays that role? We take this up in the next section.

The dispossession of African wealth at the cost of African health

Section 1 described how poverty and inequalities in wealth and social development challenge any opportunities for health, affecting coverage and access to health care in the region. Underlying this is poor households' diminishing capacity to claim their rightful share of the resources from growth and thus secure the resources for health. Despite countries' significant efforts to widen health care availability, we observed that groups with greater health needs suffer from poorer health service coverage. Sections 3 and 4 further explore this equity gap and suggest how health systems can stake claim to a greater share of national resources to effectively address these health needs.

What are the possibilities for growth with improved human development? Two challenges emerged in Section 1. The first arises from the insecure and dependent nature of growth:

> *'For most African countries, real growth rates have remained low relative to their development goals. With only four countries recording an average real gross domestic product growth rate of 7 per cent or more during 1998-2006, few African countries are positioned to achieve the Millennium Development Goals by 2015. Meanwhile, growth performance exhibits substantial disparities across the five sub-regions. North Africa recorded the highest acceleration in gross domestic product growth, followed by central Africa. There was a deceleration in growth in west Africa and southern Africa, whereas east Africa maintained the same growth rate as in 2005. Heavy dependence on primary commodities remains a common feature of production, exports and growth in all the sub-regions. This exposes the continent to external shocks and makes economic diversification a top priority for growth policies on the continent.'*

African Union, UNECA, 2007

The second challenge is in Africa's disadvantaged position in global inequality, described in Section 1 and represented graphically in figure 2.1a and b on page 38. Africa, emaciated in gross domestic product globally, is bloated in child mortality, indicating the global inequity between the demands for social protection and the resources to provide it.

Africa is not a 'poor continent'. The substantial flow of resources outwards from the continent, however, together with the inequality in wealth described in Section 1, leaves most African people living in poverty and depletes the resources essential for health.

The drain of resources dates back many centuries, beginning with the appropriation of wealth, consolidated through slavery and colonialism and intensified under current globalisation policies. It is amplified today through various measures, including debt, falling terms of trade, capital and financial market outflows, reduced foreign direct investment, human resource flows and depletion of natural resources (Bond, 2006).

Figure 2.1a Global cartogram with country sizes proportional to their gross domestic product

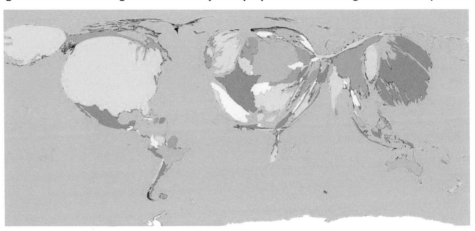

Figure 2.1b Global cartogram with country sizes proportional to their child mortality

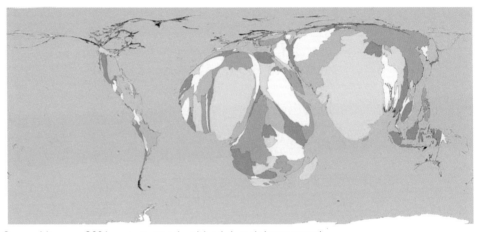

Source: Newman, 2006, www-personal.umich.edu/~mejn/cartograms/

Structural adjustment programmes in east and southern Africa removed barriers to trade, liberalised the finance sector, lowered corporate taxation, deregulated business and labour markets and privatised or commercialised state-owned enterprises. Associated with this, user charges for services increased and public sector employment and wages stagnated or fell. Far removed from the regulation and subsidies used by developed countries to promote their own industrial development and services, liberalisation was promoted by international finance institutions and developed countries as essential for economic and social development in Africa (EQUINET SC, 2004).

After two decades of such policies, the experiences of sluggish growth, highlighted by the African Union, and of growth with poor human development returns, highlighted in Section 1, contest the view that production for export invariably brings progress (African Union, UN ECA, 2007). There are many debates about the strategies needed to integrate into the global economy and the consequences of this integration (UNDP, 2005; WCSDG, 2004). In this analysis we focus on one aspect: Is this integration enabling – or disabling – control over the resources for social development in the region?

African countries obtain diminishing returns on trade

Trade in natural resources accounted for nearly 80 per cent of African exports in 2000, compared to 31 per cent for all developing countries and 16 per cent for the advanced capitalist economies (Commission for Africa, 2005). Within east and southern Africa, Angola, Botswana, Uganda and Zambia all rely upon a single product for at least 75 per cent of their export earnings. Only five countries in the region (Lesotho, South Africa, Swaziland, Tanzania and Zimbabwe) claim at least 25 per cent of export earnings from more than four products. The region is highly dependent on returns from single raw material products. Worse still, prices for these African exports have fallen sharply in recent decades (see table 2.1):

> 'Between 1995 and 2004, Europe alone has been able to increase its agricultural exports by 26 per cent, much of it because of the massive domestic subsidies it provides. Each percentage increase in exports brings in a financial gain of $3 billion. On the other hand, a vast majority of the developing countries, whether in Latin America, Africa or Asia, have in the first 10 years of the World Trade Organisation turned into food importers. Millions of farmers have lost their livelihoods as a result of cheaper imports. If the World Trade Organisation has its way, and the developing countries fail to understand the prevailing politics that drives the agriculture trade agenda, the world will soon have two kinds of agriculture systems – the rich countries will produce staple foods for the world's six billion plus people, and developing countries will grow cash crops like tomato, cut flowers, peas, sunflower, strawberries and vegetables.'

Sharma, 2005

Table 2.1: Commodity price declines, 1980–2001

Product, unit	1980	1990	2001
Coffee (Café robusta) cents/kg	411.70	118.20	63.30
Cocoa cents/kg	330.50	126.70	111.40
Groundnut oil dollars/ton	1090.10	963.70	709.20
Palm oil dollars/ton	740.90	289.90	297.80
Soya dollars/ton	376.00	246.80	204.20
Sugar cents/kg	80.17	27.67	19.90
Cotton cents/kg	261.70	181.90	110.30
Copper dollars/ton	2770.00	2661.00	1645.00
Lead cents/kg	115.00	81.10	49.60

Source: Touissant, 2005

Worsening terms of trade for primary commodities grip east and southern African producers in a price trap, demanding higher production but providing lower revenues. Northern producers obtain state subsidies, notably in agriculture, making their exports increasingly competitive. In contrast, east and southern Africa countries are pressurised to scrap subsidies, even though many producers are already undermined by rising costs and falling returns.

Developing countries lose US$35 billion annually as a result of industrialised countries' protectionist tariffs alone (Bond, 2006).

Developing countries lose US$35 billion annually as a result of industrialised countries' protectionist tariffs alone.

Effects of northern agricultural subsidies in east and southern Africa

Kenya had more than doubled its processed milk production between 1980 and 1990 but imports of milk powder soared after 1990, increasing from 48 tonnes to 2,500 tonnes by 1998. At the same time, domestic production of processed milk plummeted by almost 70 per cent. Kenya's ability to diversify into processing was undermined and small producers bore the brunt of the decline in demand for local fresh milk.

European Union beef is sold in southern Africa for 30 pence a kilogram although it costs one pound per kilogram to produce it. This has completely changed the economics of the Namibian meat canning industry which has shifted from local beef to the imported subsidised beef.

South Africa dismantled its subsidy scheme for fruit and vegetables as part of its re-entry into the international market. However the European Union retained its subsidies and placed tariffs of between 11 and 23 per cent on South African canned fruit and vegetables. This has led to many small fruit and vegetable farmers in South Africa being forced to sell or to consolidate with larger farming concerns.

Chopra, 2004

Domination of the food supply chain by transnational corporations

- Six transnational corporations account for 85 per cent of world trade in grain.

- Eight transnational corporations account for 60 per cent of global coffee sales (Madeley, 2003).

- Cargill, a transnational corporation, controls 80 per cent of grain distribution throughout the world (Kneen, 1996).

- Ten agrochemical companies control 81 per cent of the US$29 billion global agrochemical market.

- Four transnational corporations own nearly 45 per cent of patents for staples such as rice and maize (ActionAid, 2003).

- In South Africa, Monsanto controls 100 per cent of the national market for genetically modified seed, 60 per cent of the hybrid maize market and 90 per cent of the wheat market.

- Three large retailers are now responsible for over 70 per cent of total food sales in east and southern Africa

Madeley, 2003

As shown by the Kenyan experience, food production in particular has been affected by these trends. Globally, food imports have grown fastest in Africa, rising from 8 per cent of world food imports in 1986 to 18 per cent in 2001 (FAO, 2004). At the same time, the value of agricultural output per worker in Africa fell from US$424 in 1980 to about US$365 per worker (constant: 1995 US$) in the late 1990s. This happened for several reasons. Falling international prices reduced returns, while the expanding areas under production, particularly by large companies, encroached into fallow land, exhausting soils and damaging biodiversity. Agricultural yields levelled off or fell for many crops in the region (Chopra, 2004).

Meanwhile, a food supply chain increasingly controlled by a few transnational corporations was able to further drive down producer prices, increase consumer prices and shift profits to their processing and retailing operations (Chopra, 2004).

The World Trade Organisation, International Monetary Fund and World Bank have reinforced each other's policy instruments to consolidate these trends. In 2000, for example, the International Monetary Fund advised the Malawian national food reserve agency to reduce its almost full capacity stocks to a two to three month supply of food for the Malawi population, and to use the proceeds to repay its debts, to pay salaries, to cover running costs and to replenish old maize. This proved costly as Malawi was unable to import enough (more expensive) grain from the international market to prevent widespread hunger the following season (Lambrechts and Barry, 2003).

In Zambia, in an attempt to stimulate greater private sector involvement, the World Bank, through structural adjustment programmes, persuaded the Zambian government to replace the Zambian grain marketing authority with the much smaller Food Reserve Agency. However, a lack of infrastructure made it uneconomical for private traders to do business in remote areas and people have been left with no access to markets on which to sell their produce or buy inputs. An independent International Monetary Fund evaluation found that liberalisation of the state marketing board contributed to a 30 per cent increase in rural poverty between 1991 and 1994 (Lambrechts and Barry, 2003).

These policies deplete the resources for health in various ways.

Rapid trade liberalisation depletes public sector resources

The loss of public revenue caused by tariffs being removed is, reportedly, not offset by improved returns to public revenue from trade. Furthermore, there is a cost in reduced public expenditure which also means less funding available for health (Mabika *et al.*, 2007).

In a United Nations Economic Commission for Africa report, Karingi *et al.* (2005) outline, for example, the potential impacts on public revenues of the trade liberalisation measures proposed in the economic partnership agreement negotiated between the European Union and east and southern Africa in 2007. Table 2.2 shows that all the east and southern African

The loss of public revenue caused by tariffs being removed is, reportedly, not offset by improved returns to public revenue from trade. Furthermore, there is a cost in reduced public expenditure which also means less funding available for health

countries involved face lost revenue. The rapid imposition of tariff reductions is not replaced by improvements in other tax revenues which accrue much more slowly, if at all. For many east and southern Africa countries, revenue from import duties and other trade tariffs is substantial, the measures are simple to administer and they provide useful incentives for industrial policy.

Trade liberalisation has depleted household resources for production and food security, critical for health.

Trade liberalisation has depleted household resources for production and food security, critical for health.

As described in the examples from Kenya, South Africa and Zambia, smallholder producers are most affected by falling prices and rising input costs, and have lost markets to cheap subsidised imports (Chopra, 2004).

Given the economic significance of agriculture in the region, it is not surprising that these trends are associated with increased household poverty and widening inequality in wealth. The World Bank concedes that rapid trade-related integration has caused or exacerbated social inequality. In a World Bank working paper, Milanovic (2002) concludes that those who benefited most from rapid trade liberalisation were the import/export firms, transport and shipping companies, large-scale commercial farmers and financiers as well as the politicians and bureaucrats who are tapped into these commercial and financial circuits:

Table 2.2 Revenue implications of an economic partnership agreement between the European Union and east and southern Africa

Country	Revenue impacts in US$*
DRC	-24,691,828.00
Kenya	-107,281,328.00
Madagascar	-7,711,790.00
Malawi	-7,090,310.00
Mauritius	-71,117,968.00
Zimbabwe	-18,430,590.00
Uganda	-9,458,170.00
Zambia	-15,844,184.00

*Negative figures mean revenue losses
Source: Karingi et al., 2005

'*Most of the post-independence economic policies geared to long-term development were replaced by macro-economic stabilisation policies focusing on short-term goals. This reorientation of economic policies has failed to yield the expected results and it is clear that a shift in policy orientation is needed to accelerate progress towards the Millennium Development Goals.*'
UNECA and African Union, 2007:9

Small-scale coffee producers, World Social Forum, Kenya, 2007
Source: I Rusike

Trade imbalances are not the only way resources flow out of the region; there are many other sources of the haemorrhage.

Foreign direct investment has been low compared to returns and has had limited benefits for African economies. Africa's share of this investment fell from 25 per cent of all transnational corporation investment during the 1970s to less than 5 per cent during the late 1990s (Commission for Africa, 2005).

Most of the foreign direct investment flows into the region, shown in table 2.3, are related to mineral extraction, with little for value-added processing (Bond and Dor, 2003). A brief rise in foreign direct investment into sub-Saharan Africa after 1997 appears to be associated with investments in oil in Angola and Nigeria, and with South Africa's largest firms being relisted on the London market (Commission for Africa, 2005; Bond, 2006). Despite rates of return on direct investments that have generally been much higher in Africa than in other developing regions and the evident range of risk and governance environments within which investments take place, low investment continues to be attributed to high assessments of risk (Mkandawire, 2005).

Portfolio investment has mainly taken the form of 'hot money' – highly risky speculative investment in stock and currency markets:

> '*It is widely recognised that direct investment is preferable to portfolio investment and foreign investment in 'green field' investments is preferable to acquisitions. The predominance of these [portfolio and acquisition] types of capital inflows should be cause for concern.*'
>
> Mkandawire, 2005

Privatisation-related foreign direct investment (which constitutes 14 per cent of total recent foreign direct investment) has proved disappointing or even detrimental throughout the continent. In South Africa, foreign investors have had exceptionally high returns on privatised assets – for example, as high as 108 per cent on shares in the Airports Company of South Africa, which are then repatriated to their foreign headquarters.

With these disappointing trends, African countries have been challenged to raise levels of domestic investment to finance economic and social infrastructure in order to tackle poverty. With the exception of Botswana at above 30 per cent, the level of savings in east and southern Africa has been historically less than 20 per cent of gross domestic product, considerably below the average for East Asia (35 per cent) for example. With low levels of savings and limited private capital flows,

Table 2.3 Foreign direct investment inflows and outflows, Africa

	1990	1994	2000	2004
FDI inflows Africa (US$ million)	2840	6096	9627	18090
Africa FDI inflows as % total developing countries	8%	6%	4%	8%
FDI outflows Africa (US$ million)	689	2066	1573	2824
Africa FDI outflows % total developing countries	5%	4%	1%	3%

FDI = foreign direct investment
Source: Global Policy Forum, 2006

Table 2.4 Bilateral trade between Africa and China

Year	Trade level (US$ millions)
Late 1950s	12
2000	10,600
2005	40,000

Source: *Peoples Daily Online*, 2006

At the same time, greater attention also needs to be given to identifying and managing outflows. Beyond the trade losses described earlier, outflows due to transfer pricing, tax fraud, corruption and other techniques for financial extraction have significantly reduced and, in many countries, reversed the net gain from investments

domestic investment as a share of gross domestic product in the region is at a low 18 per cent, compared to 31 per cent in East Asia (African Union and UNECA, 2007). The African Union has called for improved development of domestic capital markets, including bond markets and stock exchanges, and regional integration of capital markets, especially for the smaller economies.

East and southern Africa countries have also explored alternative sources of foreign direct investment. The 2006 World Bank global development finance report showed that foreign direct investment flows between developing countries (south-south flows) are now growing more rapidly than those between developed and developing countries (north-south flows), even though the absolute amounts are not as great as for the north–south investments. Much of the foreign direct investment between developing countries originated from middle-income country firms and much is invested in the same region, such as for South African companies investing elsewhere in southern Africa (World Bank, 2006). The African Union points further to China and India as new drivers of Africa's growth through the substantial increase in trade and investment from these sources over the past ten years (see table 2.4) (African Union and UNECA, 2007).

China offers debt reduction and preferential trade treatment and finances large infrastructure investments. These large capital investments have been welcomed as they do not carry the macro-economic conditionalities of loans from western institutions.

However, while these investments represent a rapidly rising source of new capital, concerns have been raised about their returns for domestic industrial development, improved household resources or public sector revenue. They have been noted to largely exploit natural resources, offer poor working conditions, make inadequate investment in secondary processing, include weak skills transfer to Africans and to pose a threat to domestic industry due to competition from low-cost Chinese imports. So these investments do not adequately lever improved social and public spending and there is a risk of countries accumulating more debt through Chinese infrastructure and export credit loans (African Union and UNECA, 2007).

The African Union has called for greater strategic engagement and regional co-ordination to encourage investments that diversify African economies (African Union and UNECA, 2007).

At the same time, greater attention also needs to be given to identifying and managing outflows. Beyond the trade losses described earlier, outflows due to transfer pricing, tax fraud, corruption and other techniques for financial extraction have significantly reduced and, in many countries, reversed the net gain from investments (Bond, 2006). The outflow of skilled people, discussed further in Section 5, has been a major drain of public resources and capabilities.

China's investments in Zambia

China pledged in 2007 to pour US$800 million into Zambia over the following three years and to write off US$11 million worth of debt. It promised to build schools and provide agricultural training and loans for road-construction equipment. A US$200 million copper smelter is the centrepiece of an economic and trade co-operation zone in the Copperbelt province, the first of five such zones to be established in Africa with Chinese investment and the co-operation of host governments. The Zambian zone is expected to create 50,000 new jobs by 2010. Zambia offers in return: tax holidays, a low 0.6 per cent mineral royalty tax – the global norm is 3 per cent – and no duty imposed on imports of equipment and machinery.

However, the benefit of Chinese investment in Zambia is under debate. Muweme Muweme, social conditions research project officer at the Jesuit Centre for Theological Reflections, has called for China to rather 'build the capacity of the local people so that they can contribute to their own economic growth'. Emily Sikazwe, executive director of Women for Change, decried Zambia becoming: 'a provider of cheap raw resources and a market for poor-quality goods':

> *We expect China to make their investment in our country more meaningful by observing human rights, especially the right to livelihood and dignity.'*

Criticism has been made of the conditions Zambian workers experience working at these investments, including the salaries and safety conditions. In 2005, 49 miners were killed in an accident at the Chinese-owned Chambishi mine in the Copperbelt and in 2006 five miners were shot dead by police during violent protests over working conditions at the same mine.

IRIN News, 5 February 2007

Flows of private African finance shifted from a net inflow during the 1970s, to gradual outflows during the 1980s and substantial outflows during the 1990s.

Official outflows out of Africa from residents have, on average, exceeded US$10 billion a year between 1998 and 2004. The total overseas accounts of African citizens in northern banks and tax havens was estimated at $80 billion in 2003, while African countries owed $30 billion to those same banks (Bond, 2006). These outflows have been linked to economic policies (exchange rate valuation), high-risk ratings, indebtedness, political instability and corruption (Sundberg and Gelb, 2006; ECA, African Ministers of Finance, 1999; Collier *et al.*, 1999).

Flows of private African finance shifted from a net inflow during the 1970s, to gradual outflows during the 1980s and substantial outflows during the 1990s.

The depletion of non-renewable resources and the consumption by the north of the global commons represents a further loss to the region. In any fair framework of global resource allocation, the amounts owed to the continent would easily cover debt repayments.

Global commons are natural assets that are public goods, deemed important to the international community. Individual countries cannot address them adequately so they are best addressed multilaterally and collectively. They consist of, for example, the oceans, outer space and the atmosphere. They are sometimes taken to include the shared intellectual commons of the internet and culture.

The depletion of non-renewable resources and the consumption by the north of the global commons, particularly the earth's clean air, represents a further loss to the region. In any fair framework of global resource allocation, the amounts owed to the continent would easily cover debt repayments.

For example, according to the UNDP, the estimated value of minerals in South Africa's soil fell from US$112 billion in 1960 to US$55 billion in 2000. Forests in the south absorbing carbon from the atmosphere in effect provide northern polluters with an estimated annual subsidy of US$75 billion. A method used by the World Bank to measure resource depletion suggests a country's potential gross domestic product falls by 9 per cent for every percentage point increase in a country's extractive-resource dependency. This implies, for example, that in 2000 Gabon's people lost US$2,241 each, based on oil company extraction of oil resources, with little investment and few royalties provided in return (Bond, 2006). This huge continental loss through depletion of natural non-renewable resources dwarfs the estimated US$150 per capita needed to meet the Millennium Development Goals and the additional costs of AIDS prevention and treatment, discussed in Section 4. As suggested by the inequities represented in figures 2.2a and 2.2b, reclaiming the value of these resources globally could make a significant difference to organising

Figure 2.2a Global cartogram with country sizes proportional to energy consumption

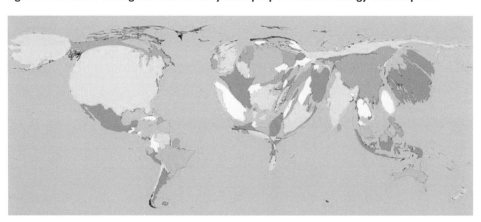

Figure 2.2b Global cartogram with country sizes proportional to population living with HIV and AIDS

Source: Newman, 2006, www-personal.umich.edu/~mejn/cartograms/

a fairer and more autonomous mobilisation of resources for African countries to respond to their health demands.

The drain of resources to debt repayments further depletes resources for health, as African countries continue to spend more on debt than on health. The continent now repays more on debt than it ever received, with debt repayment outflows equivalent to three times the inflow in loans and, in most African countries, far exceeding export earnings. As shown in table 2.5, debt repayments during the 1980s and 1990s were 4.2 times the continent's original 1980 debt and three times the current inflow of loans, with a net flow deficit by 2000 of US$6.2 billion.

This outflow of resources through debt servicing and liberalised currency markets has left significantly less discretionary public funding, including for health, with some correlation with reduced public health expenditure (see figure 2.3).

The continent now repays more on debt than it ever received, with debt repayment outflows equivalent to three times the inflow in loans and, in most African countries, far exceeding export earnings.

Table 2.5 Africa's debt and repayments: 1980 to 2002

Total foreign debt:	$61 billion (1980) ➔ $206 billion (2002)
Debt to GDP ratio:	23% (1980) ➔ 66% (2002)
Loan to repayment ratio:	$9.6 billion : $3.2 billion (1980) ➔ $3.2 billion : $9.8 billion (2000)
Net flow:	+$6.4 billion ➔ -$6.2 billion
Overall repayment: $255 billion (1980s–90s) or 4.2 times original 1980 debt	

Source: World Bank, 2002

Figure 2.3 Public expenditure on health by debt service levels, east and southern Africa

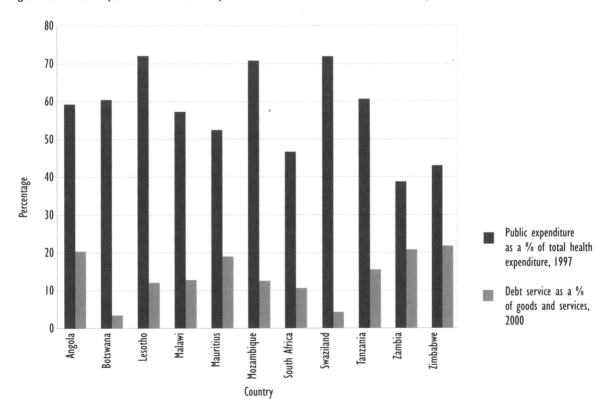

Source: World Bank, 2002b

Both globally and in the region, there has been significant pressure for debt cancellation:

> '*We, southern and northern people's movements and organisations… recognise that the accelerating processes of globalisation have only extended and exacerbated the debt crisis, one of the worst scourges afflicting humanity. … Debt is used as a tool of control over exploited and impoverished countries. Debt domination must be ended immediately. The injustice and poverty caused by debt must be ended and reparations made for its consequences. The plunder of natural resources and the exploitation of peoples carried out in order to guarantee debt servicing must be ended. The use of debt to impose policies such as neo-liberalism on the countries of the south must be ended. ….This cancellation must not be linked to externally imposed conditions.*
>
> *Cancel all illegitimate and odious debt now. Don't owe, won't pay!*'
>
> Declaration of Havana South-North Consultation on Resistance and Alternatives to Debt Domination Havana, Cuba, 28–30 September 2005, Jubilee South, 2005

Pressure from states and civil society globally has triggered a series of debt relief measures, first under the Heavily-Indebted Poor Countries initiative (HIPC), covering 32 sub-Saharan Africa countries, then, after the 2005 Gleneagles G8 Summit, through the proposal to cancel 100 per cent of outstanding debts of eligible countries to the International Monetary Fund, the International Development Association (the lending section of the World Bank) and the African Development Fund (G8 Finance ministers, 2005).

Experience from the first round of the Heavily-Indebted Poor Countries initiative suggests that while there has been increased social spending in support of poverty reduction, this has mainly benefited the education sector, with much smaller increases in expenditure in the health sector. Nevertheless, debt cancellation holds promise, as does the requirement that public revenue released through debt relief be spent on social services. There are still concerns, however, about the long period over which this will take effect (40 years) levering quite small annual reductions in debt burdens in the face of significant immediate deficits in health and the health system (Abugre, 2005):

> '*The hope that Africa's external debt will be significantly reduced under the Highly Indebted Poor Countries initiative and that economic reforms will stimulate private capital inflows has been very slow to materialise. Although Africa's debt stock declined considerably relative to gross domestic product, total debt service obligations remained unchanged in 2006 due to rising interest rates. The debt burden seriously constrains spending on public investment and ultimately retards growth and employment generation.*'
>
> African Union and UNECA, 2007

Debt cancellation holds promise, as does the requirement that public revenue released through debt relief be spent on social services.

Figure 2.4 Third world aid trends, 1965–2004: official development assistance as a percentage of gross national income

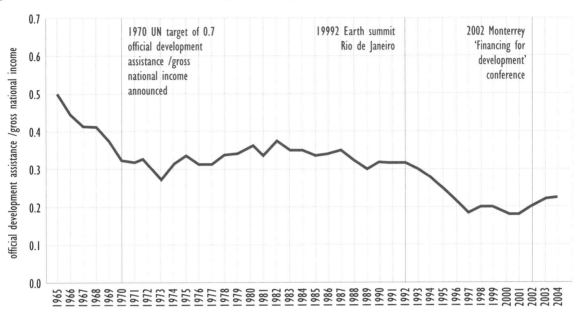

Source: ActionAid, 2005

With foreign direct investment highly concentrated in a small number of countries, official development aid is a significant source of capital inflows for many east and southern Africa countries. The rise in new sources of funds, like the Global Fund for AIDS, Tuberculosis and Malaria, in the context of these falls in public revenue have meant that external financing is now more visible in the financing of health systems. This has led to greater attention being focused on the influence and effectiveness of aid.

A recent analysis of aid in a quarterly review of the International Monetary Fund summarises the trends (Sundberg and Gelb, 2006). The real levels of aid dropped 40 per cent during the 1990s, increased up to 2005 and fell again globally in 2006. Excluding debt relief for Nigeria, real levels of aid to sub-Saharan Africa rose by only 2 per cent in 2006 (OECD DAC, 2007). With rising gross national income in many Organisation for Economic Co-operation and Development countries, average contributions of 0.3 per cent of gross national income fell well below the United Nations agreed target of 0.7 per cent of gross national income (OECD DAC, 2007; see figure 2.4). In 2006 only Sweden, Luxembourg, Norway, the Netherlands and Denmark met this commitment.

A substantial share of total official aid is directed towards administrative costs and foreign advisors or tied to exports or firms from funding countries and so does not cross the borders of the donor country. Technical co-operation and tied aid together are estimated to comprise up to a third of the bilateral aid for Africa. Removing the administrative and debt relief components leaves only 38 per cent of total aid for project and programme financing (Sundberg and Gelb, 2006). Action Aid (2005) estimated that out of total official aid of US$69 billion in 2003, only US$27 billion was finally directly disbursed as aid for poor people).

Technical co-operation and tied aid together are estimated to comprise up to a third of the bilateral aid for Africa. Removing the administrative and debt relief components leaves only 38 per cent of total aid for project and programme financing.

Levels of per capita aid have not in the past correlated well with indicators of social need, like lower human development index ratings (UNDP, 2005). Aid has been criticised for being more linked to geopolitical aims than development objectives, while conflict, corruption and instability in Africa are reported to have eroded the gains from prior external funding (Sundberg and Gelb, 2006; ECA Ministers of Finance, 1999). Recent assessment suggests that these trends are changing, with improved responsiveness to policy and poverty levels, greater focus on country ownership and mutual accountability, and with strengthened public resource management and financial monitoring (Sundberg and Gelb, 2006).

> As increasingly recognised, ... real aid inflows do not match the outflows from the continent described in this section and aid cannot substitute for measures to provide fair returns in global trade and investment. An effective response to the outflows must thus be a part of any sustainable strategy to reclaim the resources for health.

As increasingly recognised, however, including in global platforms, real aid inflows do not match the outflows from the continent described in this section and aid cannot substitute for measures to provide fair returns in global trade and investment (UNDP, 2005).

An effective response to the outflows must thus be a part of any sustainable strategy to reclaim the resources for health.

Reclaiming resources for health

Reform proposals for over two decades have suggested that African poverty can be reversed through 'a stronger climate for investment and market access', with higher levels of integration into the global economy through increasing export-led growth and increasingly liberalised trade. The evidence on the economic outcomes of these strategies, drawing on lived experience from the region, raises serious questions about this strategy and particularly about its ability to deliver on policy goals of enhanced domestic investment and savings, diversified industry and wider access to land and capital for production (African Union, UN ECAS 2007). One example of the basis for these concerns is described opposite and relates to Zambia's structural adjustment programme.

East and southern Africa countries face significant challenges to negotiate and secure fairer returns from the global economy. Equally, options are being raised for strategic management, control and use of domestic resources.

Various policy options have been raised to create negative incentives for outflows. They include the following measures:

- improving disclosure of financial flows;
- systematically defaulting on third world debt repayments;
- enforcing domestic reinvestment of pension, insurance and other institutional funds using well-tested strategies, such as prescribed assets;
- regulating financial transfers from offshore tax havens on a national scale, to control capital flight, as part of re-establishing exchange controls;
- refusing offers of tied or phantom aid;

- for trade relations, pursuing strategies and applying trade incentives that develop and protect infant industries;

- carefully calculating the costs of foreign direct investment (not simply the benefits), including natural resource depletion, transfer pricing and profit/dividend outflows;

- refusing investment where such calculations are not favourable;

- imposing taxes on currency transfers (Tobin taxes); and

- making ecological reparations.

Bond, 2006

New study attributes Zambian economic fall in 1990s to World Bank and International Monetary Fund intervention

A World Development Movement report claims that reforms forced on Zambia by the World Bank and the International Monetary Fund 'directly resulted in making tens of thousands unemployed, destroyed key industries, caused extensive social unrest and increasing poverty'. The report, 'Zambia: condemned to debt', charts the link between 'sweeping trade liberalisation, deregulation, dismantling of the public sector and massive privatisation' and a drop of 36 places in Zambia's United Nations human development ranking between 1990 and 2001.

Reduced import tariffs on textile products and used clothes resulted in large-scale import of cheap second-hand clothing, and a closure of 132 textile manufacturing firms over the decade, with a loss of 30,000 jobs. 'We used to supply retailers with three and a half thousand tonnes of clothing annually, we're down to less than 500 tonnes now,' Ramesh Patel from a textile company is quoted as saying. The firm that employed 250 people eight years ago now employs 25.

The World Bank itself acknowledged in 2000 that removal of subsidies on maize and fertilisers had led to 'stagnation and regression instead of helping Zambia's agricultural sector'. The 'one-size-fits all' privatisation programme has meant that 'many companies have collapsed, jobs have been lost and welfare programmes have not been continued by private companies'. Zambian president, Levy Mwanawasa, stated in 2003 that the International Monetary Fund privatisation programme had 'been of no significant benefit to the country. Privatisation of crucial state enterprises has led to poverty, asset stripping and job losses'. The failed policies led to widespread dissatisfaction, with government caught between social protest and pressure from the International Monetary Fund and the World Bank. The World Development Movement asserts:

> 'It is not acceptable that these institutions have effective control over policy-making in countries like Zambia. Policies need to be developed which are genuinely homegrown alternatives that put the Zambian people, especially the poor, first.'

Suri, 2004

Orange farm water crisis committee blockades the Golden Highway

Residents of Orange farm, organised under the banner of the Orange farm water crisis committee, have blockaded the Golden Highway in frustration at the way in which their local councillors are responding to their needs for decent water, sanitation, electricity and housing. They are calling for the council to take responsibility for the behaviour of the private enterprises now running these basic services. After a day of shootings and arrests, residents agreed to call off the blockade, with an agreement from the local councillors to meet. Armed with the slogan 'No peace without development', the residents demanded that the needs and voices of residents be heard in current discussions and plans for service delivery in the area.

> *'People are tired of waiting and talking. We don't want any more meetings. Our demand is simple – free basic services now. We have been waiting for too long for decent water, sanitation, houses and electricity. Our government says that it is bringing development to poor communities, but what kind of development is it when we are still living without electricity, when we get our water from tanks and when we are expected to take care of our own sanitation needs? We are fighting for the better life that we fought for under apartheid.'*

Indymedia South Africa, 2006

At grassroots level, activism has been increasing around the unacceptable exclusion that results from basic services being commercialised or sold, around trade rules that undermine access to medicines and around economic policies that undermine living wages or access to social services.

Many of these measures have greater purchase in south-south dialogue or in measures applied by specific groups of countries than in global forums. Some are being explored through regional co-operation. At grassroots level, activism has been increasing around the unacceptable exclusion that results from basic services being commercialised or sold, around trade rules that undermine access to medicines and around economic policies that undermine living wages or access to social services.

To give concrete focus to these options, in the remainder of this section we explore more closely the issues and strategies for better access to food and medicines – two areas vital for health, as shown in Section 1.

Food sovereignty as a means to improve nutrition

Food is increasingly considered just another commodity and food security is now defined in terms of the market. This is a radical departure from one of the traditional functions of states – to be in control of food production so they can feed their population (Devereux and Maxwell, 2001). As a senior United States official boldly stated to the World Trade Organisation (McMichael, 1994:127):

'The idea that developing countries should feed themselves is an anachronism from a bygone era. They could better ensure their food security by relying on United States agricultural products, which are available, in most cases, at much lower cost.'

Economic policies that promote food imports and increase the influence and power of large corporate producers were described earlier. Countries in the region are nutritionally vulnerable, with relatively high levels of underweight children. Ten of the 16 countries have more than 20 per cent of children underweight and chronic under-nutrition is up to 2.6 times higher amongst lower income groups than higher income groups (see table 2.6).

Table 2.6 Nutrition levels and inequalities across income groups in east and southern Africa

	% <5 year child under-nutrition (using weight for age) 1995-2003	Survey year for data	Ratio bottom quintile to top quintile <5 year child under-nutrition (using height for age)
Angola	31	...	n.a.
Botswana	13	...	n.a.
DRC	31	...	n.a.
Kenya	20	1998	2.6
Lesotho	18	...	n.a.
Madagascar	33	1997	1.0
Malawi	22	2000	1.1
Mauritius	15	...	n.a.
Mozambique	24	1997	1.6
Namibia	24	2000	2.0
South Africa	12	1998	n.a.
Swaziland	10	...	n.a.
Tanzania	29	1999	1.8
Uganda	23	2000	1.4
Zambia	28	2001	1.4
Zimbabwe	13	1999	1.5

n.a. = data not available

Source: UNDP, 2005

While the Millennium Development Goal target in the region is to halve the proportion of underweight children, the proportion and absolute number of malnourished children in the region has actually increased (see figure 2.5), particularly in east Africa (UN SCN, 2004).

In Lesotho, Malawi, Mozambique, Swaziland, Zambia and Zimbabwe, available large-scale nutritional survey data over the last ten years show that the slow national trend towards improved nutrition in the 1990s ceased by the end of the decade and the situation remained static or deteriorated thereafter (UNICEF, 2003). In the United Nations' *Fifth report on the world nutrition situation*, only three out of ten African countries with maternal nutrition data showed a reduction in the prevalence of severe maternal under-nutrition (BMI<16) in the last decade (UN SCN, 2004). While under-nutrition in the region halved in the 1970s and 1980s, after 1990, under a period of intensifying market reforms, it increased significantly (Chopra, 2004).

Surveillance of nutritional status is part of most demographic health surveys in the region and is also measured by distinct national surveys. These data represent a rich source of information to help identify health inequalities and monitor trends. The trends in child underweight prevalence from these sources for selected east and southern African countries (see figure 2.6) show that, until recently, Malawi, Mozambique and Zambia had about 25–30 per cent underweight prevalence, almost double that of Zimbabwe. Lesotho experienced lower rates of below 20 per cent, while Zimbabwe experienced an improvement after 2002, despite experiencing a drought (Mason *et al.*, 2006).

Figure 2.5 Trends in child malnutrition in developing countries 1990–2000

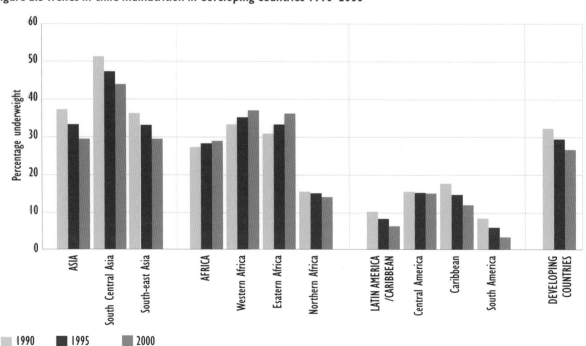

Source: UN SCN, 2004

While further analysis needs to be done of the specific determinants of these various trends, nutritional status of children has been associated with improved household food security, levels of care, maternal education, access to primary health care services and management of HIV and AIDS (Chopra, 2004; Chopra and Tomlinson, 2007). Conversely, poor nutrition exacerbates poor living and social environments, increasing the risk of disease, vulnerability to illness and the impoverishing effect of illness.

© M Ndlovu and TARSC

The evidence suggests that socio-economic conditions are an important determinant of nutritional outcomes and that worsening nutrition is likely to be a key driver for inequalities in health in east and southern Africa (Chopra and Tomlinson, 2007; UN SCN, 2004). Climate and environmental changes intensify these factors so are likely to make food security an increasing rather than a diminishing challenge in the future. While effective supplementary feeding and drought relief programmes can mitigate these impacts, they make nutritional wellbeing very dependent on emergency relief.

Improved nutrition calls for policies that will deliberately direct resources towards smallholder production and avoid the increased ownership of land, capital and other assets being vested in big corporates in the food sector, so that households are better resourced to produce their own food.

Improved nutrition calls for policies that will deliberately direct resources towards smallholder production and avoid the increased ownership of land, capital and other assets in big corporates in the food sector, so that households are better resourced to produce food.

Figure 2.6 National trends in underweight prevalence in selected east and southern Africa countries

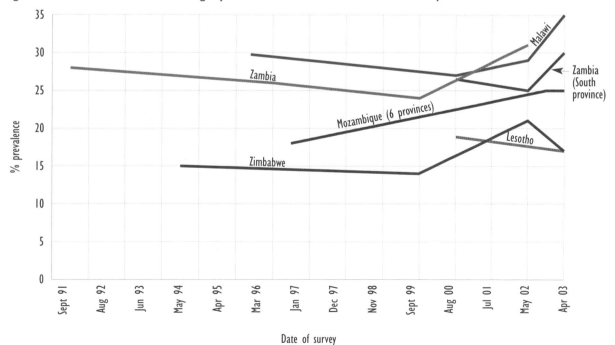

Source: Mason *et al.*, 2006

This call was made by Southern African Development Community (SADC) ministers of agriculture in 2004:

> 'Ministers reaffirmed the right of SADC citizens to have access to safe, adequate and nutritious food all the time and by all the people for an active and healthy life. Ministers also reaffirmed the importance of water for household use ...
>
> 'Ministers noted with concern that financial flows to agriculture from both public and private sources have declined over time; hence a considerable level of investment in the agricultural sector is required in order to achieve the objectives of food security and economic growth... The Maputo African Union Declaration of July 2003 called for an increase in member states' budgetary allocation of 'at least 10 per cent of national budgetary resources' to agriculture and rural development within five years. Ministers reaffirmed the need to meet this target at national level.
>
> 'Ministers encouraged SADC member states to explore innovative financing instruments that promote private and public resource mobilisation that could be used to finance agricultural activities including marketing, irrigation, agro-processing, infrastructure, rehabilitation of degraded areas, capacity building and the provision of credit at grassroots level.
>
> 'Ministers stressed that poverty reduction and food security strategies should, inter alia, include measures to increase agricultural production, productivity and food availability. Ministers expressed commitment to promote equal access for men and women, as well as child-headed households, to land, credit, technology and other key agricultural inputs. Ministers in particular, reaffirmed the need to support empowerment of women, recognising and valuing their vital role in agriculture and food security.'

SADC ministers of food, agriculture and natural resources, 2004

Local market produce at harvest time: Malawi
Source: B Goddard

The policy framework that appears to have greatest potential to address these social determinants of under-nutrition appears to be one of food sovereignty. Food sovereignty includes the following measures:

- prioritising food production for domestic and local markets, based on peasant and family farmer diversified and agro-ecologically based production systems;

- ensuring fair prices for farmers, which means the power to protect internal markets from low-priced, dumped imports;

- providing access to land, water, forests, fishing areas and other productive resources through genuine redistribution;

- recognising and promoting women's role in food production and giving women equitable access and control over productive resources with decision-making powers;

- ensuring public and community rights to use and manage land, water, seeds, livestock and biodiversity;

- protecting seeds – the basis of food and life itself – for free exchange and use by farmers, which means no patents on life and a moratorium on genetically modified crops; and

- making public investment to support families and communities' productive activities, geared towards empowerment, local control and production of food for people and local markets (Food First, 2003).

While food sovereignty approaches have many potential links to health, we explore two examples more directly linked to improved nutrition:

Nutrition improves when agricultural policies give priority to women smallholders

Women are responsible for 80 per cent of food production in Africa, including the most labour-intensive work, such as planting, fertilising, irrigating, weeding, harvesting and marketing. They achieve this despite unequal access to land (less than 1 per cent of land is owned by women), unequal inputs such as credit (less than 10 per cent of credit provided to small farmers goes to women), poor access to improved seeds and fertiliser, and unequal access to information. Their work extends to food preparation, as well as nurturing activities.

Although evidence is limited, the changes wrought by globalisation in the agricultural sector appear to widen gender inequalities. Women's involvement in harmful cash crops, such as tobacco, or the use of food crops for commercial sales where they do not control the income, such as alcohol brewing, can lead to food insecurity and undernutrition (Nangawe *et al.*, 1998). Shifts in trade and investment that support large-scale commercial farmers appear to do so at the expense of women smallholder farmers. This increases the likelihood of women becoming low-wage labour for export-orientated commercial farming concerns (Chopra, 2004). Unequal rights and obligations within the household, as well as limited time and financial resources, place much greater constraints on

Woman farmer
Source: DFID, 2007

women than men. Given equal access to resources and human capital, women farmers can achieve equal or even, as some studies show, significantly higher yields than men (Saito *et al.*, 1992). Where women's productivity improves, the household gains are also more likely to be used to improve the wellbeing of children in the household, with a positive impact on childhood nutritional status (Kennedy, 1991; Haddad and Hoddentot, 1994; Jones, 1986).

Nutrition improvements are sustained when solutions to hunger and nutritional crises reinforce local markets and household food production

Frequent drought and the acute hunger associated with drought in conditions of chronic poverty strengthened the triangle of food aid in the region: agribusiness, the shipping industry and charitable organisations. According to Jere (2007), just four companies and their subsidiaries, led by Archer Daniels Midland and Cargill, sold more than half the US$700 million in food commodities provided through the United States Agency for International Development's (USAID) food aid programme in 2004. Just five shipping companies received over half the more than US$300 million spent to ship that food. A number of large non-governmental organisations used food aid for a quarter to half of their budgets.

This form of external food aid, however, raises concerns about its effect on local food markets and production, and the extent to which it displaces local food production and reduces investment in local production. Experiences of food aid in Malawi, described opposite, suggest that negative effects of food aid on local production can be reduced with improved policy and programme co-ordination, and by making stronger links with local food markets in the investment in and procurement of food.

Food aid in Malawi

Persistent food deficits in Malawi in the past five years can be attributed to reduced maize production due to poor rains, lack of inputs and infertile soils. The deficits were bridged through a mixture of food aid, commercial imports and informal cross-border trade:

- Programme food aid was provided to the government as conditional loans or grants mainly to provide balance of payment and budgetary support for subsidised food in local markets and to build up strategic food reserves.

- Project food aid was provided as grants in support of specific development objectives and beneficiary groups through non-governmental organisations.

- Relief food aid, provided as a grant, was distributed to targeted beneficiaries to address critical food needs.

Malawi has no explicit policy framework for food aid despite its growing size and importance, although policies on economic growth and development, food security, safety nets and disasters have relevance.

Evidence from food aid programmes this decade indicate that imported food aid has had a negative effect on local production. For example, World Food Programme assessments found that free humanitarian food aid supplies reduced demand for commercial maize, resulting in unintended excess commercial maize stocks, dampening consumer and producer prices, and putting pressure on the government budget as they were financed through domestic borrowing. Response to such evidence in 2005/06 led to better co-ordination between donor, government, United Nations and non-governmental organisation responses, with increased stakeholder participation and an increase in the local procurement of food aid products.

Jere, 2007

Decisions on the design of such schemes to source food locally to fulfil aid requirements are not made in the health sector but health systems can lever approaches and partnerships with agriculture, education, social protection and other sectors to support food sovereignty. For example, an integrated approach involving home-based caregivers, orphan committees, agricultural extension agents and health workers can ensure that food, school fee relief, home gardens and health care go directly to families that most need them (IFAD, 2001).

How well are these options currently being implemented? While school feeding programmes have spread regionally, an analysis of such programmes in Malawi and South Africa indicates that despite their health, education and poverty reduction goals, the programmes are not adequately linked to wider nutritional or agrarian policies and are often localised, vertically provided and inconsistent (Tomlinson, 2007). Generally, local farmers have not been supported with the resources and opportunities to provide schools with food products. The New Economic Partnership for African Development's (NEPAD) comprehensive Africa agriculture development programme (CAADP *et al.*, 2003) includes a flagship homegrown school feeding programme that emphasises stimulating local food production but this recommendation has not been implemented (Tomlinson, 2007). Some nutrition interventions for people living with HIV and AIDS use a comprehensive approach but are often limited to specific geographical areas and need to be scaled up.

Experiences such as those described on the page opposite suggest that options are available for more effective strategic leveraging of food sovereignty approaches in east and southern Africa. These can be the bridge between strategies for mitigating immediate nutritional problems and longer-term improvement in household production and incomes. The SADC commitment to a budgetary allocation of 'at least 10 per cent of national budgetary resources' to agriculture and rural development within five years, preferentially allocated to smallholder and women's production, is an important basis for domestic financing of this. This investment will have greatest leverage value for health and nutrition if countries provide a policy framework and comprehensive guidelines linking nutrition interventions to plans to increase access to land and capital, mobilise resource inputs for local production and stimulate local market linkages, especially for smallholder and women producers.

Health centre discussion on affordable local foods for healthy nutrition
Source: B Goddard

Experiences of nutritional support for people living with HIV and AIDS in east and southern Africa

Several Ugandan ministries have initiated an AIDS control programme to strengthen AIDS education, promote nutrition standards for people living with HIV and AIDS and their families, and to reduce poverty by establishing energy and time saving agro-enterprises making people better equipped to cope with the epidemic. Support from international agencies is organised to complement this, including agricultural and market support to small-scale farmers from the World Food Programme and micro-credit support from the Belgian Survival Fund.

A number of Kenyan non-governmental organisation programmes promote household access to savings and credit, while both state and non-governmental organisation programmes offer various dimensions of support to household food production, access and nutritional sufficiency. The food for work project contributes to public infrastructures, including village roads, small-scale irrigation and planting vegetation on restored physical structures in order to minimise soil and water erosion. The Nyanza healthy water project aims to improve the quality of household drinking water. The Siaya-Busia household livelihood security project supports safe water and sanitation interventions and inputs to improve farm productivity of staple foods. The livestock marketing enterprise project assists pastoralists from north eastern Kenya in accessing and benefiting from livestock markets.

In Zimbabwe, comprehensive guidelines provide a framework for links between food security activities and interventions on HIV and AIDS, such as the connection made by the World Food Programme between nutritional support to pregnant and lactating women and prevention of mother-to-child transmission services.

The Mozambique government has plans to distribute multi-micronutrient supplements to all people living with HIV and AIDS using a clinic and community-based approach, and to provide a corn-soy blend food supplement and agreed food basket to various target groups, including patients on antiretrovirals and those HIV positive patients with chronic illnesses. The Food and Agriculture Organisation supported junior farmer field and life schools for children and young people to share agricultural knowledge, business skills and life skills with orphans and vulnerable children between 12 and 18 years of age.

Atekyereza and Panagides, 2007

Protecting health in trade agreements

Earlier in this section, we observed how trade policies can privilege countries and economic activities in ways that weaken household productivity and incomes and increase the outflow of resources from the region. Trade is thus having an increasing influence on health, not only through these effects on the determinants of and the resources for health, but more directly through the spectrum of health issues covered by bilateral and World Trade Organisation agreements (see table 2.7).

Trade agreements can foster changes in the ownership and organisation of health systems, affecting access and health outcomes (Fidler, 1999). To exemplify this, this analysis focuses on access to medicines, while noting many other areas of impact on health in table 2.7.

Patents give those who hold them a monopoly on the production and sale of an invention.

Patents are now covered under trade law, with Trade Related Intellectual Property Rights (TRIPS) rules obliging states to grant patent owners at least 20 years of exclusive commercial rights to make or sell their inventions, such as medicines. While this aims to protect research and development investments, it allows patent holders to keep patented drug prices artificially high, putting them out of reach to many. Generic medicines have been a core feature of essential drug lists in the region and, as will be described in Section 3, they are central to expanding access to health care. With mark-ups of patented drugs often a significant factor in high medicine costs, the manufacture and marketing of generic medicines can significantly reduce the cost of medicines.

Table 2.7 Health issues and relevant World Trade Organisation agreements

WTO rules	Sanitary and phytosanitary measures	Technical barriers to trade	Trade-related intellectual property rights (TRIPS)	General agreement on trade in services (GATS)
Health issues	■	■	■	■
Infectious disease control	■	■		
Food safety	■		■	■
Tobacco control		■	■	■
Environment	■	■		■
Access to drugs			■	
Health services				■
Food security	■		■	■
Biotechnology	■	■	■	
Information technology			■	
Traditional knowledge			■	

Source: Drager, 2004

Procurement of higher cost imported drugs drains resources from health systems and for many years has been a barrier to access to treatment. Public health principles were asserted over trade rules at the 2001 Doha World Trade Organisation ministerial meeting in the face of massive public health needs, clear experience of the value of generic drugs, significant treatment activism and south-south governmental pressures. The 2001 Doha Declaration (article 4) provided that the TRIPS agreement 'can and should be interpreted and implemented in a manner supportive of World Trade Organisation members' right to protect public health and, in particular, of access to medicines for all'.

This important recognition of the demand for trade to protect and promote health gave authority to use flexibilities in the TRIPS agreement in the interest of public health by:

- giving transition periods for laws to be TRIPS-compliant;
- providing in law for compulsory licensing or the right to grant a licence, without permission from the licence holder, on various grounds including public health;
- providing in law for parallel importation or the right to import products patented in one country from a country where the price is lower;
- providing for exceptions from patentability and limits on data protection; and
- providing for early working, know as the Bolar provision, allowing generic producers to conduct tests and obtain health authority approvals before a patent expires, making cheaper generic drugs available more quickly at that time.

Compulsory licences are issued by countries to import drugs without permission of the licence holder for those drugs.

Parallel importation is when governments import, without permission of the patent holder, a product manufactured under a patent held in one country but sold at lower prices in another country.

For example, after the Zimbabwe government declared a national emergency on HIV and AIDS in 2002 (as provided for in Zimbabwe law) it issued compulsory licences to three local companies to either import or produce four antiretroviral varieties at about a third of the cost of patented products, leading to price reductions in the antiretroviral, Zerit, from US$400 in 2001 to US$30 in 2002 (Musungu and Oh, 2006). Similarly, Mozambique granted a compulsory licence to a local company, Pharco Mozambique Ltd, for the local manufacture of the triple compound of generic antiretroviral drugs.

East and southern African countries need to amend their laws to use these flexibilities. All countries in the region are World Trade Organisation members and most have least developed country status (see table 2.8 on page 64). This gives them until 2016 to be TRIPS compliant. Some east and southern Africa countries have, however, still not enacted these flexibilities, won at Doha (see table 2.9 on page 64).

The legal provisions are not complex, as exemplified by the comprehensive TRIPS-compliant national laws already developed in some east and southern Africa countries.

Table 2.8 World Trade Organisation status of countries in east and southern Africa in 1995*

Country	Least developed	Developing
Angola	■	
Botswana		■
DRC	■	
Kenya		■
Lesotho	■	
Malawi	■	
Mauritius		■
Mozambique	■	
Namibia		■
South Africa		■
Swaziland		■
Tanzania	■	
Uganda	■	
Zambia	■	
Zimbabwe		■

*Least developed country status at the World Trade Organisation is negotiable at any time.

Source: United Nations OHRLLS, 2007

Table 2.9 Use of TRIPS flexibilities in east and southern Africa in 1995*

Country	LDC (to be TRIPS compliant law by 2016)	Law provides for compulsory licence	Law provides for parallel importation
Angola	YES		
Botswana		YES	
DRC	YES	YES	
Kenya		YES	YES
Lesotho	YES		
Malawi	YES	YES	
Mauritius		YES	YES
Mozambique	YES	YES	
Namibia			
South Africa		YES	YES
Swaziland		YES	YES
Tanzania	YES	YES	YES
Uganda	YES	YES	YES
Zambia	YES	YES	
Zimbabwe		YES	YES

LDC = least developed country

Source: EQUINET, SEATINI, CHP and TARSC, 2006

Legislating **TRIPS** flexibility to protect access to generic medicines in Kenya

Kenyan law permits parallel importation of patented medicines previously sold abroad and of generic medicine produced pursuant to a compulsory licence as provided for in TRIPS, article 6. Kenya applies 'international exhaustion' which implies that the exclusive right of a patent holder to import a product is exhausted and ends when that product is launched on the market.

Kenya Industrial property Act 2001 Section 58(2)

The rights under the patent shall not extend to acts in respect of articles which have been put on the market in Kenya or in any other country or imported into Kenya.

Kenya Industrial Property Act 2001 Section 80 (1) a and b

(1a) Upon exercising the powers conferred upon him under subsection (1), the Minister may, notwithstanding any of the measures set out in this section, authorise by written order the importation, manufacture or supply, or authorise the utilisation of any molecule or substance whatsoever by any individual, corporation or society as named or described by any individual, corporation or society as named or described in the order without notice to the patent holder or any other notifiable party, and such order shall remain in force until revoked by the minister in writing, after giving six months' prior notice of his intention of such revocation to the party named or described in the order.

(1b) An order made under the subsection (1a) shall not require the payment of compensation to the owner of the patent or licence holder or any other party so interested by the Minister in writing, giving six months prior notice of intention of such revocation to the party named or described in the order.

Musungu and Oh, 2006

Countries that do not yet have provisions in their laws for compulsory licensing and parallel importation are thus encouraged to:

* include these provisions in their law;
* provide deferred implementation and enforcement of pharmaceutical patents until 2016;
* specify as many of the possible grounds for issuing compulsory licences to avoid ambiguity or uncertainty;
* provide in competition law for issuing a compulsory licence on the basis of unfair competition in line with article 31(k) of TRIPS;

- include explicit provisions for the waiver of negotiations with the patent holder in cases of compulsory licensing for government use or for national emergencies;

- provide explicit provisions for the waiver of remuneration paid to the patent holder in importing countries;

- provide for time limitations for negotiation for voluntary licences in circumstances where compulsory licences are not applied, after which time the requirement shall be deemed satisfied and a compulsory licence granted;

- provide for international exhaustion of intellectual property rights;

- provide swift procedures and clear guidance in law for royalty rates so granting compulsory licences is not held up in legal appeals and royalty squabbles; and

- ensure other health and pharmaceutical laws are amended if they affect the application of these flexibilities (EQUINET, SEATINI, CHP, TARSC, 2006).

Experience shows that efforts to enact and use these laws encounter many obstacles in the wider global environment. Five years after Doha, 75 per cent of antiretrovirals in developing countries are still under monopoly, with no generics available in some countries (Act-Up, 2006). East and southern African countries implementing TRIPS flexibilities lack information about options for accessing cheaper generic medicines and about the status of patents in countries importing and exporting particular medicines. Rich countries have in the past exerted diplomatic, trade and political pressure, through trade-related technical assistance and bilateral trade agreements, to interpret TRIPS flexibilities narrowly and deter countries from using them. This occurred in the United States–Southern African Customs Union (SACU) free trade agreement negotiations. Signing agreements with TRIPS-plus rules may undermine the regulatory flexibility needed to ensure access to affordable medicines.

...east and southern African countries justifiably seek to ensure that trade partners such as the European Union explicitly commit to not push for TRIPS-plus measures, to give east and southern Africa countries the policy space to freely use TRIPS flexibilities, to provide for political and technical support to use the safeguards under TRIPS to ensure access to affordable medicines and finally to encourage development of east and southern Africa countries' pharmaceutical industries.

This has, for example, emerged as an issue in the Economic Partnership Agreement being negotiated in 2007 between the European Union and east and southern Africa. The proposed economic partnership agreement includes intellectual property rights. In the past the European Union has used free trade agreements to push for standards that go beyond those outlined by the World Trade Organisation TRIPS agreement, such as in the free trade agreement of 1999 between the European Union and South Africa. Hence while some commitment has been expressed towards respecting TRIPS flexibilities, east and southern African countries justifiably seek to ensure that trade partners such as the European Union explicitly commit to not push for TRIPS-plus measures, to give east and southern Africa countries the policy space to freely use TRIPS flexibilities, to provide for political and technical support to use the safeguards under TRIPS to ensure access to affordable medicines and finally to encourage development of east and southern African countries' pharmaceutical industries (Mabika *et al.*, 2007).

Draft text prepared by east and southern Africa countries for negotiation thus includes important safeguards for essential medicines:

- ensuring availability of legal, institutional and human resources capacities and policy frameworks for the protection of intellectual property rights whilst respecting and safeguarding the public policies of east and southern African countries;

- ensuring the implementation of the flexibilities as is provided for under the TRIPS agreement;

- providing for enhanced incentives for the development and research into new technologies, especially in pharmaceutical products, including the production of generic medicine;

- providing support to east and southern Africa countries to enable them to benefit from the relevant provisions of the TRIPS agreement and the in-built flexibilities, especially with regard to public health, including access to pharmaceutical products at a reasonable price; and

- providing support from European Union to east and southern African countries to enact appropriate laws, formulate policies and develop infrastructure for local production of pharmaceutical products, transfer of technology and the attraction of investment in their pharmaceutical sectors (cited in Mabika *et al.*, 2007).

The challenges east and southern African countries face to protect access to medicines highlights what happens when the struggle for health is directed at challenging global trends that undermine the resources for health. However, the challenges extend beyond the region. India, the largest producer of generic drugs in the world, was required in January 2005 to grant patent protection to new drugs and to drugs invented since 1995. Subsequent World Trade Organisation provisions, known as the 'August 30th decision', provide that countries that have no capacity to manufacture generics themselves (as is the case in many east and southern African countries) are permitted to import from another country (such as India) if that country issues a compulsory licence and if both parties inform the World Trade Organisation of the nature and duration of the licence and the product quantities involved. This puts the burden on east and southern African countries to carry out the legal and institutional reforms to issue compulsory licences and adds new rules to these transactions. The new challenge is for countries in the region to exert pressure internationally for simplified procedures for such exports, and to explore other sources of cheaper generic drugs that are not covered by patents, such as from Brazil and Thailand (EQUINET, SEATINI, CHP and TARSC, 2006).

The new challenge is for countries in the region to exert pressure internationally for simplified procedures for such exports, and explore other sources of cheaper generic drugs that are not covered by patents, such as from Brazil and Thailand

This calls for high levels of exchange of information, resources and expertise across and beyond the region. In Sections 3 and 6 we discuss further how state, parliament and civil society alliances can take up and have taken up these challenges. We also point to the strategic role of regional alliances and of rights to health in giving countries leverage in negotiating and implementing policies that seek to guarantee health. Working as a region, east and southern African countries can, for example, collectively issue compulsory licences for common public health problems. This was done in Latin America where ten countries combined efforts to get agreements from generic manufacturers and originators. Regional frameworks to collectively issue compulsory licences for the same drug may build a sufficient market to encourage producers to invest in generic versions of these drugs. They provide a means to address the urgent need to protect indigenous medicines from foreign patenting, while promoting their development. Regional co-operation offers opportunities for bulk procurement of drugs to reduce costs, buffer against stock-outs and stimulate generic production. It is an essential basis for building the comparative advantage, skills and markets to engage south-south co-operation to promote local production of essential drugs.

East and southern African countries are engaging in a global economy that has produced significant disadvantages in resource outflows, sluggish growth, speculative investment and household poverty. This section highlights the challenges involved and the opportunities that exist for the region to gain greater control over the outflow of resources, implement domestically-driven strategies and secure greater returns from the global economy. It highlights why this is important for public health, focusing on the food inputs for health and the medicines essential for health care. There is a resonance between the wider economic strategies needed and effective public health strategies in both these examples. In both cases, there are policies and measures that can strengthen national and household control over the resources for health, with gains for household and national production.

What role do health professionals and health workers play in advancing such win-win strategies?

As we showed in relation to nutrition and access to medicines, health systems can make a difference in these areas, and to health equity, by providing leadership, shaping wider social norms and values, providing the public health motivation for action by other sectors and supporting work across sectors in a shared approach. As we demonstrate, both in relation to nutrition and access to medicines, the health sector in the region can play a role in providing the public health basis for levering, supporting and implementing the policies and actions that reclaim the resources for health in the global economy, and in effectively directing these resources nationally to the household level.

How do health systems best do this and what kind of health system plays that role? We take this up in the next section.

Regional co-operation offers opportunities for bulk procurement of drugs to reduce costs, buffer against stock-outs and stimulate generic production. It is an essential basis for building the comparative advantage, skills and markets to engage south-south co-operation to promote local production of drugs.

Health systems are all the activities whose primary purpose is to promote, restore, or maintain health
WHO, 2000

REFERENCES

Abugre C (2005) 'G8: Hot air and little substance,' *Pambazuka News* 215, Fahamu, Oxford.

ActionAid (2003) *Going against the grain*, ActionAid, accessed 24 August 2004 at www.actionaid.co.uk.
– (2005) *Real aid: An agenda for making aid work*, Action Aid, London.

Act-Up (2006) 'Five years later the WTO deal on access to medicines is a failure: G8 leaders must step up,' mimeo, Paris.

African Union (AU), United Nations Economic Commission for Africa (UNECA) (2007) *Accelerating Africa's development through diversification*, Ethiopia.

Atekyereza P and Panagides D (2007) 'HIV/AIDS and food and nutrition security policy and programming in eastern and southern Africa', *EQUINET discussion paper* 45, EQUINET/ Medical Research Council (MRC), South Africa.

Bond P and Dor G (2003) 'Neoliberalism and poverty reduction strategies in Africa,' *EQUINET discussion paper* 3, EQUINET, Johannesburg.

Bond P (2006) 'The dispossession of African wealth: Perverse subsidies and reverse resource flows,' *EQUINET discussion paper* 30, EQUINET, Centre for Economic Justice, Harare.

Comprehensive Africa Agriculture Development Programme, New Economic Partnership for Development, World Food Programme and Millennium Hunger Task Force (2003) *Home-grown school feeding programme*, NEPAD, Abuja.

Chopra M (2004) 'Food security, rural development and health equity in southern Africa,' *EQUINET discussion paper* 22, EQUINET, Harare.

Chopra M and Tomlinson M (2007) 'Food sovereignty and nutrition in east and southern Africa: A synthesis of case study evidence,' *EQUINET discussion paper* 47, EQUINET/ MRC, South Africa.

Collier P, Hoeffler A, Pattilo C (1999) 'Flight capital as a portfolio choice', *World Bank research working paper* 2066, accessed 7 June 2007 at http://ssrn.com/abstract=569197

Commission for Africa (2005) *Our common future*, London.

Devereux S and Maxwell S (eds) (2001) *Food security in Africa*, Intermediate Technology Development Group, London.

DfID (2007) Photograph of woman farmer, *Research 4 Development*, March 2007, accessed 7 June 2007 at http://www.research4 development.info

Drager N (2004) 'Public health implications of multilateral trade agreements', *Lausanne, June 2004*, WHO, Geneva.

Economic Commission for Africa, African finance ministers (1999) *ECA briefing on the 33rd session of the commission/24th meeting of the Conference of Ministers/ 7th Conference of African Ministers of Finance, Addis Ababa, Ethiopia 6-8 May 1999*, accessed 7 June 2007 at http://www. uneca.org/ eca_resources/major_eca_websites/joint/p76.htm

EQUINET steering committee (2004) 'Reclaiming the state: Advancing people's health, challenging injustice', *EQUINET policy paper* 15, EQUINET, Harare.

EQUINET, SEATINI, CHP and TARSC (2006) *Promoting health in trade agreements: A training kit for east and southern Africa*, EQUINET/ SEATINI, Harare.

European Union-South Africa (1999) 'Agreement on trade, development and co-operation between the EC and its member states, of the one part, and the Republic of South Africa, of the other part,' *Official Journal* L311 of 4 December 1999: 0003-0297 available at http://www.bilaterals.org/ article.php3?id_article=419

EU–Syria Association Agreement (2004) 'Proposal for a council decision on the conclusion of a Euro-Mediterranean association agreement between the European community and its member states of the one part, and the Syrian Arab Republic, of the other part', COM 17 December (2004) 808 final EU, Brussels accessed 28 February 2007 at http:// www.bilaterals.org/article.php3?id_article=2549

FAO (2004) *FAOSTAT*, FAO, Rome.

Food First (2003) *Food sovereignty*, Food First, Oakland, California, accessed at www.foodfirst.org/progs/global /food/finaldeclaration.html.

Fidler DP (November 1999) 'International law and global public health', *Law Review*, University of Kansas, Kansas.

G8 finance ministers (2005) 'G8 finance ministers agree to proposal for debt relief' accessed 2 June 2007at http:// usinfo.state.gov/ei/Archive/2005/Sep/27-620259.html

Global Policy Forum (2006) *Foreign direct investment inflows and outflows in developing regions, 1990–2004*, Global Policy Forum, New York, accessed March 2007 at www.globalpolicy.org/ socecon/ffd/fdi/tables/developingregions.htm

Government of Kenya (2001) *Industrial Property Act 2001*, Nairobi.

Haddad L and Hoddentot J (1994) 'Women's income and boy–girl nutrition outcomes in the Côte d'Ivoire', *World Development* 22 (4): 543–553.

Indymedia South Africa (3 October 2006) 'No peace without development!' Independent media centre, available at http:// southafrica.indymedia. org/news/2006/ 10/11343.php

Integrated Regional Network (IRIN) (5 February 2007) 'Zambia: Cold reception for China's president,' *IRIN News*, UN-OCHA, New York.

International Fund for Agricultural Development (IFAD) (2001) *Strategy paper on HIV and AIDS for East and Southern Africa*, IFAD, Rome.

Jere P (2007)'The impact of food aid on food markets and food security in Malawi', *EQUINET discussion paper* 45, EQUINET /MRC, South Africa.

Jones C (1986) 'Intrahousehold bargaining in response to the introduction of new crops: A case study from north Cameroon' in Moock J (ed) *Understanding Africa's rural households and farming systems*, Westview Press, USA.

Jubilee South (2005) *Declaration of Havana south-north consultation on resistance and alternatives to debt domination*, Havana, Cuba, 28–30 Sept, Jubilee South, Quezon City, available at http:// www.jubileesouth. org/news/EEuppyEpF FowVacRTa.shtml

Karingi S, Lang S, Oulmane N, Perez N, Sadni Jallab M, Hammouda HB (2005) *Economic and welfare impacts of the EU–Africa Economic Partnership Agreements*, UN ECA, ATPC Work in Progress 10, Addis Ababa.

Kennedy E (1991) 'Income sources of the rural poor in southwestern Kenya', in von Braun J and Pandya-Lorch L (eds) 'Income sources of malnourished people in rural areas: microlevel information and policy implications', *Working papers on commercialization of agriculture and nutrition 5*, International Food Policy Research Institute, Washington DC.

Kneen B (1996) *Invisible giant*, Pluto Press, London.

Lambrechts K and Barry G (2003) 'Why is southern Africa hungry? The roots of southern Africa's food crisis,' *Christian Aid policy briefing*, Christian Aid, London, at www.christianaid.org.

Mabika A, Makombe P, Chizarura L, Loewenson R (2007) 'Health implications of proposed Economic Partnership Agreement between east and southern African countries and the European Union,' *EQUINET discussion paper* 41, EQUINET/SEATINI, Harare.

Madeley J (2003) *Food for all: The need for a new agriculture*, Zed Books, London

Mason J, Gillenwater K, Pugh R, Kenefik E, Collins G, Whitaker M and Volk D (2006) 'Analysis of nutritional surveys across the ESARO region,' *Practical Analysis of Nutritional Data* (PANDA), Tulane University, New Orleans.

McMichael P (ed) (1994) *The global restructuring of agro-food systems*, Cornell University Press, Ithaca.

Milanovic B (2002) 'Can we discern the effect of globalisation on income distribution? Evidence from household budget surveys', *Policy research working paper* 2876, World Bank, Washington.

Mkandawire T (2005) 'Maladjusted African economies and globalisation', *Africa Development* 30: 1-2.

Musungu SF and Oh C (2006) *The use of flexibilities in TRIPS by developing countries: Can they promote access to medicines?* South Centre, Geneva.

Nangawe E, Simwanza E, Mubanga F (1998) *Determinants of action against malnutrition in < 5 children, Kasama district, northern Zambia*, ZPC Publications, Lusaka.

Newman MEJ (2006) *Images of the social and economic world*, Dept of Physics and Centre for the Study of Complex Systems, Univ. of Michigan, Michigan, available at www-personal.umich.edu/~mejn/cartograms/

Organisation for Economic Co-operation and Development Development Co-operation Directorate (OECD DCD-DAC) (2007) 'Development aid from OECD countries fell 5.1% in 2006' accessed June 2007 at http://www.oecd.org/docu ment/17/0,3343,en_2649_34447_38341265_1_1_1_1,00.htm

Peoples Daily Online (25 April 2006) 'Africa and Aboriginal Tuesdays: China and Africa seek a win-win', downloaded 9 March 2007 from http://www.blackelectorate.com/ print_article.asp?ID=1630

Saito KA and Mekonnen H (1992) *Raising the productivity of women farmers in sub-Saharan Africa*, World Bank, New York.

SADC ministers of food, agriculture and natural resources (2004) *Communique*, 14 February 2004, Dar es Salaam, Tanzania, SADC, Gabarone.

Sharma D (27 Nov 2005) 'Farm subsidies: The report card', *ZNet commentary*, ZNet, Massachusets.

Sundberg M, Gelb A (Dec 2006) 'Making aid work in finance and development', *IMF quarterly*, Vol 43, No 4 accessed June 2007 at http:// www.imf.org/external/pubs/ft/fandd/2006/ 12/sundberg.htm

Suri S (24 May 2004) 'If the IMF could do this to Zambia…' Inter Press Service News Agency, Rome, downloaded 1 March 2007 from http://ipsnews.net/africa/interna. asp?idnews=23882

Tomlinson M (2007) 'School feeding in ESA: Improving food sovereignty or photo opportunity?' *EQUINET discussion paper* 46, EQUINET/MRC, Cape Town.

Toussaint E (2005) *Your money or your life*, Haymarket Press, Chicago.

UNDP (2005) *Human development report 2005*, OUP, New York, accessed 2 June 2007 at http://hdr.undp.org/ reports/view_reports.cfm?type=1

UNICEF (2003) *Southern African humanitarian crisis: Review of nutrition information*, ESARO, Nairobi.

United Nations Standing Committee on Nutrition (2004) 'Nutrition for improved development outcomes', *The 5th report on the world nutrition situation: Nutrition for improved development outcomes*, UN SCN, Geneva.

UN Office for the high representative for the least developed countries, landlocked developing countries and small island developing states (2007) *List of least developed countries*, UN OHRLLS, New York, available at http://www.un.org/special-rep/ohrlls/ldc/list.htm

World Bank (2002) *Global finance tables*, Washington.
– (2002b) *World health report,* at http://devdata.worldbank. org/data-query/
– (2006) 'Changing the face of development finance?' *Global Development Finance* 2006, World Bank, New York, available at http://web.worldbank.org/WEBSITE/ EXTERNAL/NEWS /0contentMDK:20935894 ~page PK:64257043 ~piPK:437376~theSitePK:4607,00.htm

World Commission on the Social Dimension of Globalisation (2004) *A fair globalisation: Creating opportunities for all*, ILO, Geneva.

WHO (2000) *World health report: Health systems improving performance*, World Health Organisation, Geneva.

WTO (Nov 2001) 'The Doha declaration,' *The 4th ministerial meeting of WTO, Doha, Quatar*, Geneva.

Building

UNIVERSAL, COMPREHENSIVE, PEOPLE-CENTRED

HEALTH SYSTEMS

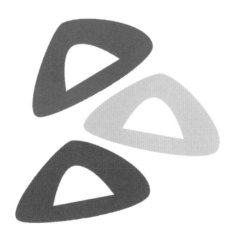

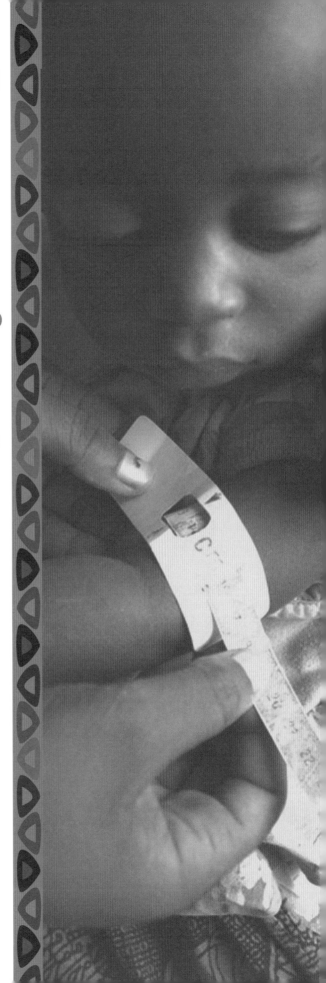

SECTION
3

KEY ISSUES

The economic and social inequality in east and southern Africa calls for health systems to play a role in redistributing resources to those with greatest health needs.

Countries in the region have done this through public sector led health systems. Increased public investment in health and comprehensive primary health care approaches have led to improved health outcomes, especially for those with greatest health needs. While such approaches spread in Africa in the 1980s, declining investment in primary health care and rising financing of vertical, disease-based programmes has occurred more recently, often in response to national resource constraints.

Economic liberalisation has been associated with commercialisation and privatisation of health services, particularly through user charges and the expansion of formal and informal for-profit services. These have had negative effects on equity and access to health care in the region, making state intervention essential to manage the market forces within health systems.

The scale of the AIDS epidemic and the limitations of vertical programmes in the context of weak health systems make the lessons learned from the roll out of prevention and treatment for HIV and AIDS strategically significant. The most enabling conditions for sustained, equitable antiretroviral therapy roll out appear to occur where treatment is free at point of delivery through adequately-staffed district health systems, with a range of services for adult and child illness and support for community outreach. These lessons signal the continued relevance of primary health care, even in the face of new challenges such as AIDS.

Rebuilding universal, comprehensive people-centred systems calls for public leadership to manage pressures to commercialise health care and use resources provided for immediate tasks, such as treatment roll out, to reinforce the longer term development of health systems. This political leadership needs backing from social action, from public–public partnerships and from rights to health written into national constitutions and laws and protected by international conventions.

What kind of health system reclaims the resources for health?

Section 2 highlighted the strategic role that health systems can play in redistributing the resources for health. Health systems, while often reduced to just health care programmes, actually incorporate all those actions whose primary purpose is to promote, restore or maintain health. They can provide a means to improve people's lives – protecting them from the vulnerability of sickness, generating a sense of human security and building common purpose and trust within society. Health systems can widen the inclusiveness of and benefits from socio-economic development (Gilson *et al.*, 2007). They are social institutions that assert and protect social values and norms. They also reflect social inequalities (Mackintosh, 2001).

This may seem paradoxical – but health systems are sites of struggle. Some interests and policies that reform health systems also help them to cope with, rather than challenge, policies that widen inequality in wealth. But there are also activities and institutions within health systems that have contested inequality and the policies that drive it, to better protect public health. In our region, we have experienced both these scenarios.

At different times in the past two decades, health systems in the region have challenged and been challenged by policies that widen inequalities in health. Yet they have made significant improvements when they use specific strategies to direct resources to those with greatest health needs:

At different times in the past two decades, health systems in the region have challenged and been challenged by policies that widen inequalities in health.

- **Promoting a comprehensive, a primary health care oriented approach and providing the public leadership to involve other sectors in health**

  There is extensive evidence that health systems in the region markedly improve health when they provide prevention, treatment and care within effective and comprehensive district-level systems, organised around primary health care (WHO Afro, 2006; Baez and Barron, 2006; De Savigny *et al.*, 2004). More recent evidence shows this is equally important in dealing with chronic illness. Most commonly this is organised through public sector led services, co-ordinated with interventions provided by non-profit organisations (WHO Afro, 2006; Baez and Barron, 2006).

- **Redistributing resources within the system**

  This is implemented through redistributing budgets towards prevention, improving rural infrastructure, strengthening primary health care approaches and providing improved quality health services free at point of use (Loewenson *et al.*, 1991; Haddad and Fourier, 1995; Kida and Mackintosh, 2005). Health outcomes have improved when health systems deploy and orient health personnel towards major health problems, using staff time effectively and balancing tasks with resources at primary care level (Haddad and Fourier, 1995). Such redistribution ensures that private sector provision complements public provision instead of competing for public funding (Makwiza *et al.*, 2006).

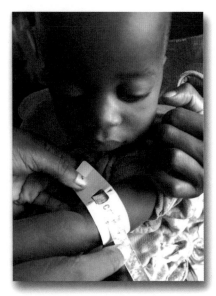

Measuring arm circumference to monitor child nutrition, Malawi
Source: B Goddard

- **Recognising and investing in the central role of people in health systems**

  Improvements in health have been made when health services are integrated with social structures and cultural systems, involving users and communities in the planning and running of services and promoting respectful and 'equal' relationships between providers, users and health personnel. Recognising social roles has meant that services do not simply focus on supply but also provide prompts to encourage the effective use of services, for example, the dissemination of information on prevention and early management of illness (Curtis, 1988; EQUINET SC and TARSC, 1998; Arblaster *et al.*, 1996; Jhamba, 1994).

This experience suggests that health systems can have impact on health and close gaps in access to health care when they provide and secure the resources for a comprehensive range of services at primary and secondary care level, with innovative action to ensure that these services reach out and are used by marginalised and disadvantaged groups. The financial, human and social resources for this are discussed in Sections 4 to 6.

Organising health systems around primary health care

The primary health care foundation of the health system is essential. The Alma Alta Declaration in 1978 defined primary health care as:

> '*Essential health care made universally accessible to individuals and families in the community by means acceptable to them, through their full participation and at a cost that the community and country can afford. It forms an integral part of the country's health system, of which it is the nucleus, and of the overall socio-economic development of the community. It includes inter-sectoral action.*'
> PAHO, 2006

Primary health care orients the whole health system towards promoting health and preventing ill health as the first line of action. It prioritises areas of health intervention that are often lost when systems are driven by the response to disease.

Primary health care is thus a strategic approach to rebuilding and organising health systems. Health systems that prioritise the commitment to promote health, prevent ill health and manage disease need to reach, involve and facilitate action in communities. This is discussed in Section 6. They also need to lever action from other sectors that are vital to health, as outlined in Section 2 (Gilson *et al.*, 2007; WHO Afro, 2006).

Orienting our health systems around primary health care implies that decisions on allocating resources are not driven by where the best level of clinical care can be found, but by how to bring the best level of prevention, promotion and treatment to where the people are, especially disadvantaged people. We discuss the means to achieve this in Section 4.

Primary health care orients the whole health system towards promoting health and preventing ill health as the first line of action. It prioritises areas of health intervention that are often lost when systems are driven by the response to disease.

The primary health care approach is strategic because it drives important choices. For example, one reason wealthier groups get better access to health care resources, as indicated in Section 1, is because our health systems spend a higher share of resources on higher level hospitals, often based in urban areas, which poor people generally do not use. Increasing the budget allocation towards primary care levels would improve the targeting of spending on health towards poor people, with adequate resources also provided for secondary referral services needed to support comprehensive primary health care (Gwatkin *et al.*, 2004; Castro-Leal *et al.*, 2000). Table 3.1 shows evidence of this in selected countries in the region where, except for Madagascar, spending at primary level provides higher benefits to poor households. If health systems ensure that poorer groups capture a larger share of spending than at present, even if richer groups continue to capture most of health spending, then the overall redistributiveness of the systems will be stronger (O' Donnell *et al.*, 2005).

© M Ndhlovu and TARSC, Ifakara 2006

There is significant experience in east and southern African countries of designing and implementing health systems that reflect primary health care approaches. A review of primary health care in the Africa region in 2003 found considerable progress in developing health care systems based on primary health care, with evidence of gains in health (WHO Afro, 2006). As 2008 is the 30 year anniversary of the Alma Alta agreement, it would be useful to have a more systematic documentation of these experiences, many of which have continued relevance.

In 1994, when the newly independent South Africa needed to address inequalities in health and in access to health care, it introduced free care for pregnant women and for children under 6 years of age and, in 1996, free primary health care for every citizen. A series of measures were introduced to support this, including an essential drugs list and an expansion of clinics in rural areas (Dept of Health South Africa, 2000). These measures led to clear health gains, such as those shown in figure 3.1 on page 79 (Solarsh and Goga, 2003). The significant fall in measles cases and deaths after the introduction of free primary health care in 1996 exemplifies the health gains from this reorientation of the health system.

Table 3.1 Poor/rich differences in benefits of health spending at different levels

Country	% of benefits received from health care services at primary-level facilities		% of benefits received from all curative* health care services at hospital and primary-level facilities	
	Poorest quintile	Richest quintile	Poorest quintile	Richest quintile
Kenya (rural) 1992	22	14	14	24
Madagascar 1993	10	29	12	30
South Africa 1994	18	10	16	17
Tanzania 1992-3	18	21	17	29

*Data based on a household's reported use of health services in response to illness or injury, thus considered curative by the study authors.

Adapted from: Carr, 2004

Community-based tuberculosis care in Namibia

The steep rise in the tuberculosis caseload due to the HIV epidemic overwhelmed the capacity of many government health services to provide quality tuberculosis care in Namibia. The country has one of the world's heaviest per capita burdens of tuberculosis at 748 cases per 100,000 people. Although case detection is high (88 per cent) only 63 per cent of new smear-positive patients were completing treatment. This called for new approaches through local health centres and communities, drawing on the decentralisation of tuberculosis control services into the primary health care system. In 1999, Omaheke region had the country's worst treatment outcomes, with success rates of less than 30 per cent. The region has a highly mobile San population in a vast and sparsely populated farming area, making patient follow-up a major challenge.

Initially hospital staff introduced direct observation of treatment on the wards. When these measures proved insufficient to improve results, tuberculosis inpatients were counselled about tuberculosis and its treatment and were given the option of treatment under the supervision of their nearest clinic or of a community treatment supporter. Community volunteers were trained on treatment observation. Each local clinic had a focal person who was trained to supervise the community treatment supporters. Clinic health committees were formed and became the link between the community, including local San chiefs and the Ministry of Health and Social Services. The programme provides transport and drivers to be used for primary health care outreach activities, including following up defaulters. Treatment supporters were also trained to refer any chronic coughers to clinics for investigation, further increasing case detection rates. The introduction of a 'Best managed clinic health committee of the year' competition based on tuberculosis control criteria generated great interest and enthusiasm.

The results were remarkable. Hospital wards were decongested. Of an initial 1,200 defaulters in the region's tuberculosis register at the outset, only two were not located, but the rest were put back on treatment, which they completed. Treatment success increased from less than 30 per cent in 1999 to 89 per cent in 2003 and the stigma associated with tuberculosis decreased.

AU, 2006

Although a decline in primary health care was noted by ministers of health at the WHO Africa regional committee meeting in 2006 (WHO Afro, 2006), positive experiences continue to emerge across the region. Primary health care oriented systems at national level have improved health practices such as breastfeeding, mother and child health and nutrition and integrated management of childhood illness, and have led to outcomes such as improved maternal mortality rates and patient satisfaction (WHO, 2003; Guyon *et al.*, 2006; Omaswa *et al.*, 1997). Despite positive experiences in the 1980s, and less well documented but continued positive experiences in recent years, a review of primary health care in Africa suggests that liberalisation policies have generally undermined countries'

Figure 3.1 Measles cases and deaths, South Africa, 1980-2003

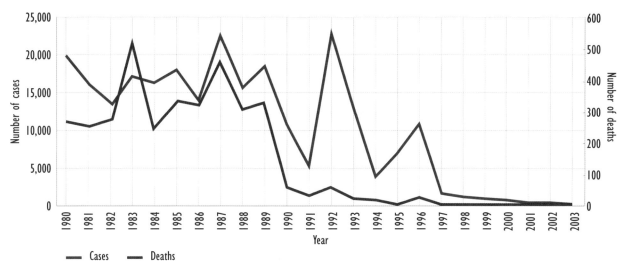

Source: Stats SA in Solarsh and Goga, 2003

plans to implement this approach and particularly the resources required for it (Chatora and Tumusime, 2004). Resource constraints rather than public health effectiveness generally drove decisions towards selective, rather than comprehensive, primary health care (Obimbo, 2003). Section 4 will further explore the financing mechanisms for primary health care oriented services.

Furthermore, an assumption that decentralised decision making would strengthen primary health care implementation was not always valid. After Uganda decentralised in the 1990s, for example, local government priorities were found to have shifted from comprehensive primary health care, and especially community-oriented prevention interventions, towards individual curative care (Hutchinson *et al.*, 2006). Organising and taking measures for equity-oriented decision making are further discussed in Section 6.

While these reversals are noted, the evidence cited earlier suggests that primary health care approaches continue to have nation-wide health impacts when organised and delivered nationally through the public sector health system, while drawing on the innovation and co-operation of non-governmental and faith-based organisations:

> *'The regional committee for Africa recalling the 1978 Alma Alta Declaration on primary health care…..noting that national health systems have deteriorated due to a number of challenges…recognising that universal access to essential health interventions requires efficient, well functioning district health systems…urges member states… to incorporate in their national and district plans the priority interventions for revitalisation of their health services, based on the primary health care approach…to reorient their hospitals to function in support of district health services … to mobilise and allocate resources giving priority to district health systems…'*

WHO Afro, 2006

…primary health care approaches continue to have health impacts that are national wide when organised and delivered nationally through the public sector health system, while drawing on the innovation and co-operation of non-governmental and faith-based organisations.

This is significant. At no time in history anywhere in the world have the major elements of health systems that promote equity been successfully organised or secured through the market. When developed countries have faced major health challenges or had the resources to afford higher levels of spending, they have turned predominantly to public initiatives and inclusive systems to improve health outcomes (Mackintosh and Koivusalo, 2005). Across a range of low and middle income countries, various health outcomes such as reduced child mortality and better care at birth were found to be associated with a higher share of gross domestic product spent on government-financed health care (Mackintosh and Koivusalo, 2005; Mackintosh, 2007).

Redistributing resources to where health needs are greater and responding to the many public health and social factors that influence health appear to be best organised through through strengthened public sector led systems and not through the market.

Rising gross domestic product and increasing national income in east and southern African countries are associated with increased public spending on health. Despite outliers, there is no evidence of a preference for increased private spending on health with rising per capita income (see figure 3.2).

Countries in the region that spend more on health also have lower income inequality (measured by Gini coefficients) (see figure 3.3). This association, supported by evidence from wider international review, suggests that countries with lower income inequality prefer public sector led investment in health, or that public spending on health may contribute

> Redistributing resources to where health needs are higher and responding to the many public health and social factors that influence health appear to be best organised through through strengthened public sector led systems, and not through by the market.

Figure 3.2 Share government spending on health by GDP/capita (PPP), east and southern Africa, 2003

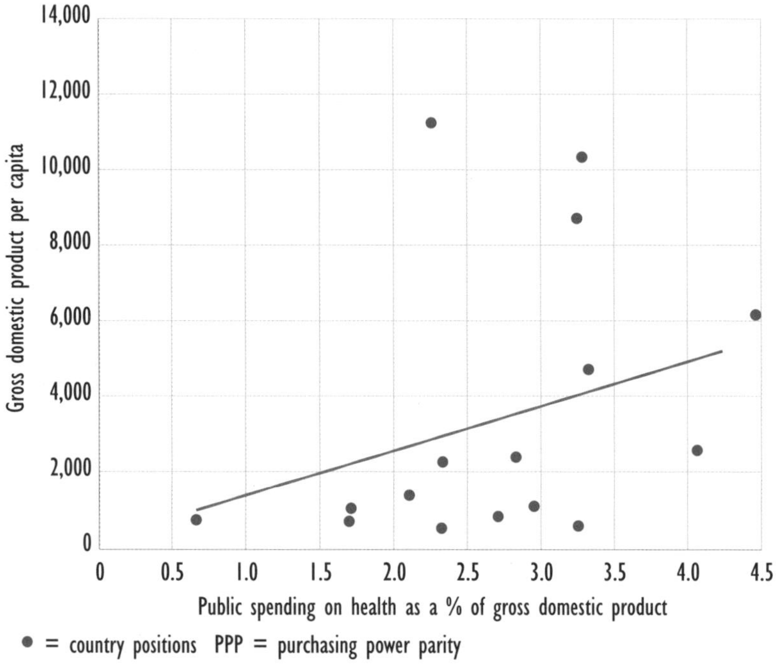

= country positions   PPP = purchasing power parity

Sources: WHO, 2006a; WHO, 2006c

Figure 3.3 Correlation between the Gini coefficient and % public expenditure of health budget among countries in SADC

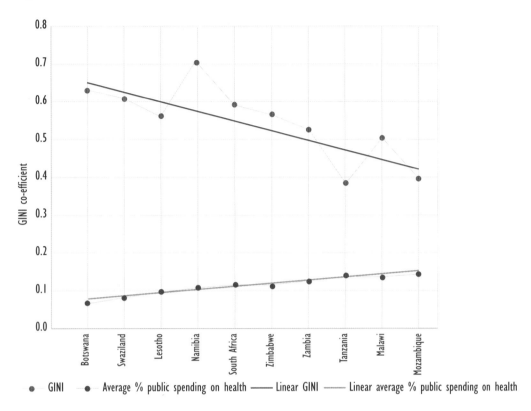

GINI co-efficient

● GINI ● Average % public spending on health ── Linear GINI ── Linear average % public spending on health

Source: EQUINET SC, 2004; WHO, 2002

to reducing poverty and narrowing economic inequality (Mackintosh, 2007). Both scenarios point to the important role of public spending in redistributing resources for health. For east and southern African countries that have made deliberate choices to increase public health investment, whether gross domestic product has grown or not, there appear to be potential positive returns in reduced inequality that merit more detailed assessment (EQUINET SC and TARSC, 2000).

Significant socio-economic differentials in maternal mortality in the region were shown in Section 1. These were reported to relate to socio-economic differentials across households and to differences in access to and quality of health services, especially at primary and secondary care level. The general improvements in maternal mortality and in child mortality with increased public investment in health, again with some outliers, suggest the importance of public investment in redistributing resources towards health services used by largely poor communities (see figures 3.4 and 3.5 on page 80). The range of maternal mortality outcomes for countries with public sector spending of 3–3.5 per cent of gross domestic product indicates, however, that this is not simply a matter of the share of public spending on health, but also relates to the adequacy and use of these resources, further discussed in Section 4.

The evidence suggests, generally, that increasing public investment in health is an important measure in improving health outcomes.

The evidence suggests, generally, that increasing public investment in health is an important measure in improving health outcomes.

Figure 3.4 Share of public spending on health as a percentage of gross domestic product (2003) and maternal mortality rate in east and southern Africa (1985–2003)

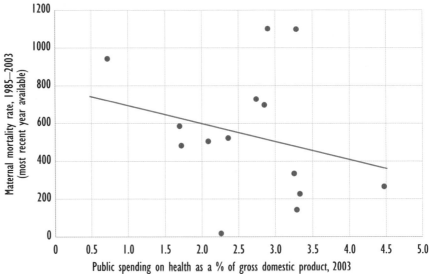

Sources: WHO, 2006a; UNDP, 2005

Figure 3.5 Share public spending on health as a percentage of gross domestic product (2003) and under 5 mortality rate (2004) in east and southern Africa countries

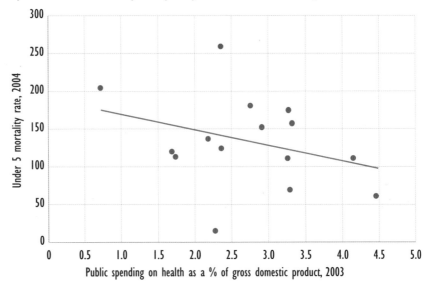

Sources: WHO, 2006a; World Bank, 2006

In east and southern Africa, public spending on health is directed largely through publicly provided or private non-profit services (discussed further in Section 4). Improved public spending on health thus appears to strengthen the strategic role of public leadership in health systems. It may do this in two ways. Firstly by direct delivery of public health services, including the training of health personnel, and secondly by giving the public sector the leverage and resources to effectively co-ordinate other sectors and providers to work towards national health goals.

New challenges are now being posed by the AIDS epidemic. Health systems that were once largely oriented towards providing prevention and treatment for acute infectious disease now need to manage treatment over lifetimes. There has been some debate about whether the policy principles governing equitable health systems in the region apply when trying to rapidly reach and treat large numbers of people living with HIV. The public sector has been seen as weak and has sometimes been bypassed by projects that go directly to community level, targeting specific services, organisations and programmes for people living with HIV and AIDS (Makwiza *et al.*, 2006; Loewenson and McCoy, 2004). Meeting equity goals may be regarded as a luxury in the efforts to address a 75 per cent shortfall in universal access targets. All these views have been voiced and acted on by international and national organisations working in the region. A review of documented experience of antiretroviral therapy roll out in the region suggests, however, that national, universal, comprehensive, people-centred and redistributive health systems are the best way to scale up and sustain access to antiretroviral treatment (Makwiza *et al.*, 2006).

> A review of documented experience of antiretroviral therapy roll out in the region suggests that national, universal, comprehensive people-centred and redistributive health systems are the best way to scale up and sustain access to antiretroviral treatment.

Lessons learned from the roll out of antiretroviral therapy

While integrating primary health care was losing its position as the central focus in health systems, vertical, disease-specific programmes gained ground (WHO Afro, 2006). Only a year after the Alma Alta Declaration, 'selective primary health care' was introduced as an 'interim' strategy to begin the process of implementing primary health care, contrasting purported 'unattainable' primary health care goals with 'feasible' and cost-effective selected medical interventions. Thus, rather than the envisioned emphasis on development and sustainability of health systems and infrastructures to improve population health, selective primary health care was focused on four vertical programmes: growth monitoring, oral rehydration therapy, breastfeeding and immunisation, and later on family planning, female education and food supplementation (Magnussen *et al.*, 2004). This sparked debate, not least because it abandoned Alma Alta's focus on social equity.

Selective primary health care has extended into a range of vertical disease-specific programmes. While these have led to large increases in service coverage for specific interventions, such as immunisation or directly observed tuberculosis treatment, they have not addressed issues of declining population coverage of essential health services and have weakened the mobilisation of resources for essential services and the co-ordination across public and private service providers, with negative effects for services and vulnerable communities (WHO Afro, 2006).

Responding to the wide gap between need and provision in antiretroviral treatment, activism in the 2000s has galvanised commitments to and significant new resources for universal access to prevention, treatment and care for HIV and AIDS (see figure 3.6 on page 84).

Figure 3.6 Share of people in need of antiretroviral therapy receiving it in east and southern Africa, 2005

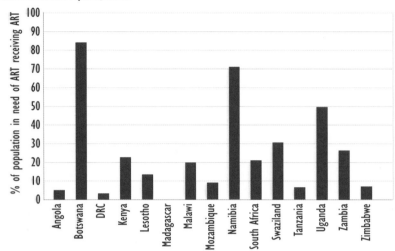

The changing country progress in treatment access, treatment regimes and funding is available at http://www.plusnews.org/aids/treatment.asp, a periodically updated site.

Source: WHO, 2006b

Global day of action for treatment access, South Africa, August 2006
Treatment Action Campaign, 2006

Mobilisation around access to treatment has given new impetus to exploring how disease-specific pro-grammes can strengthen universal health systems, particularly as constraints within health systems have become more obvious obstacles to universal access to prevention, treatment and care. For antiretroviral therapy roll out this is a learning by doing process.

The roll out of antiretroviral therapy in the region has taught us lessons about how to reach communities and points to areas where health systems either facilitate or impede the roll out. Country experiences show how scaling up treatment can strengthen social factors that support roll out, such as literacy or women's social power, that are also critical for other health gains (EQUINET, 2004c).

District-based approaches and extending outreach to primary care and community levels seem to have combined coverage and equity. These approaches use the resources of the hospital and community outreach to improve and sustain access to treatment and use treatment resources to strengthen these elements of the health system.

These approaches have had the following positive features:

- directly strengthening leadership, planning and management capacities, district and primary care level health worker training, conditions, re-engagement and retention based on clear planning;
- integrating antiretroviral therapy programmes with programmes for prevention of mother to child transmission and for prevention and management of tuberculosis and sexually-transmitted infections;
- removing community fee barriers; and
- co-ordinating with and, where relevant, subsidising large, district-level providers such as church services.

Scaling up antiretroviral therapy in Malawi

Scaling up antiretroviral therapy in Malawi started in 2004 and the treatment has since been provided free in all public and Christian Health Association of Malawi facilities. In 2004 it was estimated that only 5.1 per cent of people in need of antiretrovirals were actually receiving them and most districts did not have access to the therapy. Antiretroviral therapy was introduced into an already overstretched health system with high vacancy rates among clinical officers, nurses and pharmacists. Statistically, over half the 29 districts had fewer than 1.5 nurses per facility and five districts had fewer than one.

Recognising this situation, government and key players made the effort to integrate antiretroviral therapy services into the broad health system and built co-operation between the public and private sectors. The goal was set that by the end of 2005, all districts should have at least one health centre providing antiretrovirals and measures implemented to strengthen the services at this level to manage this, while also building synergies with existing services. Antiretroviral therapy services were also integrated with tuberculosis programmes.

Additional staff needs and resources were estimated and integrated into funding proposals and plans. A six-year human resources emergency relief plan costing US$273 million was developed and the HIV and AIDS crisis was used to focus attention and show the need for the improvements in this plan. Investments were made in training capacity, in retention and re-engagement incentives and programmes, and in management capacities within the Ministry of Health. Health workers themselves were considered a priority group for receiving antiretrovirals.

In Malawi, antiretroviral therapy is provided to health facilities if they are assessed as 'ready' to provide treatment. The health team has to have had formal training and done a successful clinical attachment in an antiretroviral therapy clinic and a qualified nurse has to draw up a report assessing the site as satisfactory.

Evidence from monitoring indicates that by the end of 2005 more women than men accessed antiretroviral therapy in every region and children had relatively less access to the therapy than adults. Gender equity was difficult to assess in the absence of gender and age sensitive prevalence rates in the country. In rural communities and among children, access was still limited and antiretroviral therapy services were less integrated with related services, such as prevention of mother to child transmission and treatment of sexually-transmitted infections. Limited human resources further limited the expansion of antiretroviral therapy services.

Makwiza et al., 2005; Schouten, 2006

Integration within wider primary care and district services is important on both public health and organisational grounds. It is estimated, for example, that about 80 per cent of tuberculosis patients are co-infected with HIV and eligible for antiretrovirals. Joint tuberculosis and HIV activities have been adopted in many sub-Saharan African countries and, as tuberculosis programmes are mainly decentralised, they have the potential to support decentralisation of antiretroviral services (Makwiza *et al.*, 2006; Chakanyuka, 2005). Women's high access to antenatal care services in the region provides an important entry point for prevention of mother to child transmission programmes, if effectively integrated. The low coverage of prevention of mother to child transmission (only 11 per cent of eligible pregnant women) suggests that these synergies are not yet effectively tapped (WHO *et al.*, 2007).

> Women's high access to antenatal care services in the region provides an important entry point for prevention of mother to child transmission programmes, if effectively integrated. The low coverage of prevention of mother to child transmission (only 11 per cent of eligible pregnant women) suggests that these synergies are yet to be effectively tapped

The lessons learned from antiretroviral therapy roll out more generally inform the actions needed to ensure that health systems reach out to all marginalised groups. In a context of universal district health systems, experience across the region suggests that access for groups with high health needs and low income or social power has been improved by:

- selecting points of entry in district or catchment areas based on, for example, their poverty levels or particular public health or gender equity concerns;

- locating antiretroviral therapy (or other needed interventions) at health service points used by low income groups;

- operating on a first come, first served basis but putting in place explicit measures to overcome barriers to access, such as income and travel support or female empowerment (this can include specific measures for tracing and follow-up of people on treatment, as done with tuberculosis, to enhance compliance);

- providing antiretroviral therapy (or other needed interventions) free at the point of delivery in the public health system;

- prioritising treatment access for service providers, such as health workers and teachers, who significantly contribute to wider epidemic control and poverty reduction; and

- involving communities in setting criteria for patient selection and monitoring to prevent the development of patronage or corrupt practices (Makwiza *et al.*, 2006; Loewenson and McCoy, 2004).

Nevertheless, problems persist. In 2007, there was still an urban bias in service provision in many countries, low paediatric access to antiretroviral treatment, social and cost barriers, as well as unmet transport and other needs (Makwiza *et al.*, 2006):

> '*So the problem that is there is that we men are selfish, selfish in the way that we are only buying medicines for ourselves and denying our partners to buy the medicine as well. Maybe if it were halved but K2500, how much money do we get?*'

Community member Malawi, communication, REACH Trust, 2004

Making difficult choices where antiretroviral therapy is rationed: Khayelitsha, Western Cape, South Africa, 2003

Khayelitsha is a slum area in Cape Town where Médecins Sans Frontières has been working since 1999. Antiretroviral therapy eligibility is based on:

- clinical criteria – someone at WHO stage III or IV who has a CD4 count less than 200/mm;

- social criteria – someone who attends HIV clinics regularly and lives in Khayelitsha;

- an anticipated ability to adhere to the antiretroviral therapy programme, assessed against adherence to co-trimoxazole and tuberculosis treatment (where relevant); and

- disclosure to at least one person who will act as a treatment assistant.

The anonymous dossiers of potential candidates are presented to a committee of community members, people living with HIV and AIDS and clinicians who are not affiliated with Medecins Sans Frontières. This process of involving community representatives and people living with HIV and AIDS in decisions appears to enhance 'fair process'. Preference has been given to those who:

- have a number of dependents;

- are very sick;

- are perceived as very poor and unlikely to afford treatment in the future;

- are open about their status and are involved in AIDS activism.

Adapted from: WHO, 2003 in Makwiza et al., 2006

There are also inadequate health workers employed to expand programmes, even where other resources are mobilised. This is discussed further in Section 5.

Large bilateral funds and those from Global Fund for AIDS, Tuberculosis and Malaria have been central to antiretroviral therapy roll out in the region. This too has taught us lessons about fair financing for health, further discussed in Section 4. While these funds have provided potentially invaluable new resources for health systems, the funders have been reluctant to make investments in systems and there have been barriers to uptake. Systems have faced multiple bureaucratic and reporting demands, and have had to try to meet timeframes and targets for impacts that may not match their real capacity to absorb, use and produce effects from resources. This has led to pressure for 'islands of excellence' able to produce more rapid change, weakly integrated with national health systems and, in some cases, drawing personnel from these systems. This has compromised sector-wide approaches and given impetus to vertical programmes, weakening efforts to build comprehensive integrated services (Kemp et al., 2003; Makwiza et al., 2006; Stillman and Bennet, 2006). East and southern African countries are more vulnerable to these pressures when domestic planning and resource mobilisation are weaker. There are, however, some examples of national resource mobilisation for AIDS, such as Zimbabwe's AIDS levy of 3 per cent levy on taxable income to government and the Zambian levy on financial transactions.

Antiretroviral therapy roll out has made clearer the constraints to universal access and equity in existing health systems, such as: the urban and tertiary care biases in resource flows; the inadequacy of trained and supported health workers at primary care and district level; the weak integration with existing services (unless actively organised); and the fragmentation and segmentation of donors and providers, especially private providers. If these weaknesses can be dealt with, health systems will benefit from an increased capacity to reach all marginalised groups.

The lessons learned from antiretroviral therapy roll out are relevant for improving health systems, while strong health systems are essential for antiretroviral therapy roll out. Strategic information is vital to inform and exchange this learning and to inform planning. The SADC business plan on AIDS calls for monitoring of the equity and health system impacts of antiretroviral therapy roll out. Indicators of equity and health systems strengthening in antiretroviral therapy roll out have been developed and are being piloted within national monitoring systems (EQUINET, 2004b; EQUINET *et al.*, 2004). It would be desirable to have regular public reporting at regional level on progress on these key national and regional goals, as implemented at global level (WHO *et al.,* 2007).

The experience of antiretroviral therapy roll out in east and southern Africa suggests the continued relevance of comprehensive, primary health care oriented district health systems. The features sustaining equitable roll out appear to include:

The experience of antiretroviral therapy roll out in east and southern Africa suggests the continued relevance of comprehensive, primary health care oriented district health systems.

- free services at point of delivery;

- provision of community outreach;

- links with other sectors for support like food and transport inputs;

- comprehensive and integrated prevention and care services close to communities; and

- social and community action to demand service outreach, participate in decisions on new developments and facilitate uptake and effective use of services.

Rather than reducing the commitment to public sector led, national health systems, AIDS and the challenges of universal access to treatment further reinforce the demand for delivery on this commitment.

Threats to equity-oriented health systems

There have, however, been times in east and southern African countries when health systems have had limited effect on improving health or closing up inequalities in health, or when specific measures have been introduced that have worsened access to health care. Falling overall budgets and reduced relative allocations to primary and preventive care have reduced coverage and quality of care, particularly at primary care level (UNICEF and MoHCW, 1996). Poorly designed cost recovery systems have led to declining access to services (McIntyre *et al.*, 2005). Quality of care has been affected by poorly functioning referral systems, staffing constraints, poor conditions of service and inadequate resources for health workers to implement tasks effectively. This has left communities commuting between providers to access care and has increased costs (Loewenson *et al.*, 1991; McIntyre *et al.*, 2005; Padarath *et al.*, 2003).

The most marked turn-around in health policies came with the World Bank structural adjustment programmes implemented in the 1980s. These programmes laid the groundwork for policy shifts that have since been extended to wider liberalisation and privatisation policies.

> '*By the end of the 1990s, the health systems in most sub-Saharan countries had virtually collapsed. Few people could afford annual check-ups, medicines or user fees at hospitals. One result was the resurgence of infectious diseases such as malaria, tuberculosis and cholera. A WHO study revealed that in some developing countries, malaria deaths tripled in the first four years of the reform, partially due to the collapse of curative health services and the soaring prices of antimalarial drugs. Such was the impact of structural adjustment programmes on the health systems of most African countries.*'
>
> E Samba, WHO Regional director for Africa, December 2004

Liberalisation policies and market reforms affected health systems profoundly:

- They moved from public sector driven national health systems to promoting provision by a 'mix' of public, private and voluntary providers, downplaying the public sector role.

- They redirected government away from direct service provision towards a mainly regulatory and 'stewardship' role, funding provision by others.

- They promoted corporate autonomy of the tertiary and quaternary hospital sector.

- They shifted from tax-based financing towards insurance schemes, managed care, pre-paid schemes, local resource mobilisation and user charges (World Bank, 1987, 1993, 1997; WHO, 1997, 2000; Preker and Harding, 2003; OECD, 2003, all cited in Mackintosh and Koivusalo, 2005).

Source: Anti-War Committee, 2000

Kenya's experience of structural adjustment in health

Kenya's health care crisis has been 20 years in the making. Its dimensions are spelled out in the 2004 *Poverty reduction strategy paper*, a government document written in consultation with the International Monetary Fund and the World Bank and approved by both bodies' boards. Life expectancy declined from 57 in 1986 to 47 in 2000; infant mortality increased from 62 per thousand in 1993 to 78 per thousand in 2003; and under-five mortality rose from 96 per thousand births to 114 per thousand births in the same period. The percentage of children with stunted growth increased from 29 per cent in 1993 to 31 per cent in 2003 and the percentage of Kenya's children who are fully-vaccinated dropped from 79 per cent in 1993 to 52 per cent in 2003.

Why this deterioration? As in most African countries, Kenya's health care system was hit hard by International Monetary Fund and World Bank structural adjustment policies introduced in the 1980s. As usual with such programmes, the emphasis was on cutting budgets. As a result, local health clinics and dispensaries had fewer supplies and medicines, and user fees became more common. Standards of care fell in the public hospitals and the largest public facility, Kenyatta National Hospital in Nairobi, began to ask patients' families to provide outside food and medical supplies. Professional staff took on jobs – some part-time, others full-time – at private health care facilities or migrated to Europe or North America in search of better pay.

Between 1991 and 2003, the Kenyan government reduced its workforce by 30 per cent – hard-hitting cuts. A World Bank group document from November 2003, written to justify waiving a loan condition calling for a workforce reduction, noted:

> *This condition required retrenching 32,000 personnel from the civil service over a period of two years. In practice, 23,448 civil servants were retrenched in 2000/01 before the programme was interrupted by lawsuits. [...] A specific commitment in the updated [agreement] is to reduce the size of the civil service by 5,000 per year through natural attrition.'*

Ironically the very same document supports Kenya's Assistant Minister Kibunguchy's assessment of the sector's current needs: 'the health sector currently experiences a staff shortage of about 10,000 health workers'.

These effects were cited recently by Member of Parliament, Alfred Nderitu, as the primary motivation for his motion of censure against the International Monetary Fund and World Bank in the Kenyan parliament. He insisted that any future loans from these institutions get parliamentary approval.

Ambrose, 2006

Proponents of commercialisation and privatisation of health systems have argued that these measures will improve equity and efficiency of services, enhance sustainable health care financing and improve accountability to clients as consumers (Turshen, 1999). Arguments for privatisation have also been made in the face of declining public funding in health, as a means to draw increasing private sector resources into health. Substantive reviews of health service privatisation in Africa (Turshen, 1999) and commercialisation of health services globally (Mackintosh and Koivusalo, 2005) explore these assumptions in the face of empirical evidence on user charges, self financing insurance, investment in private services and use of market incentives to motivate staff and allocate resources. Both reviews question the claims of the proponents, pointing to market failures and negative consequences for access to quality health services, particularly in poor communities.

Privatisation and commercialisation of services has had negative effects on equity and access.

A review of evidence on user fees and price increases in health services found that they had led to falling use of services, especially in poor households, resulting in increased child mortality and disease burden (Gilson, 1997). These outcomes are not limited to health services only, but apply in relation to other essential services for health. Inequalities in access to safe water and sanitation in east and southern Africa were described in Section 1, despite the importance of these inputs for health. Research on privatisation and commercialisation of water services in southern Africa found that privatised water services have led to increased user fees and falling use (McDonald and Ruiters, 2005). The case study in Dar es Salaam on page 90 exemplifies this. While user charges may appear cost effective, if falling use of services increases the rate of disease and demand for curative care, the returns can be negative.

Privatisation and commercialisation of services has had negative effects on equity and access.

Poorly maintained water services, South Africa
Source: Municipal Services Project, 2005

Effect of user charges for water in Dar es Salaam

Mrs Hassan lives in Tabata, a low income area of Dar es Salaam. She is the chairperson of the Tabata Women's Group. Her household is large, with four children living at home and four other dependent relatives. Mrs Hassan is one of the lucky ones because she has a water connection in her house. However, she does not receive any water through it. In her view, there may have been a change of name from DAWASA to City Water but the service is as bad as it was before. But now, bills are being delivered. She received a bill for 400,000 Tanzanian shillings ($400) even though she had not received any water. She complained to City Water but had no response. They later came to try to disconnect her water because she had not paid the bills. Eventually they left without removing the pipes.

Because she cannot get water through her connection, Mrs Hassan has to buy water from a well dug by a private individual. She has to pay 800 Tanzanian shillings (80 US cents) per day for this. Water delivered through her connection would be cheap but since it does not come, she has to collect water from a well instead. This is much more expensive, and she is not sure whether it is safe and clean but she has no choice. Mrs Hassan doubts whether water will ever come through her connection.

Families in her area that can't pay for water have to go to shallow, contaminated wells. People are forced to drink the water because they have no money and no working water connection. If they bath in it, water from shallow wells makes people itch. It also makes them ill and this costs money because they then have to buy medicines to treat the illness.

Greenhill and Wekiya, 2006: 17

© M Ndhlovu and TARSC, Ifakara 2006

As further discussed in Section 4, countries in the region have used various options to control negative effects of privatisation and commercialisation, including subsidies, regulation and partnerships. These have had varying degrees of effectiveness. Evidence from analysis of countries in the region indicates the following:

- Regulation can be effective but there are difficulties in sustaining enforcement (Hongoro and Kumaranayake, 2000; Kumaranayake et al., 2000).

- Accreditation and certification systems have worked well for hospitals in wealthy and middle-income countries but have had scant success in poor developing countries, with little impact on private practitioners working solo. Government initiatives to encourage contact and referrals between private and public health care providers, even offering private practitioners access to subsidised medication, have worked in limited settings, such as tuberculosis control (Prata et al., 2005).

- Contracted HIV testing and counselling services in Zimbabwe supported by community health workers led to increased monthly visits and improved generic drug access (Prata *et al.*, 2005).

- Voucher systems increased affordability of specific health care treatments but are prohibitively expensive to manage through large numbers of service-delivery points (Mushi *et al.*, 2003).

- While postgraduate education for private providers led to improved quality of clinical care, the benefits declined over time in the absence of systems for continued regular engagement with public and private systems (Prata *et al.*, 2005).

Commercialisation of health services has thus created problems for coverage and access to vital services, while a fall in public sector funding at the same time has depleted public services. Privatisation and commercialisation have led to multiple, smaller providers, fragmented systems, weakened risk pooling and cross-subsidisation in health service financing and weakened public sector ability to meet health obligations (EQUINET, SEATINI, CHP, TARSC, 2006; Muroyi *et al.*, 2003). The implications of this for rebuilding universal coverage are discussed in the next section.

Cuts in the size of the civil service, declining morale and reduced real wages have exacerbated salary differentials between private and public sectors. This led to attrition of skilled health professionals from the public to the private for-profit health sectors, later turning into a flow of health workers to higher income countries. With falling resources in public sector health systems in the 1990s, the World Bank promoted 'essential packages of care' to target the main causes of the burden of disease and combine various vertical interventions for those judged to be cost-effective (World Bank, 1993). While intended as 'pro-poor', this approach underestimated needs and the investment required to extend services to vulnerable groups and populations in remote areas (Bond and Dor, 2003). The combination of interventions did not adequately reflect the comprehensive district and primary health care systems needed to adequately provide health for such groups and did not adequately invest in the system-wide processes necessary for the interventions to work. The relatively low estimated cost of the packages was used to justify further cuts in public health spending.

Countries and communities struggling to deal with the consequences of these policies also need to see how they are realigning values and policy principles. Equitable health systems are framed on values of equity and solidarity, goals of human development and justice and on public health principles. While proposals for reduced public sector roles, privatisation and commercialisation did not make their values explicit and were presented as purely technical in content, they were driven by explicit market values. In March 2002, the World Bank's *Sourcebook on community-driven development in the Africa region* made the World Bank's position clear on essential services such as water:

Risk pooling refers to grouping people with different health risks so that the costs of meeting individual risks are shared across many people. The larger the risk pool the more risks are shared.

Cross-subsidisation refers to the use of resources paid by lower risk groups to support costs of higher risk groups within a risk pool, for example, between healthy, younger and more wealthy groups and sick, elderly and poorer groups.

'Work is still needed with political leaders in some national governments to move away from the concept of free water for all... promote increased capital cost recovery from users. An upfront cash contribution based on their willingness-to-pay is required from users to demonstrate demand and develop community capacity to administer funds and tariffs and ensure 100 per cent recovery of operation and maintenance costs.'

Bond, 2002

These policy shifts profoundly affected our policy values and commitments. They gave excessive weighting to economic efficiency and market behaviours over public health considerations, delegitimised the state (a major source of health intervention for poor communities), transformed people from citizens with social rights to individual consumers with(out) purchasing power and demoralised communities. (Mackintosh and Koivusalo, 2005; Bond and Dor, 2003).

The liberalised growth of private care under conditions of declining access to basic public services has led to parallel worlds, where those with wealth and connections have access to the highest technology while many poor people cannot even secure or afford tuberculosis drugs or safe water supplies. Many of these changes reflect the fact that macro-economic and health sector reforms have enabled more powerful medical and middle class interest groups to exact concessions at the cost of the poorer, less organised rural health workers or the urban and rural poor (Van Rensburg and Fourie, 1994; Bennett *et al.*, 1995; Kalumba, 1997; LaFond, 1995; Storey, 1989).

Cutbacks in public funding were inevitably followed by increased dependency on external resources and policy influence, raised in Section 2 (see figure 3.7).

> These policy shifts profoundly affected our policy values and commitments. They gave excessive weighting to economic efficiency and market behaviours over public health considerations, delegitimised the state (a major source of health intervention for poor communities), transformed people from citizens with social rights to individual consumers with(out) purchasing power and demoralised communities.

Figure 3.7 External resources share of health financing, east and southern Africa, 1999-2003

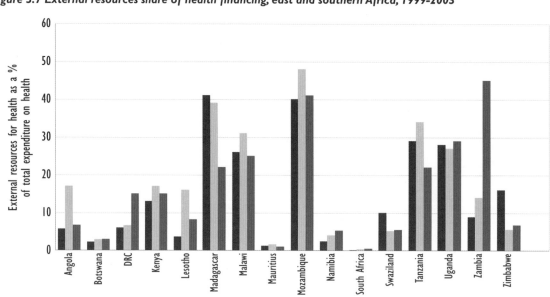

Source: WHO, 2002

One effect of the combination of increased external influence and cost efficiency perspectives has been the drive for more immediate and focused returns to spending in health, motivating vertical disease control programmes and targeted approaches. Disease control programmes, referred to earlier, are essential within health systems and provide specific measures to reach particular vulnerable groups. However, with reduced public roles and resources, these elements become more high profile than the systems they are located within. Instead of health systems integrating such focused programmes to deliver additional benefits to specific groups or to enhance performance on specific priority areas, these elements draw resources to themselves, segmenting resources and leaving the wider health system increasingly fragile (Lewis, 2005).

© M Ndhlovu and TARSC, Ifakara 2006

A review in Benin, Ethiopia and Malawi of one of the most substantial sources of external financing, the Global Fund for AIDS, Tuberculosis and Malaria found that most of these funds appear to be aligned with overall national health policies and plans. This was especially the case where the Global Fund was filling in gaps, that is where it provided the financial support to scale up activities envisaged in national plans, with proposals to the fund culled from existing but unfunded national plans. This was the case in Malawi, for example, where a comprehensive and costed national plan to address HIV and AIDS and malaria had been developed. A scaled-down version of this national plan was used as the basis for its proposal. Malawi has a sector-wide approach for planning and programming in the health sector. Although the sector-wide approach was signed in November 2004, after the Global Fund for AIDS, Tuberculosis and Malaria grant agreement had been signed, the activities programmed with the fund's support were linked to the sector-wide approach through the 'essential health package' – under which malaria, HIV and AIDS and tuberculosis services are integrated with other health services at the service delivery point. The review found, in contrast, that the Global Fund's resources were less supportive of wider health systems where plans for fund-supported activities were not integrated with the Ministry of Health's plans and where these funds were channelled separately, thus creating a parallel system to the sector-wide funding pool. Debates about how these global funds should flow are reported to have contributed to delays in signing grants in some cases (Stillman and Benett, 2006).

As discussed earlier, the lessons from antiretroviral therapy roll out point to the importance of system-wide investments. As noted from the review of experiences with the Global Fund for AIDS, Tuberculosis and Malaria, these investments are more likely to be effective when their focus areas are integrated within comprehensive and costed national plans for health services. The overall public investment and strategic leadership discussed earlier is thus important in ensuring that specific programmes are integrated within national policies for universal, comprehensive primary health care oriented health systems.

Reasserting public interest in health systems

This section presents and gives evidence around two scenarios: publicly-driven national health systems organised around principles of public health, equity and solidarity or commercialised, segmented health systems, organised around market and cost-efficiency principles. The evidence points to the former being preferred politically and socially and having better health outcomes in the region, particularly when accompanied by measures to redistribute resources to primary health care oriented services that reach into communities and address areas of greatest health need. These lessons have been reinforced by experiences of antiretroviral therapy roll out.

The experience of the last two decades draws attention to the importance of not only what policy choices are made but *how* these choices are made. When economic policies are profoundly affected by global pressures for austerity and liberalisation, how does the health system hold its ground on a different set of principles and values, maintain its space and even influence these policies? How do we reassert public interest in health?

In Section 4 we explore how the financing of health systems enables or disables the assertion of public interest in health. Section 5 examines how we can value and involve health workers. The common term, 'human resources for health' signals that health workers have become commodified and need to be repositioned as actors – people who shape the functioning of health systems. In Section 6 we explore the ways in which popular involvement, control and support within health systems can be strengthened to develop the social power to advance equity and promote public interests.

Public interests are asserted through the public partnerships developed to strengthen and sustain health systems. For example, countries have pursued partnerships with the not-for-profit private sector or with public authorities in health, rather than with for-profit providers. The Tsumeb market project in Namibia, described opposite, is one such example. Such public–public partnerships offer opportunities for capacity transfers across public agencies and for stronger community support and accountability for services (Hall *et al.*, 2005). Partnerships between different public sector health agencies within countries (universities, local authorities, central government) blend different skills and capacities for mutual benefit. Those between public sector health agencies and local communities can make the planning and delivery of health services better informed by the needs of local communities.

Development partnerships between public sector health agencies in high-income countries and public health care agencies in low-income countries provide opportunities for two-way learning, while those between public sector agencies at international level, such as local authorities working in partnerships to promote healthy cities, provide room for sharing information and experience, for training and capacity-building.

The experience of the last two decades draws attention to the importance not only of what policy choices are made, but of *how* those choices are made. When economic policies are profoundly affected by global pressures for austerity and liberalisation, how does the health system hold its ground on a different set of principles and values, maintain its space and even influence these policies? How do we reassert public interest in health?

Public interests are asserted through the public partnerships developed to strengthen and sustain health systems.

Developing trust and respect are essential to such partnerships (Dowling *et al.*, 2004; Hall *et al.*, 2005). Where there are sharp inequalities in income, cooperative inter-municipal arrangements may facilitate more equal redistribution of resources and promote economic development better than privatisation (Hall *et al.*, 2005).

Asserting public interest demands that states regulate and limit commercial interests that are harmful to health. Countries in the region have taken positions on the activities of private business when this is harmful to public health, even if this confronts economic activities. This is evident in relation to tobacco control, control of breastmilk substitutes (discussed in Section 6), control of hazardous chemicals, regulating pricing

> Asserting public interest demands that states regulate and limit commercial interests that are harmful to health.

Tsumeb market development project, Namibia

Tsumeb municipality in Namibia and Chesterfield Borough council in the United Kingdom have had an official twinning relationship since 1993. The aim of the partnership was to develop Tsumeb's informal local market into a well-managed market with good amenities. This would contribute to improved standards in food safety and public health.

At the beginning of the market development project, the informal market (at Nomtsoub) was the largest income generator for poor people in the town, providing a living for 234 families. The market was a focal point for the local community and it provided a source of affordable food and other services. However, hygiene standards were poor and the market lacked basic amenities. The capacity-building project involved three groups of players: the market community; Tsumeb municipality and Chesterfield Borough council. The exchange group (two environmental health officers) from Chesterfield, the market committee and a field worker from the Urban Trust of Namibia formed the Okapana Action Force and set up the 'Let's build a sink' project. Negotiations took place between the Urban Trust of Namibia, Tsumeb municipality and the market committee on the increased role of the committee and the creation of a community-based organisation, Tulongeni Pamwe, which would take over the roles of the market committee. The project has led to a number of public health improvements: sanitation has improved; food hygiene training continues; legal power connections are now available and sharing power connections is banned; and meat is inspected every morning. Traders take pride in the cleanliness of the market and welcome public health advice, the municipality understands the needs of the traders and communication has improved.

One of the most significant factors in the success of this initiative was the change in culture in the town that enabled the municipality to allow the market traders to take action and to respect their views about how to develop the market. This led to the market committee developing a sense of ownership of the market. This has ensured the sustainability of the public health improvements.

Didcock, 2002; Hall, *et al.*, 2005

South Africa squeezes big tobacco

Rapidly increasing tobacco consumption in many parts of Africa has led to an epidemic of tobacco-related disease and death. It is projected that this will overtake AIDS in Africa in terms of cumulative deaths by the year 2010. In South Africa, prior to 1994, a third of all South Africans smoked, excise taxes were low and there were few tobacco control measures. In 2005, there were 25,000 deaths from tobacco-related disease.

From 1991, civil society action on tobacco grew. A tobacco action group, a coalition of various anti-tobacco lobbies, raised public awareness about smoking hazards and drove tobacco control to the forefront of the political agenda. From the early 1990s action by government ensued. A Tobacco Products Control Act controlled smoking in enclosed public areas, ensured health warnings on tobacco products and prohibited sales to children under 16. The Act was further strengthened over the decade with restrictions on smoking in government buildings and in some private businesses, while government also moved to increase cigarette taxes.

These actions attracted a response from the industry, with claims of job losses, loss of tax revenue and loss of foreign exchange earnings. Research by the South African Medical Research Council and the University of Cape Town contradicted the industry claims and the measures were further strengthened. Between 1994 and 1999 tobacco consumption went down 21 per cent. Although overall smoking rates declined, targeted advertising on radio (still exempt from the ban on advertising) was associated with rising smoking rates among coloured and black people. In response, radio airtime was used to broadcast health messages and shift public opinion in favour of tobacco control. By 1998, a poll showed that 90 per cent of non-smokers and 70 per cent of smokers supported a stronger ban on smoking in public places. This strong public backing gave the health minister the political room to propose one of the world's strongest tobacco control laws.

Industry reacted, arguing that tourism and small businesses could not afford the changes required by the law and that advertising was not aimed at influencing non-smokers to take up the habit but at competing over market share. Some groups, scared by the supposed economic threat, testified against the Bill. The contestation led to over two years passing between the Tobacco Products Control Bill being passed by South African parliament in December 1998 and its eventual approval into law in 2000.

Stronger legislation in South Africa could simply cause the industry to redouble its efforts in other countries in the region. The WHO Framework Convention on Tobacco Control, adopted in 2003 with over 40 countries ratifying it through their domestic processes by 2004, came into force in early 2005, making the principles of the South African law a legally binding public health treaty at global level. For countries in the east and southern Africa region, this means putting the WHO convention clauses into domestic law, closing any legal loopholes, such as definitions of 'public place' and 'tobacco product', and using systems of enforcement, strict penalties and social monitoring to ensure that the control of tobacco is implemented.

Independent Online, 2006; Schwarz, 1999; White, 2001

practices in the pharmaceutical sector and using trade flexibilities for public health (described in Section 2). When states take on transnational corporations, they may be taking on corporates with turnovers larger than their gross domestic product, with extensive links and power. Where actions are taken in defence of public health, they need support from international public health conventions and civil society, such as in the case of tobacco control opposite.

Health demands some 'bottom lines' of what rights and obligations must be secured, particularly in an environment of powerful market forces. Health has long been regarded as a universal human right:

> *'The enjoyment of the highest attainable standard of health is one of the fundamental rights of every human being without distinction of race, religion, political belief, economic or social condition.'*
>
> World Health Organisation, May 1948

The political choices made to protect public interests and public health are not so easily challenged or reversed when they are embedded in a rights framework, especially in international charters and national constitutions and laws, and protected by social action (London, 2003). There are instruments that express these bottom lines at international, regional and national level but they are often hardly known or seldom used to protect public health.

The African Charter on Human and Peoples' Rights (1981) in article 16 states, for example, that every individual has the right to enjoy the best attainable state of physical and mental health and that countries shall take the necessary measures to protect the health of their people and to ensure that they receive medical attention when they are sick. Specific groups are further catered for in other charters, for example, children's health in the African Charter on the Rights and Welfare of the Child (1999) and women, including their sexual and reproductive health, in the Protocol to the African Charter on Human and Peoples' Rights on the Rights of Women in Africa (2003).

These African charters reflect wider global commitments. For example, 150 countries are signatories to the International Covenant on Economic, Social and Cultural Rights (1976). Article 12 of this covenant provides for state parties to recognise the right of everyone to the enjoyment of the highest attainable standards of physical and mental health.

Health demands some 'bottom lines' of what rights and obligations must be secured, particularly in an environment of powerful market forces.

Boystown South Africa
Indymedia, November 2005

Table 3.2 Ratification of human rights treaties in the region as of 2005

TREATY	ANGOLA	BOTSWANA	DRC	KENYA	LESOTHO	MADAGASCAR
African Charter on Human and Peoples' Rights (1990) (1)	1986	1982	1983	n.a.	1988	n.a.
African Charter on the Rights and Welfare of the Child (1990) (2)	1988	1997	—	1996	1995	2001
Protocol to the African Charter on the Rights of Women in Africa (2003) (2)		—	2003*	2003*	2000	2004*
International Covenant on Economic, Social and Rights (1966) (3)	1992a	—	1976a	1972a	1992a	1971a
International Covenant on Civil and Political Rights (1966) (3)	1992a	1996	1976a	1972a	1992a	1967
International Convention on the Elimination of all forms of Race Discrimination (1966) (3)	—	1974a	1976a	1901a	1971a	1965
Convention on the Rights of the Child (1989) (3)	1986	1995a	1986	1986	1988	1987
Convention on the Elimination of all forms of Discrimination Against Women (1979) (3)	1986a	1996a	1982	1984a	1991	1985
Convention against Torture and Other Cruel, Inhuman and Degrading Treatment or Punishment (1984) (3)	—	1996	1996a	1997a	2001a	2001
International Convention on the Protection of the Rights of all Migrant Workers and Members of their Families (1990) (4)	—	—	—	—	2001	—
Convention on the Prevention and Punishment of the Crime of Genocide (1948) (3)	—	—	1962d	—	1974a	—
Convention on the Prohibition and Immediate Action for the Elimination of the Worst Forms of Child Labour (1999) (5)	1997	1996	1997	1997	1997	1997

KEY: − = country has not acted yet; Date = year ratified only; Codes after dates as follows: * = signatory only   a = accession   d = succession
(1)–(5) = sources (see below)

Sources:
(1) Kamupira and London, 2005;
(2) African Union, 1981, at http://www.africa-union.org/official_documents/Treaties_%20Conventions_%20Protocols/Banjul%20Charter.pdf;
(3) UN OHCHR, at http://www.ohchr.org/english/countries/ratification/3.htm;
(4) UN, 2007
(5) ILO, 2006

MALAWI	MAURITIUS	MOZAMBIQUE	NAMIBIA	SOUTH AFRICA	SWAZILAND	TANZANIA	UGANDA	ZAMBIA	ZIMBABWE
1985	1988	1985	1988	1992	1991	1980	n.a.	1980	1986
1995	1988	1994	2000	1996	1992*	1999	1990	1992*	1991
2001	2005*	2003*	2000	2000	2004*	2003*	2003*	2005*	2003*
1993a	1973a	—	1994a	1994*	2004a	1976a	1987a	1984a	1991a
1993a	1973a	1993a	1994a	1994	2004a	1976a	1995a	1984a	1991a
1996a	1972a	1983a	1982a	1994	1969a	1972a	1980a	1968	1991a
1991a	1996a	1990	1986	1991	1991	1987	1986	1987	1986
1987a	1984a	1997a	1992a	1991	2004a	1981	1981	1981	1991a
1996a	1992a	1999a	1994a	1994	2004a	—	1986a	1998a	—
—	—	—	—	—	—	—	1995a	—	—
—	—	1983a	1994a	1998a	—	1984a	1995a	—	1991a
1995	1996	1999	1996	1996	1998	1997	1997	1997	1997

This is stated as extending beyond medical care and treatment, and includes access to underlying determinants of health, such as safe and potable water, adequate sanitation, an adequate supply of safe food, housing, healthy occupational and environmental conditions and health-related education and information, including on sexual and reproductive health. In relation to health care it calls for: health facilities, goods and services to be accessible to all, especially the vulnerable or marginalised among the population; health facilities to be within safe physical reach for all sections of the population; facilities to be affordable for all with payment based on the principle of equity; and for access to information on health issues.

The Committee on the International Covenant on Economic, Social and Cultural Rights, tasked with monitoring the implementation of the treaty obligations, noted that states parties have a core obligation to ensure the satisfaction of minimum essential levels of each of the rights enunciated in the covenant, including essential primary health care. Read in conjunction with more contemporary instruments, they concluded in 2000 that the Alma Alta Declaration provides compelling guidance on the core obligations arising from article 12. Accordingly, the committee suggested that these core obligations include at least the following obligations to:

- ensure the right of access to health facilities, goods and services on a non-discriminatory basis, especially for vulnerable or marginalised groups;

South African constitutional provisions on health

South Africans have the right to:
- bodily and psychological integrity;
- make decisions concerning reproduction;
- secure and control over one's body and not to be subjected to medical or scientific experiments without consent [Section 12(2)];
- an environment that is not harmful to their health or wellbeing [Section 24];
- access to health care services, including reproductive health care [Section 27(1a)];
- access to sufficient food and water [Section 27 (1b)];
- guaranteed emergency medical treatment [Section 27(3)].

South African children have the right to:
- basic nutrition, shelter, basic health care services and social services [Section 28 (1c)].

The state must take reasonable legislative and other measures, within its available resources, to realise these rights.

Government of South Africa, 1996

- ensure access to the minimum essential food which is nutritionally adequate and safe, to ensure freedom from hunger for everyone;

- ensure access to basic shelter, housing and sanitation, and an adequate supply of safe and potable water;

- provide essential drugs, as from time to time defined under the WHO action programme on essential drugs;

- ensure equitable distribution of all health facilities, goods and services; and

- adopt and implement a national public health strategy and plan of action, on the basis of epidemiological evidence, addressing the health concerns of the whole population. The strategy and plan of action shall be devised, and periodically reviewed, on the basis of a participatory and transparent process (London, 2003).

As shown in table 3.2 on pages 100 and 101, most countries in the region have ratified these treaties. Some have embedded rights to health and health care in their constitutions, as a point of reference for official policies and to establish the protection of public health as a condition for curtailing individual rights and commercial interests.

Constitutional provisions vary across the region and generally cover:

- the prohibition of conduct injurious to health (for example, limiting alcohol exposure);

- provision for specific programmes and services (for example, medical services and emergency care);

- provisions for the production of health resources (for example, drugs);

- provisions for social financing of health;

- regulation of the quality of care; and

- regulation of the rights and relationships between health professionals and community or state (EQUINET SC and TARSC, 1998).

Embedding the provisions of article 12 of the International Covenant on Economic, Social and Cultural Rights in east and southern African country laws and constitutions would appear to be fundamental to protecting the right to health. Where constitutional rights place an obligation to protect the health and health care of the population, and specifically of vulnerable groups like children, they strengthen the hand of states and communities to assert public interest.

We also need the mechanisms to deliver on those values and entitlements and the social action to implement and defend them. We discuss these in the following sections.

> Embedding the provisions of article 12 of the International Covenant on Economic, Social and Cultural Rights in east and southern African country laws and constitutions would appear to be fundamental to protecting the right to health ... they strengthen the hand of states and communities to assert public interest.

REFERENCES

African Union (1999) *African Charter on the Rights and Welfare of the Child*, AU, Addis Ababa.
– (2003) *Protocol to the African Charter on Human and Peoples' Rights on the Rights of Women in Africa*, AU, Addis Ababa.
– (1981) *African (Banjul) Charter on Human and Peoples' Rights* (adopted 27 June 1981), OAU Doc. CAB/LEG/67/3 rev. 5, 21 I.L.M. 58 (1982), accessed June 2007 at www.africa-union.org/official_documents/Treaties_%20Conventions_%20Protocols/Banjul%20Charter.pd
– (2006) 'Community-based TB care in Namibia', *Special Summit of African Union on HIV/AIDS, Tuberculosis and Malaria, 2-4 May 2006, Abuja, Nigeria*, AU, Addis Ababa, available at www.africa-union.org/root/au/ conferences /past/2006/may/summit/doc/en/ SP_PRC_ATM6I_Best%20Practices.pdf.

Ambrose S (June 2006) 'Preserving disorder: IMF policies and Kenya's health care crisis', *Pambazuka News*, Fahamu, Oxford.

Anti-war Committee (2000) 'Structural adjustment anti-war committee, USA', accessed Dec 2006 at http://www.antiwarcommittee.org/images/clipart/ economics/SAP.jpg

Arblaster L, Lambert M, Entwistle V, Forster M, Fullerton D, Sheldon T and Watt I (1996) 'A systematic review of the effectiveness of health service interventions aimed at reducing inequalities in health', *Journal of Health Services Research and Policy* 1(2):93-103.

Baez C and Barron P (2006) 'Community voice and role in district health systems in east and southern Africa: A literature review', *EQUINET discussion paper 39*, EQUINET, Harare.

Bennett S, Russell S and Mills A (1995) 'Institutional and economic perspectives on government capacity to assume new roles in the health sector: A review of experience', *Health Economics and Financing Programme working paper*, London School of Hygiene and Tropical Medicine, London.

Bond P (2002) *Unsustainable South Africa: Environment, development and social protest*, Merlin Press, London.

Bond P and Dor G (2003) 'Neoliberalism and poverty reduction strategies in Africa', *EQUINET discussion paper 3*, EQUINET, Johannesburg.

Carr D (2004) 'Improving the health of the world's poorest people', *Health Bulletin 1*, Population Reference Bureau, Washington DC, accessed 6 Dec 2006 at http://www.prb.org/pdf/ImprovingtheHealth World_Eng.pdf

Castro-Leal F, Dayton J, Demery L, Mehra K (2000) 'Public spending on health care in Africa: Do the poor benefit?', *Bulletin of the World Health Organisation* 78(1): 66-74.

Chakanyuka C (2005) 'Update of the antiretroviral therapy programme in Zimbabwe', unpublished report, Zimbabwe.

Chatora R and Tumusime J (2004) 'Primary health care: A review of its implementation in sub-Saharan Africa', *Primary Health Care Research and Development* 5: 296-306.

Curtis C (1988) 'Botswana: Reaching out to a scattered population', *People* 15(2): 1-3.

Dept of Health, South Africa (2000) *Primary health care progress report 2000*, South African Govt, Pretoria, available at http://www.doh.gov.za/docs/ reports/2000/dhis 2000.pdf.

De Savigny D, Kasale H, Mbuya C and Reid G (2004) *Fixing health systems*, IDRC, Ottawa.

Didcock S (2002) *Tsumeb market development project*, Namibia 1999–2002, sponsored by Chesterfield Borough Council and the Commonwealth Local Government Forum, London.

Dowling B, Powell M and Glendinning C (2004) 'Conceptualised successful partnerships', *Health and Social Care in the Community* 12(4):309–317.

EQUINET steering committee and TARSC (1998) 'Equity in health southern Africa: Overview and issues from an annotated bibliography', *EQUINET policy paper 2*, EQUINET, Harare.
– (2000) 'Turning values into practice: Equity in health in southern Africa,' *EQUINET policy paper 7*, EQUINET, Harare.
– (2004) 'Reclaiming the state: Advancing people's health, challenging injustice', *EQUINET policy paper 15*, EQUIINET, Harare.

EQUINET (2004b) 'Expanding treatment access and strengthening HIV/AIDS programmes in ways that strengthen the broader health systems agenda: Issues for the Global Fund to fight HIV/AIDS, Tuberculosis and Malaria', mimeo, EQUINET and IDRC Research Matters, Harare.
– (2004c) 'Principles, issues and options for strengthening health systems for treatment access and equitable responses to HIV and AIDS in southern Africa', *EQUINET discussion paper 15*, EQUINET, Harare.

EQUINET, SEATINI, CHP, TARSC (2006) *Promoting health in trade agreements: A training kit for east and southern Africa*, EQUINET/ SEATINI, Harare.

EQUINET, Equi TB and TARSC (2004) 'Strengthening health systems for treatment access and equitable responses to HIV and AIDS in southern Africa', *Meeting report, 16-17 Feb 2004*, EQUINET, Harare.

Gilson L (1997) 'In defence and pursuit of equity', mimeo, London School of Hygiene and Tropical Medicine, London.

Gilson L, Doherty J, Loewenson R, Francis V (2007) *Final report of the Knowledge Network on Health Systems,* WHO Commission on the Social Determinants of Health, Geneva.

Global Fund to Fight AIDS, Tuberculosis and Malaria (2006) 'Disbursement details report', Geneva, accessed 3 Dec 2006 at: http://www. theglobalfund.org/en/funds_raised/ commitments/

Greenhill R and Wekiya I (2006) *Turning off the taps: Donor conditionality and water privatisation in Dar es Salaam, Tanzania*, Action Aid International, UK.

Guyon A, Quinn V, and Hainsworth M (2006) 'Using the essential nutrition actions approach to improve the nutritional practices of women and children at Scale in Antananarivo and Fianarantsoa provinces of Madagascar: Results and trends 2000 to 2005', Ministry of Health, Govt of Madagascar, Linkages, Antananarivo, at http://www. linkagesproject.org/publications/Madagascar_Final_Report_2006.pdf

Gwatkin DR, Bhuiya A, Victora CG (2004) 'Making health systems more equitable', *The Lancet* 364: 1273-1280.

Haddad S and Fourier P (1995) 'Quality, cost and utilisation of health services in developing countries: A longitudinal study', *Zaire Social Science and Medicine* 40(6): 743-53.

Hall D, Lethbridge J and Lobina E (2005) 'Public-public partnerships in health and essential services', *EQUINET discussion paper* 23, EQUINET and MSP, Harare.

Hongoro C, Kumaranayake L (2000) 'Do they work? Regulating for-profit providers in Zimbabwe', *Health Policy and Planning* 15:368-77.

Hutchinson P, Akin J and Ssengooba F (2006) 'The impacts of decentralisation on health care seeking behaviours in Uganda', *International Journal of Health Planning and Management* 21(3):239-70.

Independent Online (21 September 2006) 'Second tobacco Bill is on the way', at http://www.int.iol. co.za/general/news/newsprint.php?art_id=qw1158872581125B231&sf=

Indymedia South Africa (18 November 2005) Photograph: Boystown housing protest, Indymedia Cape Town, accessed Dec 2006 at www.sa.indymedia.org

International Labour Organisation (2006) *Convention No. C182 was ratified by 163 countries*, ILO International Labour Standards Department, Geneva.

Jhamba T (1994) 'Mortality determinants in Zimbabwe: Policy implications,' mimeo, UZ Sociology Dept, Harare.

Kalumba K (1997) 'Towards an equity-oriented policy of decentralisation in health systems under conditions of turbulence: The case of Zambia', *EQUINET discussion paper* 6, EQUINET, Harare.

Kamupira M and London L (2005) 'Human rights commitments relevant to health made by states in southern Africa: Implications for health equity', *EQUINET discussion paper* 25, EQUINET, South Africa.

Kemp J, Aitken JM, LeGrand S, Mwale BI (2003) 'Equity in health sector responses to HIV/AIDS in Malawi', *EQUINET discussion paper* 6, EQUINET and OXFAM GB, Harare.

Kida T and Mackintosh M (2005) 'Public expenditure allocation and incidence under health care market liberalisation: A Tanzanian case study,' in Mackintosh and Koivusalo (eds) *Commercialisation of health care: Global and local dynamics and policy responses*, Palgrave Macmillan, Basingstoke.

Kumaranayake L, Mujinja P, Hongoro C and Mpembeni R (2000) 'How do countries regulate the health sector? Evidence from Tanzania and Zimbabwe', *Health Policy and Planning* 15: 357-67.

LaFond AK (1995) 'Improving the quality of investing in health: Lessons on sustainability', *Health Policy and Planning* 10 (Supplement): 63-76.

Lewis M (2005) 'Addressing the challenge of HIV/AIDS: Macroeconomic, fiscal and institutional issues', *Working paper* 58, Centre for Global Development, Washington DC.

Loewenson R, Sanders D and Davies R (1991) 'Challenges to equity in health and health care: A Zimbabwean case study', *Social Science and Medicine* 32(10): 1079-1088.

Loewenson R and McCoy D (2004) 'Access to antiretroviral therapy treatment in Africa: New resources and sustainable health systems are needed', *British Medical Journal* 328: 241–2.

London L (2003) 'Can human rights serve as a tool for equity?', *EQUINET policy paper* 14, EQUINET, Harare.

Mackintosh M (2001) 'Do health care systems contribute to inequalities?', in Leon D and Walt GT (eds) *Poverty, inequality and health: An international perspective*, Oxford Medical Publications, Oxford.
– (2007) 'Planning and market regulation: Strengths, weaknesses and interactions in the provision of less inequitable and better quality health care', paper prepared for the WHO CSDH Health Systems Knowledge Network, WHO CSDH, Geneva.

Mackintosh M and Koivusalo M (2005) *Commercialisation of health care: Global and local dynamics and policy responses*, Palgrave Macmillan, Basingstoke.

Magnussen L, Ehiri J and Jolly P (2004) 'Comprehensive versus selective primary health care: Lessons for global health policy', *Health Affairs* 23(3): 167-176, at http://content.healthaffairs.org/cgi/content/full/23/3/167

Makwiza I, Nyirenda L, Bongololo G, Loewenson R, Theobald S (2005) 'Monitoring equity and health systems in the provision of antiretroviral therapy: Malawi country report', *EQUINET discussion paper* 24, EQUINET, Harare.

Makwiza I, Nyirenda L, Goma F, Hassan F, Chingombe I, Bongololo G, Theobald S (2006) 'Equity and health systems in antiretroviral therapy roll out: An analysis from literature review of experiences from east and southern Africa, Malawi', *EQUINET discussion paper* 38, EQUINET, Harare.

McIntyre D, Gilson L, Mutyambizi V (2005) 'Promoting equitable health care financing in the African context: Current challenges and future prospects', *EQUINET discussion paper* 27, EQUINET, Harare.

McDonald DA and Ruiters G (2005) *The age of commodity: Water privatisation in southern Africa*, Earthscan, London.

Municipal Services Project (MSP) (2005) 'Poorly maintained water services, South Africa', photograph, Cape Town.

Muroyi R, Tayob R and Loewenson R (2003) 'Trade protocols and health: Issues for health equity in southern Africa', *EQUINET discussion paper* 6, EQUINET, Harare.

Mushi AK, Schellenberg JR, Mponda H, Lengeler C (2003) 'Targeted subsidy for malaria control with treated nets using a discount voucher system in Tanzania', *Health Policy Planning* 18:163-171.

Obimbo EM (2003) 'Primary health care: Selective or comprehensive, which way to go?' *East African Medical Journal* 80(1):7-10.

O'Donnell O, Van Doorslaer E, Rannan-Eliya R, Somanathan A, Adhikari SR, Harbianto D, Garg CC, Hanvoravongchai P, Huq MN, Karan A, Leung GM, Ng CW, Pande BR, Tin K, Tisayaticom K, Trisnantoro L, Zhang Y, Zhao Y (2005) 'Who benefits from public spending on health care in Asia?', *EQUITAP project working paper* 3, Erasmus Univ. and IPS, Rotterdam and Colombo, at www.equitap.org/publications/ wps/EquitapWP3.pd.

Omaswa F, Burnham G, Baingana G, Mwebesa H and Morrow R (1997) 'Introducing quality management into primary health care services in Uganda', *Bulletin of the World Health Organisation* 75(2): 155-161, WHO, Geneva.

Pan American Health Organisation (2006) 'Renewing primary health care in the Americas', a *PAHO position paper* of the Pan American Health Organisation.

Padarath A, Chamberlain C, McCoy D, Ntuli A, Rowson M and Loewenson R (2003) 'Health personnel in southern Africa: Confronting maldistribution and brain drain', *EQUINET discussion paper* 3, EQUINET, Harare.

PlusNews (2007) *Country profiles/ Treatment map*, IRIN, New York, at http://www.plusnews.org/aids/treatment. asp

Prata N, Montagu D and Jefferys E (2005) 'Private sector, human resources and health franchising in Africa', *Bulletin of the World Health Organisation* 83: 4, WHO, Geneva.

SADC (1999) *SADC Health Protocol*, Gabarone, accessed 6 Aug 2006 at http://www.sadc.int/english/documents/ legal/protocols/health.php#article3

Samba EM (Dec 2004) 'African health care systems: what went wrong?', *Editorial*, WHO, Geneva, at http://www .afro.who.int/regionaldirector/ emeriti/samba/reports/ afrhealthsys200412en.doc

Schouten E (2006) ' The Malawi government's emergency human resources programme', *Joint Consultation on AIDS and Human Resources for Health, Geneva, May 2006*, WHO, IOM and ILO, Geneva.

Schwarz T (1999) 'Tobacco economics: South Africa, a case study', *Bulletin von Medicus Mundi Schweiz* 72, at http://www. medicusmundi.ch/mms/services/bulletin/bulletin199901/ kap02/09southafrica.html

Solarsh G and Goga A (2003) 'Child health,' in Ijumba P, Day C and Ntuli A (eds) *South African Health Review 2003/4*, Health Systems Trust, Durban.

South African Government (1996) *Constitution of the Republic of South Africa*, accessed 2 June 2007 at http:// www.info.gov.za/ documents/constitution/index.htm

Stillman K and Bennet S (2006) *System-wide effects of the global fund: Preliminary findings from three country case studies*, ABT Associates, Maryland.

Storey P (1989) 'Health care in South Africa: The rights and responsibilities of the community', *Medicine and Law* 7(6): 649-655.

Treatment Action Campaign (24 Aug 2006) photograph, South Africa, at http://www.tac.org.za

Turshen M (1999) *Privatising health services in Africa*, Rutgers University Press, New Jersey.

UN Commission on Economic, Social and Cultural Rights (1966) *International Covenant on Economic, Social and Cultural Rights*, UNHCHR, Geneva, at http://www.unhchr.ch/html/ menu3/b/a_cescr.htm

UNDP (2005) *Human development report 2005*, UNDP, New York, accessed 2 Dec 2006 at http://hdr.undp.org/

UNICEF and Zimbabwe Ministry of Health and Child Welfare (1996) 'District health service costs, resource adequacy and efficiency: a comparison of three districts', mimeo, Harare.

United Nations (2007) *United Nations treaty collection*, New York, at http://untreaty.un.org

United Nations Office of the High Commission on Human Rights (2007) 'Reservations and ratifications: International Covenant on Economic, Social and Cultural Rights, New York 16 Dec 1966', UN, New York, at http://www.ohchr. org/english/countries/ ratification/3.htm

Van Rensburg HC and Fourie A (1994) 'Inequalities in South African health care', *South African Medical Journal* 84(2):95-103.

White A (2001) 'The great South African smoke-out', *Multinational Monitor* 22:1-2, at http://multinationalmonitor. org/mm2001/01jan-feb/corp8.html

World Bank (1993) *World Bank development report 1993: Investing in health*, OUP, New York.
– (2002) *Sourcebook on community-driven development in the Africa region*, World Bank, New York.
– (2006) *World development indicators database*, World Bank, New York, accessed 3 Dec 2006 at http://devdata.worldbank. org/wdi2006/contents/Section4.htm

World Health Organisation (1948) *Constitution of the World Health Organisation* accessed 2 June 2007 at http://www. who.int/gb/bd/PDF/BDenglish/Constitution.pdf
– (1981) 'International code of marketing of breast-milk substitutes', WHO, Geneva, accessed 6 Dec 2006 at http://www.who. int /nutrition/publications/ infant feeding/en/index.html
– (2002) *World health report 2002*, WHO, Geneva, accessed 1 Dec 2006 at http://www.who.int/whr/2002/en/ whr2002_ annex5.pdf
– (2003) *Community-based strategies for breastfeeding promotion and support in developing countries*, WHO, Geneva, at http://www. who.int/child-adolescent health/New_Publications/ NUTRITION/ISBN_92_4_ 159121_8.pdf
– (2006a) *World health report 2006: Working together for health*, WHO, Geneva, accessed 6 Dec 2006 at: http://www.who.int/ whr/2006/annex/en
– (2006b) *Progress on global access to antiretroviral therapy: A report on '3 by 5' and beyond,* WHO, Geneva, accessed 25 Nov 2006 at: http://www.who.int/hiv/mediacentre /news57/en/index. html
– (2006c) *Core indicators database*, WHO, Geneva.

WHO Afro (2006) 'Revitalising health services using the primary health care approach in the African region', WHO Regional Committee for Africa, Aug/ Sept 2006, Brazzaville.

WHO, UNAIDS and UNICEF (2007) *Towards universal access*, WHO, Geneva.

FAIR
FINANCING OF
HEALTH
systems

KEY ISSUES

Health systems and households are better able to reclaim resources for health when countries have adequate health financing, mobilised though progressive means, organised within a framework of universal coverage and allocated on the basis of need.

Based on estimates detailed in this section, the real costs of financing a health system are at least US$60 per person per year, with the most basic interventions for major public health burdens costing US$34 per capita. There are additional demands from AIDS and the Millennium Development Goals, costing up to US$150 per capita. Yet nearly half the countries in the region have not attained these levels overall and twelve countries fall below these levels in the public sector, the major source of health care for the low income majority.

Addressing this gap calls for governments to increase their own financing to health to at least the 15 per cent commitment made in Abuja, excluding external financing. However, we argue for 'Abuja plus' – for cancelling debts, releasing the resources going to debt servicing and allocating these funds to health, with dialogue between international agencies and governments to address the remaining shortfall.

No one who needs health services should be denied access due to inability to pay and the costs of health care should not threaten anyone's livelihood. High levels of out-of-pocket financing for health should thus be replaced by increased progressive tax revenues and measures to bring various forms of health insurance into a framework of universal coverage. Those with greater ability to pay should contribute a higher proportion of their income than those with lower incomes.

Government allocations are a critical way of offsetting disparities, if these disparities are explicitly taken into account when allocating public funds across areas and levels of the health system. Resource allocation formulae should include equity measures, with increased allocations to district and primary health care systems, and use of tax and regulatory measures to improve efficiency and equity in the private health sector.

Adequate resources for national health systems

The features of equity-oriented health systems described in Section 3 call for adequate, fair and sustainable health funding and an allocation of resources in response to need.

The basis for any dialogue on fairness in health is adequacy of funding (Doherty *et al.*, 1996). If public financing is inadequate, poor households pay more for a poorer quality of service and care (Aday and Anderson, 1981). We assess adequacy of national funding for health in three ways: health funding as a share of gross domestic product; health funding as a share of government spending; and per capita financing for health.

The United Nations Commission on Social Development recommended that countries should spend 5 per cent of their gross domestic product on health. Public spending on health in the region varies from 0.7 per cent of gross domestic product in DRC to 3.3 per cent in Malawi (see table 4.1). Private expenditure on health generally has relatively larger shares than public expenditure. Per capita spending on health ranged in 2003 from US$14 in DRC to US$669 in South Africa. Of this a range of only US$1 in DRC to US$258 in South Africa is spent in the public sector. Public spending has fallen relative to other sources of funds in the east and southern African region, except in Botswana, Uganda and Tanzania (see figure 4.1).

Table 4.1: Health financing in east and southern Africa

	GDP per Capita, US$ 2005	Per-capita expenditure on health US$ 2003	Public sector/capita expenditure on health US$ 2003	Expenditures on health as % of GDP (2003)*		% of GDP from external funding, 2004 (ODA)**
				Public	Private	
Angola	1227	40	22	2.4	5.9	5.9
Botswana	5297	375	135	3.3	0.4	0.4
DRC	121	14	1	0.7	27.4	27.4
Kenya	525	65	8	1.7	3.9	3.9
Lesotho	810	106	25	4.1	7.8	7.8
Madagascar	271	24	5	1.7	28.3	28.3
Malawi	161	46	5	3.3	26.8	26.8
Mauritius	5166	430	7	2.2	0.6	0.6
Mozambique	335	45	101	2.9	20.2	20.2
Namibia	3016	359	114	4.5	3.1	3.1
South Africa	5314	669	258	3.2	5.2	0.3
Swaziland	2415	324	7	3.3	4.9	4.9
Tanzania	316	29	5	2.4	16.1	16.1
Uganda	302	75	11	2.2	17	17
Zambia	622	51	14	2.8	20	20
Zimbabwe	259	132	22	2.8	4	4

GDP = gross domestic product; ODA = official development assistance
Sources: World Bank 2006; WHO 2006 from National Health Accounts, OECD DAC, 2006

Figure 4.1 Government expenditure as a % of total expenditure on health, east and southern Africa, 1998-2003

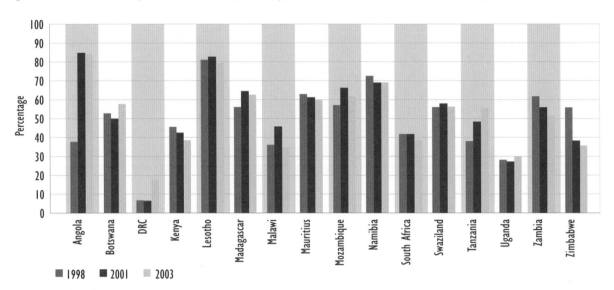

■ 1998 ■ 2001 ■ 2003

Source: WHO, 2006

In principle, government spending on health should be counter-cyclical to economic trends. Increased growth has certainly been associated with reduced public spending on health. However, this reduced spending has accompanied widening economic inequality and poverty, depleting the resources for rising health needs. As described in Section 2, an export-led and often speculative growth path has produced little gain for health sectors. The health sector does not earn from exports, faces the high costs of imported drugs and technology and tends to allocate a large share of budgets to wages.

Using the average per capita gross domestic product for the region of US$1,171, a 5 per cent share of gross domestic product represents an average of US$59 and 2.5 per cent represents an average of US$29 spent on health. Is this enough? What does a health system cost?

It is impossible to cost a health system precisely and international estimates tend to ignore national perceptions of how comprehensive or integrated the system should be. These estimates take little account of the social norms involved or the social consensus on what constitutes fair and actionable proposals. Many estimates are based on a package of services or discreet interventions rather than a functional health system which presents additional complications:

> '*Applying unit costs [for achieving the health-related Millennium Development Goals] to the treatment population could lead to both an over- and an under- estimate of the costs of reaching the health goals. It could be an over-estimate because the diseases are inter-related: tuberculosis spreads much more rapidly in the presence of AIDS; AIDS has an impact on infant and maternal mortality; and malaria kills a large number of young children. At the same time, it could be an under-estimate because of the many 'weak links in the chain' going from public health spending to health outcomes.*'

Devarajan *et al.*, 2002: 7

Using the average per capita GDP for the region of US$1171, a 5 per cent share of GDP represents an average of US$59, and 2.5 per cent represents an average of US$29 spent on health. Is this adequate financing for health? What does a health system cost?

However, the range of estimates made indicates the costs of a national health system that encompasses promotive, preventive, curative and rehabilitative care from primary care to referral levels:

- The WHO Commission on Macroeconomics and Health in 2003 estimated the cost of services to meet basic health needs of the poor as between US$34 and US$38 per capita per year.

- A costing study in Ghana in 2001 estimated that a district health system costs US$45 per capita per year.

- A WHO report in 2000 estimated a comprehensive functioning health system as costing between US$60 and US$80 per capita per year.

The 2003 Commission on Macroeconomics and Health estimate was calculated to ensure a minimally adequate set of interventions for HIV and AIDS, tuberculosis, malaria and early childhood and maternal illnesses, with the infrastructure necessary to deliver them in sub-Saharan Africa (WHO CMH, 2004). The estimated US$34 (2007) to US$38 (2015) per person per year would cover direct costs of medicines and health services, capital investments, complementary management and institutional support. Further investments in training new personnel would come mainly from the public sector (WHO CMH, 2004). The figure excludes elements such as family planning, tertiary hospitals and emergency care – part of any operational health system.

In 2001, the cost of scaling up the high-quality mission-hospital sector in Ghana was estimated as US$45 per person per year for recurrent costs, excluding initial capital costs for physical infrastructure (Arhin-Tenkorang and Buckle, 2001).

The 2000 WHO *World health report* made a more inclusive estimate of US$60 per capita for a comprehensive health system, including a minimally adequate set of interventions and the infrastructure to deliver them (Dodd and Cassels, 2006; Verheul and Rowson, 2002). In 2001, this estimate was revised up to US$80 per capita per year, based on a positive relationship between efficiency and health expenditure per capita up to that amount, 'suggesting there seems to be a minimum level of health expenditure below which the system simply cannot work well' (Evans *et al.*, 2001: 309).

Few countries meet the most basic level of US$60 per capita. Figure 4.2 shows the gap for the eleven countries whose total per capita spending on health falls below US$300.

- The WHO Commission on Macroeconomics and Health in 2003 estimated the cost of services to meet basic health needs of the poor as between US$34 and US$38 per capita per year.

- A costing study in Ghana in 2001 estimated that a district health system costs US$45 per capita per year.

- A WHO report in 2000 estimated a comprehensive functioning health system as costing between US$60 and US$80 per capita per year.

Figure 4.2 Per capita expenditure on health US$, east and southern African countries, 2003*

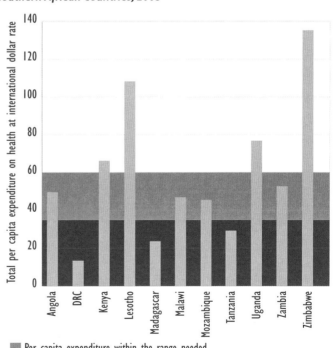

Per capita expenditure within the range needed
Per capita expenditure below the range needed
Actual per capita expenditure

*Excludes countries with per capita expenditures over US$300 (Botswana, Mauritius, Namibia, South Africa and Swaziland).

Source: WHO, 2006a

Seven of the sixteen countries in the east and southern African region are attempting to run health systems with inadequate resources of below US$60 per capita and three countries do not even have the US$34 per capita required for the most basic programmes.

This under-funding takes place in the context of additional annual demands due to AIDS and the region's commitment to meet the Millennium Development Goals for health, estimated to cost about US$146 per capita.

Seven of the sixteen countries in the east and southern African region are attempting to run health systems with inadequate resources of below US$60 per capita and three countries do not even have the US$34 per capita required for the most basic programmes. Since these figures include private spending, which goes largely to a minority for high-cost curative services, the public sector situation is likely to be worse.

This under-funding takes place in the context of additional annual demands due to AIDS and the region's commitment to meet the Millennium Development Goals for health, estimated to cost about US$146 per capita.

HIV and AIDS prevention and treatment demands between US$2.6 and US$4.2 billion annually, a further US$138 per capita (Devarajan *et al.*, 2002). Access or lack of access to low-cost generic antiretrovirals affects this figure, as discussed in Section 2 (Boulle *et al.*, 2003). Health systems need to invest an estimated extra US$3 to US$12 per capita between 2002 and 2015 (updated to current prices) to reverse health declines and meet the Millennium Development Goals for health (see table 4.2).

Current public sector spending of about US$29 per capita in the region reflects a shortfall of US$31 on WHO's estimated minimum needed for a functional health system meaning that countries need to almost double their current spending. Overall, current per capita spending in the region is US$177 per capita less than the level needed to prevent and treat HIV and AIDS and meet the Millennium Development Goals for health.

Clearly, this calls for more than minor adjustments to health spending. The two potential sources for large inputs into health financing, government spending and global public financing, both give emphasis to the need to control resource outflows from the region (as discussed in Section 2). While outflows and significant under-funding continue, fulfilling global commitments like the Millennium Development Goals will not be possible without international transfers into the region – as a matter of economic equity and public health obligation:

> '*For the avoidance of any doubt, the Committee wishes to emphasise that it is particularly incumbent on states parties and other actors in a position to assist, to provide 'international assistance and cooperation, especially economic and technical' which enable developing countries to fulfill their core and other obligations.*'
>
> UN Committee on Economic, Social and Cultural Rights, 2000

Table 4.2 Per capita demands of Millennium Development Goals for health in selected countries, 2002

| | Additional financing demands for health (in US$ millions) | | | | Additional financing demands for HIV/AIDS (in US$ millions) | | | |
| | 2002 | | 2015 | | 2002 | | 2015 | |
	Total	per capita	Total	per capita	Total	per capita	Total	per capita
Cameroon	607	39.28	n.a.	n.a.	77	4.98	n.a.	n.a.
Uganda	117	4.51	170	10.63	127	4.89	184	11.50
Tanzania	101	2.79	134	2.94	n.a.	n.a.	n.a.	n.a.
Malawi	1210	100.25	n.a.	n.a.	2500	207.13	n.a.	n.a.

Source: UNDP, 2002; World Bank, 2006b population estimates; UNDP, 2005

Recognising the declines in health resources and the need to prioritise health in government spending, African heads of state who met in Abuja in 2001 committed their countries to devoting 15 per cent of total government expenditure to the health sector:

'WE PLEDGE to set a target of allocating at least 15 per cent of our annual budget to the improvement of the health sector...

WE CALL UPON donor countries to complement our resource mobilisation efforts... to, among others, fulfill the yet to be met target of 0.7 per cent of their gross national product as official development assistance to developing countries...

WE UNDERTAKE to mobilise all the human, material and financial resources required to provide care and support and quality treatment to our populations infected with HIV/AIDS, tuberculosis and other related infections, and to organise meetings to evaluate the status of implementation of the objective of access to care...

WE ALSO RESOLVE to take immediate action to use tax exemption and other incentives to reduce the prices of drugs and all other inputs in health care services for accelerated improvement of the health of our populations.

WE, within the framework and spirit of our Sirte Declaration of 9 September 1999, renew the mandate of our brothers, President Bouteflika of Algeria, President Mbeki of South Africa and President Obasanjo of Nigeria, to continue discussion with our debt creditors on our behalf, with a view to securing the total cancellation of Africa's external debt in favour of increased investment in the social sector.'

AU Heads of state, Abuja, Federal Republic of Nigeria, 27 April 2001

How well have we performed on this commitment?

Performance so far is not impressive. As shown in figure 4.3 on page 113, when the Abuja commitment was made in 2001, total government spending on health was below 10 per cent for most east and southern African countries, having fallen after 1997. By 2004, while health spending had risen in five countries it had fallen in eleven countries. Despite renewed public attention directed at the issue, by 2005 evidence presented to the African Union showed that only five countries had increased their health spending, only one country had met the commitment (Botswana) and the remaining five (Angola, DRC, Kenya, Mauritius and Swaziland) continued to commit 8 per cent or less of their government budgets to health – just over half the share committed in Abuja.

Furthermore, given the rising share of external funding, performance on the 15 per cent target would need to exclude external funds to accurately reflect African governments' commitment. These funds are not always clearly differentiated in reported figures.

Despite renewed public attention directed at the issue, by 2005 evidence presented to the African Union showed that only five countries had increased their health spending, only one country had met the commitment (Botswana) and an equal number (Angola, DRC, Kenya, Mauritius and Swaziland) continued to commit 8 per cent or less of their government budgets to health – just over half the share committed in Abuja.

Using 2003 figures, ten of the sixteen countries would have had more than the Commission on Macroeconomics and Health basic level of US$34 per capita if they had met the Abuja public financing target. Eight of these countries would have had the WHO defined level of US$60 per capita. As figure 4.2 showed, six countries in the region are already above these levels but for Kenya, Angola, Zimbabwe and Mozambique, attaining the 15 per cent target makes the difference between reaching or not reaching these minimum per capita thresholds. For the other six countries, even reaching the Abuja target will not achieve these per capita thresholds.

While meeting the Abuja commitment does not meet the financing shortfall for many countries, it moves towards this goal. More importantly, it indicates that health has priority within public spending which is necessary for levering private and international financing for health and redressing poor households' high out-of-pocket spending.

The ability to provide adequate domestic financing is threatened by resource outflows, as discussed in Section 2. High levels of external debt consume a large share of government budgets in interest and debt repayments (see table 4.4).

Debt servicing exceeds health spending in five countries in the region. For example, Lesotho, with an estimated 29 per cent of adults living with HIV and AIDS, spent US$38 on debt which could have financed the basic Commission on Macroeconomics and Health interventions, while the health budget had only US$25 per capita (see table 4.4).

> While meeting the Abuja commitment does not meet the financing shortfall for many countries, it moves towards this goal. More importantly, it indicates that health has priority within public spending which is necessary for levering private and international financing for health and redressing poor households' high out-of-pocket spending..

Table 4.3 Health as a share (percentage) of government expenditure, east and southern Africa, 2003

Country	Per capita government expenditure on health (US$)	Health as % of total government expenditure	Per capita spending needed to meet the Abuja target (US$)	Additional per capita spending needed to meet the target (US$)
Angola	41	5.3	116	75
Botswana	218	7.5	436	218
DRC	3	5.4	8	5
Kenya	25	7.2	52	27
Lesotho	84	9.5	133	49
Madagascar	15	9.3	24	9
Malawi	16	9.1	26	10
Mauritius	261	9.2	426	165
Mozambique	28	10.9	39	11
Namibia	252	12.4	305	53
South Africa	258	10.2	379	121
Swaziland	185	10.9	255	70
Tanzania	16	12.7	27	3
Uganda	23	10.7	22	9
Zambia	26	11.8	33	7
Zimbabwe	47	9.2	77	30

Source: WHO, 2006b

Figure 4.3 Health as a percentage share of government expenditure, east and southern Africa, 1998–2005

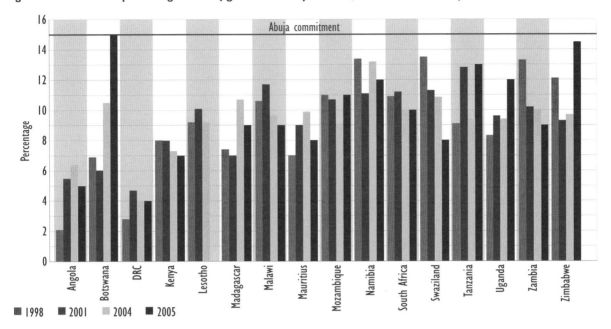

Source: WHO, 2006; 2005 data from AU reported in Atim, 2006

Table 4.4 Debt, debt service and health spending in east and southern African countries

Country	Total external debt 2003 (US $mn)*	Total debt service 1970–2003 (US$ mn)*	Debt service per capita expenditure 2002 (US$)*	Health per capita expenditure 2002 (US$)[i]	Estimated % adults living with HIV and AIDS[ii]
Angola	9,698	13,037	106	38	4
Botswana	514	1,653	36	171	37
DRC	11,170	7,322	18	4	4
Kenya	6,766	16,999	17	19	7
Lesotho	706	805	38	25	29
Madagascar	4,958	3,818	4	5	2
Malawi	3,134	2,388	3	14	14
Mauritius	2,550	4,391	207	113	n.a.
Mozambique	4,930	1,846	4	11	12
Namibia			0	99	21
South Africa[iii]	37,200	42,965	103	206	22
Swaziland	400	758	19	66	39
Tanzania	7,516	9,180	3	13	9
Uganda	4,553	3,161	3	18	4
Zambia	6,425	11,173	28	20	17
Zimbabwe	4,445	10,752	8	118	25
TOTAL	104,965	130,248			

*World Bank, World development indicators, 2005.
[i] WHO, World health report, 2004 [ii] UNAIDS, 2004, Report on the global AIDS epidemic
[iii] Debt figures for South Africa are drawn from the annual reports of the South African Reserve Bank, 1970–2003.
Adapted from: Africa Action, 2005

Debt relief in Uganda

In 2000 Uganda accessed debt relief under an enhanced Heavily Indebted Poor Countries debt relief initiative, with total debt relief initiatives saving approximately $90 million annually on Uganda's repayments of foreign debts. The Uganda government met with 45 civil society organisations in a consultative meeting with World Bank officials. The Uganda Debt Network, formed in 1996 to campaign for debt relief under the Jubilee 2000 campaign, led the civil society input.

The Uganda Debt Network's priority was to ensure that savings from debt relief were spent on poverty eradication – especially on education and health. The government set up a poverty action fund, ring-fencing a set of costed expenditures for 'directly poverty reducing' areas. The costs of these investments were compared with spending in the 2000/01 budget and the Government of Uganda re-prioritised expenditures in line with the findings. Hence the primary health care budget increased by 50 per cent and the water and sanitation budget increased by more than 40 per cent, in both cases using debt relief funds through the poverty action fund.

In this case, research and information, a political commitment to poverty reduction and civil society involvement ensured that debt relief savings were targeted towards meeting key poverty reduction goals.

Freer, 2002

Over the past three decades, east and southern African countries have paid on average US$14 per capita annually in debt servicing. Even in the 1990s, under the Heavily Indebted Poor Countries and debt relief programmes, when payments fell, debt servicing dwarfed government spending on health, and grant aid and tax revenue also fell, despite the clear returns to health of debt cancellation, exemplified in the Uganda case study above (UNDP, 2002).

Health financing thus calls for 'Abuja plus' – 15 per cent government spending on health accompanied by international support and debt cancellation.

Health financing thus calls for 'Abuja plus': 15 per cent government spending on health accompanied by international support and debt cancellation.

Fair financing of health systems

It is not simply the adequacy of health funding that is important but also its fairness. If health systems are to be national (nationally determined and managed), comprehensive (adequately financed across all priority health needs), universal (covering and accessible to all) and people-centred (ensuring inclusion and not raising barriers to health care), then resource mobilisation needs to:

If health systems are to be national, comprehensive, universal and people centred then resource mobilisation needs to: be obtained fairly ; avoid further impoverishing poor people through increased health service charges; and allocate resources towards areas of highest health need and greatest health impact.

- be obtained fairly (generally from those who are wealthier);
- avoid further impoverishing poor people through increased health service charges; and
- allocate resources towards areas of highest health need and greatest health impact.

Examining the different sources of health financing (see tables 4.5 and 4.6) shows that most countries in the region have high levels of tax funding but also often high and rising private, out-of-pocket financing, variable levels of external financing and limited social security expenditure. The efficiency and equity of these measures depends on the size of the risk pool they create and how far they provide for cross subsidy between rich and poor, and between the healthy and ill (McIntyre *et al.*, 2005).

General tax funding creates the largest risk pool and potential for cross subsidy. But overall tax rates in most African countries are well below 20 per cent of gross domestic product, compared to the 40 per cent found in developed countries. Technical capacity gaps, administrative bottlenecks, a large share of informal employment, inefficient tax collection systems and already high tax burdens limit tax rates in east and southern African countries (DFID Health Resource Centre, 2007). Adding to the limited tax base, there has been a shift towards indirect taxes through value added tax and general sales tax. Indirect taxes are regressive, with the exception of high tax rates on luxury goods and exemptions of value added tax on basic foodstuffs and food in local, informal markets which escape the indirect tax net (McIntyre, 2007).

Table 4.5 Sources of health financing in east and southern Africa, 2004

Country	Government health expenditure as % of total health expenditure	Private health expenditure as % of total health expenditure	External resources for health as % of total health expenditure	Social security expenditure on health as % of government health expenditure	Private prepaid plans as % of private health expenditure	Out-of-pocket expenditure as % of private health expenditure
Angola	84.8	15.2	4.5	0	0	100.0
Botswana	64.2	35.8	2.2	0	20.9	28.3
DRC	21.3	78.7	16	0	n.a.	100.0
Kenya	40.0	60.0	14.8	9.4	6.0	82.4
Lesotho	80.2	19.8	6.5	0	n.a.	18.2
Madagascar	69.5	30.5	27.6	n.a.	8.2	91.8
Malawi	36.3	63.7	25.9	0	1.6	42.4
Mauritius	61.1	38.9	0.9	7.8	n.a.	100.0
Mozambique	60.5	39.5	32.7	0	0.5	37.3
Namibia	70.6	29.4	5.0	1.8	76.3	19.1
South Africa	38.6	61.4	0.4	4.6	77.5	17.2
Swaziland	56.5	43.5	5.8	0	21.9	41.2
Tanzania	50.5	49.5	21.3	4.5	5.2	81.5
Uganda	31.4	68.6	30.1	0	0.2	54.1
Zambia	50.4	49.6	22.2	0	n.a.	69.4
Zimbabwe	45.3	54.7	5.0	0	23.0	55.3

NB: External resources include all grants and loans passing through government or private entities for health goods and services, in cash or in kind. n.a. = data not available

Source: WHO, 2006b

Table 4.6 Per capita spending on health financing in east and southern African, 1998 and 2004

	Per capita US$ spending on health 1998				Per capita US$ spending on health 2004			
	Public sources	Donor sources	Private sources	Overall	Public sources	Donor sources	Private sources	Overall
Angola	15	1	26	41	44	2	8	52
Botswana	122	6	108	230	316	11	176	492
DRC	1	1	13	14	3	2	11	14
Kenya	31	9	37	68	25	9	38	63
Lesotho	77	4	19	96	90	7	22	112
Madagascar	11	7	8	19	19	7	8	27
Malawi	15	13	27	42	18	13	31	49
Mauritius	176	4	105	281	299	4	190	489
Mozambique	16	9	12	28	29	16	19	48
Namibia	227	8	87	314	273	19	113	386
South Africa	252	1	350	602	275	3	439	714
Swaziland	186	62	143	329	176	18	135	311
Tanzania	7	6	12	19	15	6	14	29
Uganda	13	14	31	44	26	25	58	84
Zambia	32	12	19	51	27	12	26	53
Zimbabwe	152	48	120	272	68	8	82	150

Sources: National Health Accounts Network, ESA NHA, 2001; WHO, 2006

In the past two decades, as described in Section 2, wider liberalisation was accompanied by support for a mix of public, private and voluntary providers, local resource gathering, user charges, as well as a shift towards liberalised private insurance arrangements and away from more equitable tax-based financing mechanisms (Mackintosh and Koivusalo, 2005).

The increase in private (usually out-of-pocket) financing in most east and southern African countries raises concerns about fairness of financing and of the size of risk pools and opportunities available for cross subsidies. This section explores the opportunities for improved progressive tax funding and enhancing the equity and efficiency of other financing sources.

Mobilising resources for health through progressive revenue

> In progressive tax systems personal income tax is complemented by a reasonably substantial company income tax component, with value-added tax contributing a low proportion of general tax revenue.

In progressive tax systems personal income tax is complemented by a reasonably substantial company income tax component, with value-added tax contributing a low proportion of general tax revenue.

East and southern African countries can consider a range of wealth taxes, including taxes on financial transaction flows, luxury airline travel and currency exchanges (McIntyre *et al.*, 2005). Zimbabwe has, for example, introduced a 3 per cent levy on top of the existing personal and company income tax rates to fund AIDS interventions.

Countries can limit the percentage of profits that foreign corporations are allowed to relocate – such companies have tended to relocate profits leading to minimal tax revenue and benefit for African governments from these foreign investments (Bond, 2006).

Internationally, new income streams have been proposed, including an airline ticket levy, a stamp duty on currency transactions, an international financing facility for immunisation and a global lottery. The tax on currency transactions or 'Tobin tax' has been implemented in France and Belgium. The revenue potential of these types of taxes is significant. The worldwide application of the stamp duty on currency transactions alone would generate about US$35 billion (Hillman, 2006).

While many of these options for tax revenue are still under-explored, new attention has turned to health insurance. Private insurance of any magnitude is largely restricted to southern Africa (Botswana, Madagascar, South Africa, Swaziland, Zimbabwe) and Kenya, mainly through private voluntary coverage of formal sector employees. Community health insurance (pre-payment) schemes have expanded in the region, and we discuss this later. They remain, however, a small component of overall health care financing (see table 4.5). The experience of private voluntary health insurance has not been positive, with limited coverage, fragmentation of risk pools and rapid, uncontrolled cost spirals threatening sustainability (McIntyre *et al.*, 2005). Nevertheless, their expansion calls for measures to regulate these schemes and to provide incentives for them to integrate, increase their risk pool, cover low income populations and contribute to public health services.

The experience of private voluntary health insurance has not been positive, with limited coverage, fragmentation of risk pools and rapid, uncontrolled cost spirals threatening sustainability

Several countries in the region are considering mandatory social health insurance, compulsory by law for all or some citizens. Tanzania, South Africa, Kenya and Zimbabwe are exploring or introducing social health insurance schemes. While South Africa and Tanzania have vowed to extend insurance to a larger section of the population, no country in the region has declared an intention to move towards universal coverage, an explicit goal in Ghana, for example.

The Zimbabwe parliamentary committee on health's consultations on the proposed mandatory national health insurance suggested that such schemes are likely to be contested where employment levels are falling, where tax levels are already high and where medical aid societies are relatively well established. High inflation further complicates the costing of the benefits package (Rusike, 2007). Where health insurance covers selected groups, there have been criticisms of a resulting two-tier health system, creating a divide between those who are insured (with access to a range of high quality health services) and those who are uninsured (often consigned to under-resourced public sector services). Tax funding is required to cover the costs of care for groups who are hard to reach through insurance, such as those in the informal sector or the self-employed. If civil servants are amongst the first group to be covered, limited government funds can be diverted for these payments from tax funding for public health services (Kutzin, 1998).

Levering contributions from private financing for public health care in South Africa

The way health care is currently financed in South Africa contributes to the inequity between public and private health sectors. Most health care funds in South Africa (62 per cent) flow via private sector financing intermediaries, the largest share of these being medical aid schemes. Public sector providers receive about a third (39 per cent) of all health care expenditure while private sector providers receive 61 per cent. This is inequitable when one considers the number of people treated by the public sector.

Recognising the inequities between the public and private sectors, the South African government initiated a process to develop a health sector charter. This charter is an agreement between the public, private and non-governmental organisation sector to transform the health sector in South Africa.

The charter has four pillars:

1 **Access** to health services

2 **Equity** in health care

3 **Quality** of health services

4 **Empowerment** – broad-based black economic empowerment.

The charter is almost complete and has drawn all stakeholders together to address these issues. An innovative strategy in the charter is the implementation of the public health enhancement fund which sees the private sector contributing a percentage of their funds to strengthen the public health sector.

Chetty, 2007

Mandatory health insurance in Kenya

Kenya is explicitly pursuing the introduction of mandatory insurance through national health insurance. This will provide a mechanism to move away from user fees, given their adverse consequences, and to reduce other out-of-pocket payments made to private providers. The insured will have access to a range of providers accredited on the basis of adequacy and quality of care and their willingness to accept insurance scheme reimbursement rates. Accreditation will include public and private not-for-profit facilities, like those run by missions. Private for-profit facilities may be accredited if they are willing to charge the reasonable insurance company rates. This approach will limit out-of-pocket payments to services outside of the benefit package. The scheme is paying careful attention to improving drug procurement, distribution and stock control during implementation to ensure that out-of-pocket payments are reduced effectively.

McIntyre *et al.*, 2005

An example of mandatory health insurance as the basis for universal coverage

The Ghanaian government has made an explicit commitment to achieve universal coverage under a national health insurance scheme, aiming to enrol 60 per cent of citizens within 10 years of its inception. Two aspects of the scheme's design make the commitment to universal coverage possible. Firstly, the insurance explicitly includes those in both the formal and informal sectors from the outset. Secondly, although there are different sources of funding for the formal and informal sectors, they will belong to one, unified scheme.

The basis of the national health insurance system will be district-wide 'mutual health insurance schemes' – a form of community-based health insurance. The *National Health Insurance Act*, introduced in 2003, requires that every citizen joins either a district-wide mutual health insurance scheme or a private mutual or commercial insurance scheme. However, government subsidies will only be provided to district-wide mutual health insurance schemes, thus creating a strong incentive for people not to 'opt-out' of the integrated system by purchasing cover through private insurers.

Those employed in the formal sector will be covered through payroll-deducted contributions to the Social Security and National Insurance Trust Fund. Those outside the formal sector are expected to make direct contributions to their district mutual health insurance scheme, with different levels for low, middle and high income groups. The national health insurance fund will fully subsidise the contributions of the indigent, drawing funds from a national health insurance levy of 2.5 per cent sales tax on almost all goods and services, a 2.5 per cent payroll deduction for formal sector employees as part of their contribution to the Social Security and National Insurance Trust Fund and government allocations (including both general tax revenue and donor funding). The Social Security and National Insurance Trust Fund will allocate funds to each district mutual health insurance scheme, partially subsidising contributions for low-income households and fully subsidising contributions for the indigent.

There is considerable government and external support to promote successful implementation of the national health insurance scheme. The scheme was an election promise which the government is committed to fulfilling.

McIntyre, 2007

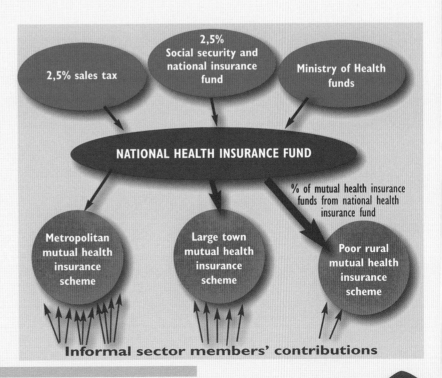

Experience of health insurance in and beyond the region suggests that the introduction and operation of mandatory national health insurance must be put in the context of a political and policy commitment to universal coverage and a clear strategic plan to achieve this.

Experience of health insurance in and beyond the region suggests that the introduction and operation of mandatory national health insurance must be put in the context of a political and policy commitment to universal coverage and a clear strategic plan to achieve this.

Progressive tax funding provides the most effective means of ensuring equity and universality, suggesting that it is the best financing mechanism for countries in the region that face high levels of poverty and inequality.

However, many countries are already grappling with multiple, often fragmented financing arrangements with a wide range of benefit packages and contribution schedules. In these conditions, moving towards universal coverage calls for action plans to include:

- proposals for a steady increase in tax funding as the core of universal coverage;

- safeguards and provisions to ensure that employer contributions for civil servants do not divert government resources from tax funding of public sector services;

- proposals for tax funding to partially subsidise contributions for low-income households and fully subsidise contributions for households living below the poverty line;

- commitments to avoid co-payments;

- legal and administrative options for harmonising multiple benefits packages and contribution schedules across voluntary insurance schemes towards a common benefit package and contribution schedule;

- proposals for increasing the risk pool and building subsidies across voluntary insurance schemes;

- legal provisions to ensure that all schemes use a progressive, or at least proportional, contribution structure and avoid flat rate contributions; and

- proposals for funds collected to be applied so that they improve geographic distribution of services and equitable access to benefit packages, ensuring entitlements equate to real access.

Reducing out-of-pocket spending, including user fees

Out-of-pocket spending on health has escalated sharply in east and southern African (see figure 4.4). It exceeds 25 per cent of total health care expenditure in more than three-quarters of east and southern African countries, and countries with high levels of inequality also have high out-of-pocket spending on health. Six of the nine countries in the region with a human poverty index higher than 40 (a high level of poverty) also have high shares of out-of-pocket spending (more than 40 per cent). Botswana, Lesotho and Mozambique, with high levels of poverty, are the exceptions. Of eight countries with Gini coefficients higher than 50, seven have high out-of-pocket spending (above 40 per cent of total) (see table 4.7).

Figure 4.4 Comparison of out-of-pocket, government and external funding levels in African countries

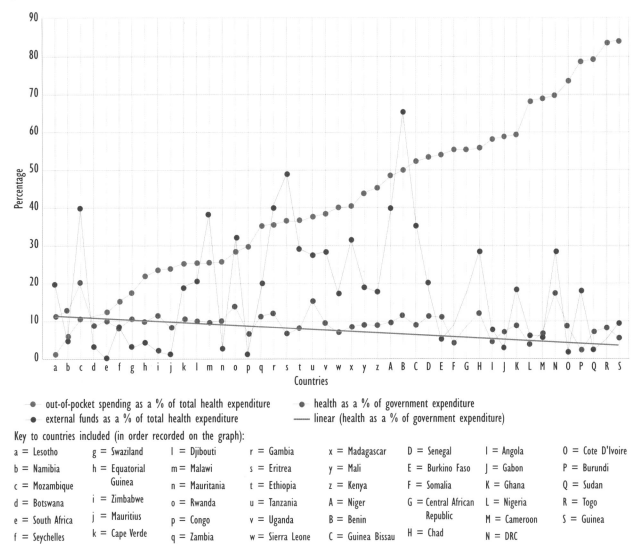

● out-of-pocket spending as a % of total health expenditure   ● health as a % of government expenditure
● external funds as a % of total health expenditure   —— linear (health as a % of government expenditure)

Key to countries included (in order recorded on the graph):

a = Lesotho	g = Swaziland	l = Djibouti	r = Gambia	x = Madagascar	D = Senegal	I = Angola	O = Cote D'Ivoire
b = Namibia	h = Equatorial	m = Malawi	s = Eritrea	y = Mali	E = Burkino Faso	J = Gabon	P = Burundi
c = Mozambique	Guinea	n = Mauritania	t = Ethiopia	z = Kenya	F = Somalia	K = Ghana	Q = Sudan
d = Botswana	i = Zimbabwe	o = Rwanda	u = Tanzania	A = Niger	G = Central African	L = Nigeria	R = Togo
e = South Africa	j = Mauritius	p = Congo	v = Uganda	B = Benin	Republic	M = Cameroon	S = Guinea
f = Seychelles	k = Cape Verde	q = Zambia	w = Sierra Leone	C = Guinea Bissau	H = Chad	N = DRC	

Generated from WHO NHA database (2002 estimates);Source: McIntyre *et al.*, 2005

Out-of-pocket spending largely derives from user fees charged by public and private providers (including informal drug sellers and traditional healers), payments in kind and payments in advance for services. Households also spend significant sums on transport and other indirect costs and face opportunity costs such as lost work time.

For the private sector, user fees provide revenue and are linked to profit motives. In the public sector the rationale for user charges ranges from the fees being a means of generating revenue and creating incentives for patients to use the referral system correctly to the fees increasing community involvement and providers' responsiveness to patients (McIntyre *et al.*, 2005). It is also argued that those who can afford to pay should pay, to ease the burden on government who can then concentrate its resources on the poor (McIntyre *et al.*, 2005). However, studies in east and southern African have encountered problems, even with low fees, motivating a review of policy.

Out-of-pocket spending in Tanzania

In one rural district of Tanzania, health workers found a growing trend of severe malaria between 1998 and 2002. Community members reported that poverty and the use of traditional medicines meant that people delayed going to health services:

> 'Leave alone the issue of fees, some households find it difficult to raise even 1000 shillings in a month and end up opting for paracetamol from kiosks or just use mitishamba (local herbs).'

Health workers and some community leaders found that during long rainy seasons (March-May and October-December), malaria in under fives peaked since villagers were busy preparing their rice and maize *shambas* (farms), with little time to take care of their children. This period was reported to be the time when households have little cash because they have not yet harvested and what they have is spent either on fertilisers and other farm inputs or on food like maize flour. From October each year, most households tend to start saving for the December Christian and Islamic holidays, new-year celebrations and school fees for their children. This leaves little or no money for health care, including for the costs of transport to health services for those living very far away.

Mubyazi and Hutton, 2003

Out-of-pocket spending on tuberculosis in Malawi

A recent analysis of the costs of obtaining a tuberculosis diagnosis in urban Lilongwe also highlighted the high cost of accessing public health care for the poor (Mann *et al.*, 2002). Patients on average spent 972 Malawi kwacha (US$13) and lost up to 22 days work while accessing a tuberculosis diagnosis. For non-poor patients, the total costs equated to 124 per cent of total monthly income or 174 per cent after food expenditure. For the poor, this cost rose to 248 per cent of monthly income or 584 per cent after food.

The study reportedly found that men spent more than women for their diagnosis and women took longer to access care than men. As patients were seeking care, 12.7 per cent of all activities were done by children – and mostly by female children (11.5 per cent). For poor women, female children were found to replace activities for 65 days – possibly days lost from school. Various studies report the coping strategies households use to pay for tuberculosis care, including: missing meals, taking on high interest local loans, selling assets (water buckets and cooking utensils), stopping the purchase of clean water or not paying school fees.

Mann *et al.*, 2002; Govt of Malawi Ministry of Health and Population, 2002

Table 4.7 Poverty, inequality and out-of-pocket spending on health in east and southern Africa, 2003/04

Country	Human Poverty Index 2003	GINI co-efficient 2003	Government expenditure on health as % of total health expenditure 2004	Private prepaid plans as % of private health expenditure 2004	Out-of-pocket expenditure as % of private health expenditure 2004
Angola	41.5	n.a.	84.8	0	100
Botswana	48.4	63.0	64.2	20.9	28.3
DRC	41.4	n.a.	21.3	n.a.	100
Kenya	35.4	42.5	40	6	82.4
Lesotho	47.6	63.2	80.2	n.a.	18.2
Madagascar	35.3	47.5	69.5	8.2	91.8
Malawi	43.4	50.3	36.3	1.6	42.4
Mauritius	11.4	47.5	61.1	n.a.	100
Mozambique	49.1	39.6	60.5	0.5	37.3
Namibia	33.0	70.7	70.6	76.3	19.1
South Africa	30.9	57.8	38.6	77.5	17.2
Swaziland	52.9	60.9	56.5	21.9	41.2
Tanzania	35.8	38.2	50.5	5.2	81.5
Uganda	36.0	43	31.4	0.2	54.1
Zambia	46.4	52.6	50.4	n.a.	69.4
Zimbabwe	45.9	56.8	45.3	23	55.3

n.a. = data not available
Sources: WHO, 2006b; UNDP, 2005

Fee charges have been found in studies to:

- encourage inappropriate self-treatment and incomplete drug doses;
- discourage early use of health facilities, with dramatic declines in service use (over 50 per cent in Kenya and 33 per cent in Zambia) particularly among the most vulnerable groups (Blas and Limbambala, 2001; Frankish, 1986; Hussein and Mujinja, 1997; Kipp *et al.*, 2001; Mwabu *et al.*, 1995; Waddington and Enyimayew, 1989 and 1990);
- have poorly designed and ineffective exemption mechanisms to protect poor people (Gilson *et al.*, 1995; McPake *et al.*, 1992; Willis and Leighton, 1995);
- contribute to poverty in vulnerable households (Gilson and McIntyre, 2005);
- generate less than 5-10 per cent of operating costs on average and be expensive to collect (Witter, 2005; Creese, 1991; Gilson, 1997);

- compel use of poverty-inducing coping mechanisms, like borrowing, cutting essential expenses and selling productive assets (Verheul and Rowson, 2002); and

- have weak or temporary impacts on the referral system without corresponding changes in the quality of care (McCoy and Gilson,1997; Lennock, 1994; Hongoro and Chandiwana,1994; Zigora *et al.*, 1996; Wang'ombe, 1997).

'*When my elder sister was sick, first of all she paid for her own medical care with the money she earned from where she worked in Dar es Salaam. Her condition didn't improve. She was then brought here from Dar es Salaam. Our family later decided that our brother should go to Dar es Salaam and sell all her belongings so that we could get money to take her to Ndanda hospital. The money brought was used up but my sister didn't recover. My father put his coconut plantation in pawn and we took her to a traditional healer but she still didn't recover. Finally, we just took her home and waited for her days to finish as there was nothing left to sell to help her. In the end she died and my father lost his plantation as he couldn't afford to reclaim it within the agreed time.*'

Focus group discussion in Lindi, Tanzania, Save the Children, 2005

A review of user fees in Africa found that they contributed little to public service revenue and offered arguable relief for ministries of finance trying to improve health budgets (Yates, 2006). In contrast, abolishing user fees has resulted in significant increases in the use of services, especially by the poor. In Uganda, for example, service use rose from 41 per cent in 1999 to 84 per cent in 2002 (Uganda Debt Network, 2004; Hutton, 2004) (see figure 4.5). This positive impact has also been found in relation to other user charges – free net retreatment policies in Malawi, for example, boosted community participation and improved coverage of insecticide treated bednets (Govt of Malawi MoHP, 2005).

South Africa, Zambia and Uganda, among other countries, have removed user fees for some or all public health services and there is pressure for other countries to adopt a similar policy. Existing experience demonstrates that fee removal needs to be undertaken carefully, given the substantial and sustained increases in use which could lead to drug shortages, staff difficulties and lower quality of care. Health worker consultation is important. On the one hand, fees have been used by communities to supplement resources at district level and help compensate health workers (as further discussed in Section 5, health workers value this contribution). On the other hand, health workers are put in a difficult position when patients cannot afford services because of charges. Simply removing user fees without improving basic services can leave health workers unable to offer the services people need.

Figure 4.5 Health service utilisation in Uganda before and after abolition of user fees, Kisoro district

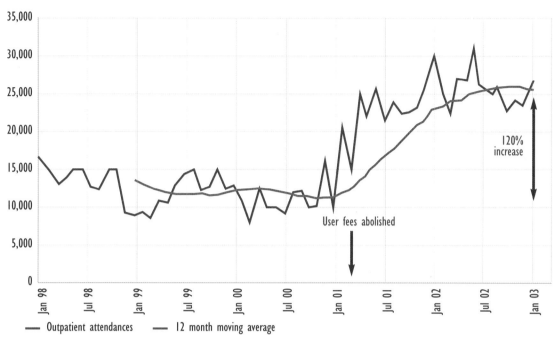

Source: Hutton, 2004: 48

> '*Aaa, you know, rural life is tough, most of the villagers have low income, have limited earnings. Now, if a facility like ours cannot serve them by ensuring that drugs are available, it is going to be difficult for them to purchase every kind of medicine from shops. And we don't feel comfortable to consult a patient and fail to provide him or her with appropriate medicines. In that sense I don't feel that I have done my job in the way I would like it to be done.*'
> Health worker in Tanzania, Manzi et al., 2004

Removing fees thus needs to take place with increased public funding for health – especially at primary care level, accompanied by provisions for community level funds, and in consultation with health workers and the public (Pearson, 2005).

While we have focused on user fees in public services, user charges in the private sector are often higher, with wider income differentials in the use of care. Private sector use in South Africa was heavily concentrated in the higher income groups (83 per cent of the highest income quintile compared with 37 per cent in the lowest income quintile). The variation in use across income groups was much lower in Zambia (22 per cent in the highest income quintile and 16 per cent in the lowest income quintile) (Makinen et al., 2000). Increasing costs and charges in the private for-profit sector make these services unaffordable for most.

Community-based health insurance schemes, community pre-payment schemes or mutual health organisations have been promoted as an alternative to out-of-pocket payments. Evidence suggests these schemes may provide financial protection against unexpected health care costs for their members and improve access to services (Schneider and Diop, 2004). However, their coverage is relatively low, they do not incorporate the most vulnerable households, giving them small risk pools and limited cross-subsidies, and they generate limited revenue (Chee *et al.*, 2002). Furthermore, the poorest and most vulnerable groups seem to be excluded from these schemes due to cost barriers (Ekman, 2004; Jakab and Krishnan, 2004).

Claims that these schemes are the new 'one size fits all solution' to the

Removal of user fees in Uganda

Uganda introduced user fees on a universal basis in 1993. Although revenue generation was relatively low (generally less than 5 per cent of expenditure), it was an important source of funds for supplementing health worker salaries, maintaining facilities and purchasing additional drugs. However, there was a dramatic decline in the use of health care services and there were growing concerns about the impact on the poor.

User fees at public sector facilities were abolished in March 2001, with the exception of private wards. Various studies showed that health services use increased immediately and dramatically. Two years after the abolition of fees, sustained increases in use of 77 per cent were recorded. Evidence from the *Ugandan national household surveys* (1999/2000 and 2002/03) and from the health management information system highlighted how poor people had benefited from the removal of fees. While the incidence of reported illness did not change significantly, ill people were more likely to seek professional care and lose fewer days from work. Cost was a less frequent cause cited for not seeking care (down from 50 per cent to 30 per cent). These gains were most marked in the poorest quintile.

However, the evidence also indicates that gains in use and in health care coverage could not have been achieved without an increase in the resources available for public sector health services. Of particular importance was the pro-active provision of a US$5.5 million buffer fund by the Ministry of Health to offset the potential impact on availability of drugs arising from the loss of fee revenue and increases in use. External funders set up a sector-wide approach support to the Ministry of Health which doubled the budget between 1999/2000 and 2002/03. The Ministry of Health directed the additional resources preferentially to primary health care services and district budgets increased seven-fold after 1999. There was some loss in staff morale related to a loss of fee revenue used to supplement staff salaries and an increase in workload of about 47 per cent. Health workers and health facility management committees also indicated that maintenance of health facilities and cleanliness had declined. While the sustained improvements in access for poor people were triggered by removing user fees, sustaining the effect was a product of increased and well directed funding (above and beyond the loss of fee revenue). The experience also highlights the negative effects on health workers' pay and workloads that need to be taken into account.

Pearson, 2005 ; McIntyre, 2007

health care financing gap in the region should thus be treated with caution. As raised earlier in relation to social health insurance, considering the end goal of universal coverage, we need to consider how to integrate these schemes into the overall health system and specify measures to ensure consistency in their contribution levels and benefit packages (Bennett *et al.*, 1998). However, even with the options to widen pre-payment, integrate price discrimination and exempt poor and vulnerable groups from fees, the gains to health equity are greatest when fee charges are removed.

The Tanzania community health fund

In the Tanzania community health fund, government and external funds are used to provide 'matching grants' according to the amount of revenue generated by each scheme. This is intended as an incentive for the scheme to register as many members and generate as much revenue from scheme contributions as possible. It does mean, however, that areas with less poverty which are likely to generate the largest revenue from contributions, generally secure the largest share of subsidies from government and external funds, raising equity concerns.

Previous evaluations of community health fund schemes in Tanzania have identified four main causes of low enrolment in the schemes: inability to pay membership contributions, low quality of health care provided by community health fund facilities, lack of trust in community health fund managers and community members not understanding the rationale of the risk covered by the schemes. A study in 2004 found that these barriers were related to the performance of district managers. District managers made little effort to address the problem of ability to pay, ignored exemption guidelines from the central government and demands for exemption from the communities, and responded ineffectively to requests to improve health care from the communities. They made little effort to educate communities about the benefits and rationale of risk-sharing and prepayment concepts. This resistance in the district managers was found to stem from the top-down execution of the community health fund in the districts.

The equity concerns and study findings indicate that the design of prepayment schemes needs to be more effectively addressed. In particular, an equitable injection of public funds is needed to protect access to care in low income areas and policy makers should consult district governments and communities to better understand implementation constraints, including those affecting improvements in the quality of health care

McIntyre *et al.*, 2005; Kamuzora and Gilson, 2006

A win-win situation is achieved, enhancing equity and effective coverage of health services, when user fees are removed, as long as this is accompanied by a clear statement of the benefits or essential health services people are entitled to and adequate funding to secure this package.

A win-win situation is achieved, enhancing equity and effective coverage of health services, when user fees are removed, as long as this is accompanied by a clear statement of the benefits or essential health services people are entitled to and adequate funding to secure this package.

Predictable external financing

As noted earlier, while mobilising more domestic resources is central for adequate health financing, in many countries the significant resource outflows, highlighted in Section 2, and low discretionary budgets make external financing essential. Given this central role, the variability and unpredictability of these funds (see figure 4.6) and their short-term nature is cause for concern. External funds also have the potential to distort national health priorities (EQUINET SC, 1998). The impact of spending caps imposed by medium-term expenditure frameworks stipulated when accepting external funding is discussed in Section 5.

Sector-wide approach (SWAp), mechanisms were established to provide opportunities for joint financing of different components within the health sector and for pooling funds. Through coordinated management of external finances and planned resource allocation, sector-wide approaches enabled external funds to be used in line with domestic policy priorities (McIntyre *et al.*, 2005; Walford, 2002; Govt of Malawi MoHP, 2002). An assessment of sector-wide approaches in east and southern Africa found that government capacity to plan and implement programmes had increased, as had ownership of programme policy and management, and international agency co-ordination (Brown, 2001).

Despite evidence of gains, east and southern African countries have faced difficulties in negotiating for global initiatives like the Global Fund for AIDS, Tuberculosis and Malaria to use the sector-wide approach and some partners insist on maintaining parallel projects or programmes. Managing sector-wide approach funds has also been beset by difficulties, for example, in obtaining financial reports from local levels, in accessing funds from finance ministries, in reconciling

Figure 4.6 Externally funded expenditure on health as a % of total health expenditure for selected east and southern African countries, 1998-2004

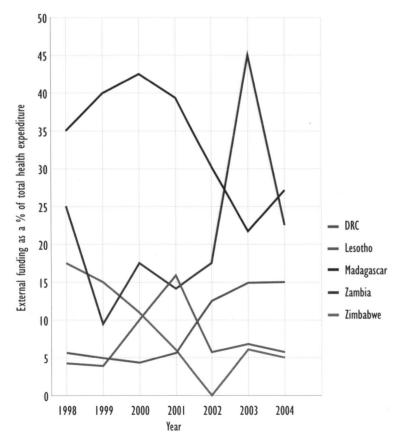

Source: WHO, 2006b

expenditure figures between finance and health ministries and with different reporting periods for external funders and government (SIDA, 2003). A 2001 study on integrating vertical programmes into the sector-wide approach in Zambia found that programmes encountered problems in reorganising technical responsibilities and procurement arrangements, and making the necessary changes in government and international agency relationships (Brown, 2001). Experience thus suggests that the sector-wide approach can play an important role in co-ordinating domestic and external financing but needs to be treated as a process, with mechanisms and evidence to support regular strategic planning and review and the capacity building to facilitate these complex management issues (Govt of Malawi MoHP, 2002). Confidence in the process demands shared vision and understanding of the essential package of health benefits that the approach is seeking to secure across all districts. This means that the design of such approaches needs to include processes to develop this shared understanding, with mechanisms to widen partnership (including with civil society) and for monitoring and reporting on progress.

More recently, a general budget support approach has been used by some external funders to channel their funds through the central Ministry of Finance. The ministry then allocates the funds to the sectors, in consultation with key stakeholders, including the external funders. The United Kingdom's Department for International Development adopted a

SWAp in Tanzania

After two years of implementation, significant results have been achieved under the sector-wide approach (SWAp) in Tanzania. An integrated financial management system means that external funds are merged into a holding account with the Central Bank of Tanzania (commonly referred to as 'the basket'), released to the consolidated fund and allocated to the spending units on a quarterly basis, following the approval by the basket financing committee. A joint audit by the Office of the Auditor General and an external audit company is performed annually, within six months of the end of the Tanzanian fiscal years (June for central government and December for local government). Despite the weaknesses of the health management information system as data provider, an overall monitoring system is progressively emerging. An interim set of input, output, outcome and process indicators have been selected to prepare the sector profile for the annual reviews. The indicators are based on existing information and are devised by measuring six key sectoral areas and six priority dimensions, thus serving as a priority-setting framework to plan resource allocation for the next fiscal year. Embedded in the production of the annually revolving medium-term expenditure framework, this process offers a practical example of the performance budgeting concept introduced by the Ministry of Finance. It also provides external funders with the output and outcome-oriented plans needed for budget support.

McIntyre et al., 2005

general budget support approach (2004 cited in McIntyre *et al.*, 2005) known as the 'poverty reduction budget support approach', identifying it as 'the aid instrument most likely to support a relationship between external funders and developing country partners which will help to build the accountability and capability of the state.'

The factors motivating external funders to shift to general budget support include:

- increased ownership and an alignment of external funds with the national budget process and national priorities;
- improved policy dialogue between governments and external funders on key expenditure priorities, measures and ways to implement the funding programmes;
- increased harmonisation of external funder activities, with clear benchmarks, reporting requirements and conditionalities;
- increased predictability of external funding over the medium term, allowing for comprehensive planning of service delivery activities;
- decreased transaction costs in the medium term as internal agencies begin to use government's own accounting and reporting systems for monitoring;
- improved efficiency in public expenditure management, expanded and more effective service delivery and more robust delivery institutions; and
- potential for increased democratic accountability as the budgeting and planning system becomes more transparent (McIntyre *et al.*, 2005).

When external funders gain policy leverage over treasuries and finance ministries through general budget support, ministries of health face new challenges to their policy authority and power (EQUINET SC, 2004). Ministries of health are obliged to argue the case for health resources within ministry of finance budget processes and are not always fully prepared for this task. The challenge is more easily met when countries have aligned wider priorities to pro-poor service delivery and where specific targets for heath care financing and delivery are set, publicly known and monitored (McIntyre *et al.*, 2005). There is still limited feedback on the impact of the general budget support approach in east and southern African countries. Uganda, one of the first countries to institute this approach, found that while there was increased government control over external funds and improved budget allocations in line with government priorities, administrative costs remained high and external funding was still unpredictable (OPM and ODI, 2003).

Generally, experience from the region calls for predictable external funding, linked to sectoral financing and national health policy priorities, and managed through domestic government-led decision making, involving wider stakeholders.

While direct investments in communities can support demand and use of services to promote equity, external funding needs to flow through and provide incentives for equity-oriented allocations within the overall system of health financing.

Equitable allocation of resources for health

A greater share of available resources needs to reach those with greatest health need, if households are to benefit from improved levels of health financing. This is affected to some extent by choices made on how to mobilise the resources. Figure 4.7 below, for example, compares the possible situation in a rural and urban area (McIntyre *et al.*, 2005).

The bars represent the level of funding from alternative sources on a per capita basis. The bottom block in each bar indicates that government has allocated its resources on an equal per capita basis. The next bar indicates that more user fee revenue is generated in the urban district than the rural one, due to greater ability to pay among urban dwellers working in the formal or informal sectors. The same applies to community-based health insurance contributions. Assuming that government matches such contributions on a 'dollar for dollar' basis, this again preferentially benefits the urban district. The block second from the top of the right-hand bar (and top of the left-hand bar) represents external programme funds, such as the Global Fund for AIDS, Tuberculosis and Malaria, discussed in Section 3, which may still be concentrated in urban area hospitals. Finally, the top block of the right-hand bar represents revenue that public sector facilities, particularly hospitals, may generate in the form of mandatory health insurance reimbursements when their members use these facilities, again more likely to be concentrated in urban areas (McIntyre *et al.*, 2005).

The diagram shows how significant inequities in the allocation of health care resources may arise, even when government allocates its tax resources on an equal per capita basis. It emphasises the importance of taking a comprehensive view of health financing in terms of equity within each mechanism and across the overall health financing system. Government allocations are a critical way of offsetting disparities arising from other health care financing mechanisms, so these disparities need to be taken into account when allocating government and pooled external funds across geographical areas (McIntyre *et al.*, 2005).

Generally, experience from the region calls for predictable external funding, linked to sectoral financing and national health policy priorities, and managed through domestic government-led decision making, involving wider stakeholders.

Figure 4.7 Equitable access to public facilities: Seeing all pieces of the puzzle

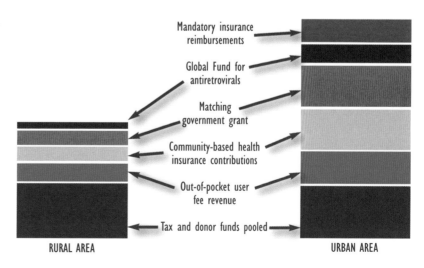

Mandatory insurance reimbursements

Global Fund for antiretrovirals

Matching government grant

Community-based health insurance contributions

Out-of-pocket user fee revenue

Tax and donor funds pooled

RURAL AREA

URBAN AREA

Source: McIntyre *et al.*, 2005

Table 4.8 Comparison of geographical equity in expenditure: South Africa, Kenya and Mozambique, 1997/98

Per capita public expenditure on health in US$ 1997/98:	South Africa	Kenya	Mozambique
Mean	105.49	2.63	2.43
Standard Deviation	28.28	1.04	1.72
Coefficient of variation	0.268	0.396	0.706
Range	81.87	2.84	6.02
Highest per capita public health expenditure	Gauteng 145.76	North eastern 4.43	Maputo city 6.96
Lowest per capita public health expenditure	Mpumalanga 63.90	Western 1.59	Zambesia 0.94

Source: National Health Accounts Network, ESA NHA, 2001: 23

Section 1 highlighted that resources are still inequitably allocated. An analysis in 1997/98 of differences across districts in three countries in east and southern Africa found, for example, variation in health spending across urban and rural areas in all countries, with Mozambique having the widest coefficient of variation (see table 4.8).

Expenditures in east and southern African countries tend to be higher in urban areas than in rural areas. External funders can exacerbate these inequalities in spending across districts when they target specific regions for their programmes. Governments do the same when they allocate public resources on the basis of existing infrastructure and historical spending patterns, despite varying regional health needs (National Health Accounts Network, ESA NHA, 2001).

Until quite recently, government resources were distributed according to existing supply and demand patterns through historical incremental budgeting and similar processes (Pearson, 2002). More recently, risk-adjusted, needs-based, resource allocation mechanisms have included indicators of relative need for health care, such as:

- population size;
- demographic composition, as young children, the elderly and women of childbearing age tend to have a greater need for health services;
- levels of ill-health, with mortality rates usually being used as a proxy for morbidity; and
- socio-economic status, given the strong relationship between ill-health and low socio-economic status and considering that the poor rely most on publicly funded services (McIntyre, 2007).

Resource allocation formulae aim to avoid prejudicing people's access to essential health care on the basis of residence and to promote access on the basis of need.

Examples of resource allocation formulae in east and southern Africa

Tanzania

The Tanzanian formula for the allocation of basket funds to districts includes population size, under-five mortality as a proxy for disease burden and poverty level, and adjusts for the differential cost of providing health services in rural and low-density areas. A basket financing committee approved the use of a revised resource allocation formula from January 2004, using the following variables:

- population size (with a 70 per cent weighting);
- under-five mortality rate as a proxy for burden of disease (10 per cent weighting);
- mileage covered for service supervision and distribution of supplies (10 per cent weighting); and
- poverty levels (10 per cent weighting).

Uganda

The primary health care budget is allocated between districts using a formula based on population size, the inverse of the human development index, the inverse of per capita external funding and non-governmental organisation spending and supplements for districts with difficult security situations and those with no district hospital. In this formula, the human development index component includes both measures of socio-economic status and ill-health, while taking account of external and non-governmental organisation funding which ensures that the full resource envelope for each district is considered when determining the allocation of government funds.

Namibia

Making decisions about allocating resources has been based on historical budgeting processes and substantial differences in health and socio-economic status are evident between geographic areas, despite the improvements in health status in the 1990s. There are particularly vulnerable groups, such as the San, and other groups with specific health needs. Resources need to be allocated more in line with these needs and with greater transparency surrounding the process of resource allocation and spending levels in different geographic areas. Research in Namibia has indicated that allocation tends to be inverse to need. This research suggested that, in the short term, allocations should aim to equalise expenditure per capita and promote the principle of vertical equity, moving away from incrementalist budgeting towards needs-based allocation. This has to be gradual as, in the short run, most of the resources are fixed and a rapid reduction of resources in some areas may adversely affect performance. The requisite capacity also needs to be built up to absorb the injection of more resources.

Zambia

Initially, a simple per capita formula was used in Zambia because of the scarcity of accurate data on other needs-based indicators. However, weightings for remoteness and disease patterns have recently been included in the formula. A resource allocation formula for determining the distribution of recurrent budgets was introduced a few years ago. This formula was based on the population size in each district, with adjustments for rural tenure and other relevant indicators. Work on revising the formula was initiated in 1998. There is a desire to include a wider range of indicators of need, including the distribution of the burden of ill-health between districts.

MoHSS, Namibia and WHO, 2005; Semali and Minja, 2005; McIntyre, 2007

It is not only across geographical areas that more equitable allocation is needed. A comparison of public sector expenditure on hospitals and primary care in selected east and southern African countries, including some central African countries, found skewed spending towards hospitals in five of the seven countries, particularly in South Africa, Rwanda and Kenya (see figure 4.8).

As these countries have relatively high levels of private, insurance and out-of-pocket spending on health, the large private sector may be the factor leading to increased public spending on hospitals. Yet, as shown in Section 3, health systems in the region have greatest impact on disease burdens and protection of poor households at the district and primary health care level. Although not in the region, Ethiopia provides useful experience. Its highest expenditure is at outpatient level and, while the country had the lowest per capita expenditure on health among all the countries in this study, its health indicators were better than in many countries in the region. This suggests that despite lower levels of spending, investing more resources at this care level yields better outcomes (ESA NHA, 2001).

The Global Health Watch 2005 presented targets for allocation within health systems to address national priorities and Millennium Development Goal targets:

- Allocations to district health services (up to and including level one hospital services) should be at least 50 per cent of total public health expenditure, of which half (25 per cent of total) should be on primary level health care.
- Allocations to district health services should be at least 40 per cent of total public and private health expenditure.
- Allocations of total expenditure on district health services in the highest spending district compared to the lowest spending district should have a ratio of no more than one to five (Global Health Watch, 2005: 85).

It is difficult to get a clear picture of the distribution of health spending across levels of care in the region. Many financial systems do not capture primary care as a specific cost centre in budgets. They include clinics and primary health care centres under district hospitals, or even under the central level departments. In different east and southern African countries funds for primary level health care, channelled through district hospitals, have also been found to leak to other uses, often at higher levels of the health system (Conticini, 2004; Lewis, 2005). Making the primary care level a specific cost centre is important to improve and monitor resource allocations to this level.

Ensuring positive discrimination in favour of disadvantaged communities also calls for inputs from community representatives and resources to develop communities' capacity to demand and benefit from any additional resources. This is further discussed in Section 6.

While there are clearer mechanisms to improve equity in the resource allocation within the public sector, work on national health accounts in the region is exposing the hidden and open subsidies from public to private care, the concentration of high-cost personnel and facilities in the private sector and the lack of private sector investment in preventive and promotive care.

A study in Zimbabwe carried out in 2000 mapped these subsidies between private and public sectors and found, for example, that a greater share of subsidies flowed from the public to the private sector than from private to public, taking into account the training, tax, grants, exemptions,

...work on national health accounts in the region is exposing the hidden and open subsidies from public to private care, the concentration of high-cost personnel and facilities in the private sector and the lack of private sector investment in preventive and promotive care.

Figure 4.8 Comparison of hospital and primary care expenditure as a share of total health expenditure in selected countries in east and southern African, 1997/98

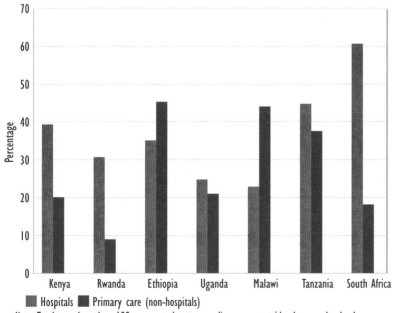

Note: Totals are less than 100 per cent due to spending areas outside the care levels shown (for example, administration and central level, research and teaching.)

Source: National Health Accounts Network, ESA NHA, 2001: 20

and use of public and private facilities and personnel (Mudyarabikwa, 2000). Only subsidies directly provided to private not-for-profit providers (churches and non-governmental organisations), consumers and to the public sector were judged to have a high impact on equity and to benefit communities.

For the private sector, government has a mix of measures from tax incentives to regulatory tools to deter rising costs to consumers and promote national health policy goals and equity. Some of these have been highlighted in Section 3 and earlier in this section. For example, discussion on tax reforms in South Africa have pointed to opportunities for tax measures to promote efficiency, coverage and equity. These include:

- making sure that tax benefits only extend to an efficiently covered basic benefit package;

- achieving a better balance in the resources available to medical scheme members and those dependent on tax-funded health services, relative to the population served by each;

- limiting tax-free medical scheme contributions to cover only the prescribed minimum benefit package, with an additional allowance for routine primary health care;

- avoiding tax benefits for additional medical expenses outside this basic coverage; and

- making subsidy payments from tax revenue towards the contributions of those below the tax threshold who elect to become medical scheme members (McIntyre *et al.*, 2005b).

These measures aim to ensure that available resources target those with greatest health needs. In the discussion on resource mobilisation, we argued that those with greater ability to pay should contribute a higher proportion of their income than those with lower incomes. In relation to allocation, we propose that countries in the region need to institute explicit measures to positively discriminate in favour of disadvantaged communities.

This section suggests policy tools that governments can use for risk adjusted, needs-based resource allocation that promotes equity and efficiency between private and public sectors. Governments can use regulations and tax measures, for example, to ensure that resources are allocated to district and primary health care systems that have the greatest impact on population health.

In resource mobilisation, we argued that those with greater ability to pay should contribute a higher proportion of their income than those with lower incomes. In relation to allocation, we propose that countries in the region need to institute explicit measures to positively discriminate in favour of disadvantaged communities.

Mobilising support for fair financing

The economic policy trends outlined in Sections 1 and 2 have had an impact on health financing in the region, as described in this section. If east and southern African countries are to provide the kind of health system suggested in Section 3 for households with greatest needs, they need a basic set of principles to shape and adjudicate trends and options in reclaiming the resources for health, whether from central or local budget processes, external funding relationships or new forms of domestic resource mobilisation.

Fundamental to these principles is financial protection – no one in need of health services should be denied access due to inability to pay and households' livelihoods should not be threatened by costs of care. There are further principles:

- **Progressive health care financing** implies that contributions are distributed according to ability-to-pay and those better able to pay should contribute a higher proportion of their income.

- **Cross-subsidies** from the healthy to the ill and from the wealthy to the poor should be promoted in the overall health system. Fragmentation between and within individual financing mechanisms should be reduced and mechanisms put in place to allow cross-subsidies across all financing mechanisms.

- **The package of benefits people are entitled to should be clear**, so they are aware of and can claim these entitlements, and so that parliaments can monitor them. The essential health package outlined in Section 3 is one such example.

- **Individuals should not be prejudiced in accessing essential health care** due to their place of residence, income or other factors. Government allocations are critical in offsetting disparities arising from other factors; and it should take these disparities into account when allocating resources across areas and levels of the health system.

Protecting these principles under current economic and social conditions calls for political leadership, health worker support, public understanding and social action. The importance of strategic information was raised in Section 3. Government management and information systems need to track and report on expenditures in relation to national goals and targets (we discuss this further in Section 7). Recognising this, there have also been civil society initiatives to monitor resources and engage with parliaments on budgets, as discussed in Section 6. Measures to improve equity in health financing can challenge the interests of articulate and powerful private for-profit businesses and high-income consumers. This section has examined how these interests can be managed within processes that effectively engage different actors, provide clear policy leadership and involve health workers and communities – issues further explored in the next three sections.

...no one in need of health services should be denied access due to inability to pay and households' livelihoods should not be threatened by costs of care.

REFERENCES

Aday LU and Andersen RM (1981) 'Equity of access to medical care: A conceptual and empirical overview', *Medical Care* 19 (12 supp.): 4–27.

Africa Action (2005) *Africa Action statement on 100 per cent debt cancellation for Africa*, Washington DC, at www.africaaction.org newsroom/docs/AfricaActionDebt Statement2005Final. pdf

African Union Heads of State (2001) 'Abuja declaration on HIV/AIDS, tuberculosis and other infectious diseases and plan of action', *African summit on HIV/AIDS tuberculosis and other infectious diseases, 24–27 April* OAU, Addis Ababa, at http://www.un.or/ga/aids/pdf/abuja_declaration.pdf

Arhin-Tenkorang D and Buckle G (2001) 'Cost of scaling up provision of primary and secondary health care services in Ghana', unpublished paper.

Atim C (2006) 'Financial factors affecting slow progress in reaching agreed targets on HIV/AIDS, tuberculosis and malaria in Africa', DFID Health Resource Centre, prepared for AU, Addis Ababa, downloaded on 7 March 2007 from: www.africa-union.org

Bennett S, Creese A and Monasch R (1998) 'Health insurance schemes for people outside formal sector employment', *Analysis, research and assessment paper* 16, Division of Analysis, Research and Assessment, WHO, Geneva.

Blas E and Limbambala M (2001) 'User payment, decentralisation and health service utilisation in Zambia', *Health Policy and Planning* 16.

Bond P (2006) 'The dispossession of African wealth: Perverse subsidies and reverse resource flows', *EQUINET discussion paper* 30, EQUINET, Centre for Economic Justice, Harare.

Boulle A, Kenyon C, Abdullah F (2003) 'A review of antiretroviral costing models in South Africa', *Economics of AIDS and access to HIV/AIDS care in developing countries: Issues and challenges*, Agence Nationale de Recherches sur le SIDA, Stockholm, at http://www.iaen.org/papers/anrs.php

Brown A (2001) 'Integrating vertical programmes into sector-wide approaches: Experiences and lessons', *The pros, cons and consequences of shifting from programme-based aid to sector-wide approaches in the health sector*, HLSP Institute, London.

Chee G, Smith K and Kapinga A (2002) *Assessment of the community health fund in Hanang district, Tanzania*, Partnerships for Health Reform, Bethesda, MD.

Chetty KS (2007) 'Equity promoting health care policies in South Africa', WHO CSDH Health Systems Knowledge Network, WHO, Witwatersrand Univ., Centre for Health Policy, Johannesburg.

Creese A (1991) 'User charges for health care: A review of recent experience', *Health Policy and Planning* 6: 309-319.

Conticini A (2004) *Macroeconomics and health in Malawi: What way forward?*, WHO, Geneva.

Devarajan S, Miller MJ, Swanson EV (2002) 'Goals for development: History, prospects, and costs', *Policy Research working paper* 2819:7, World Bank, New York.

DfID Health Resource Centre and AU (2007) *Financial factors affecting slow progress in reaching agreed targets on HIV/AIDS, TB and malaria in Africa*, AU, Addis Ababa, downloaded 7 March 2007 at HYPERLINK http://www.africa-union.org

Doherty J, McIntyre D, Bloom G (1996) 'Value for money in South African health care: Findings of a review of health expenditure and finance', *Central African Journal of Medicine* 42(1):21-24.

Dodd R and Cassels A (2006) 'Health, development and the Millenium Development Goals', *Annals of Tropical Medicine and Parasitology* 100 (5 and 6): 379-87.

Ekman B (2004) 'Community-based health insurance in low-income countries: A systematic review of the evidence', *Health Policy and Planning* 19: 249-270.

EQUINET steering committee (1998) 'Bibliography and overview: Equity in health in the SADC region', *EQUINET policy paper* 2, EQUNET, Harare.
– (2004) 'Reclaiming the state: Advancing people's health, challenging injustice', *EQUINET policy paper* 15, EQUINET, Harare.

East and Southern Africa National Health Accounts Network (ESA NHA)(2001) *National health accounts in eastern and southern Africa: A comparative analysis*, ESA NHA, Cape Town.

Evans D, Tandon A, Murray C and Lauer J (2001) 'Comparative efficiency of national health systems: Cross national econometric analysis', *British Medical Journal* 323:307-310.

Frankish J (1986) 'Day hospital fees and accessibility of essential health services', *South African Medical Journal* 70.

Freer M (2002) 'Debt relief in action: Uganda,' *Tearfund advocacy case study*, Tearfund/tilz, Teddington, downloaded 2 March 2007 at http://tilz.tearfund.org/ webdocs/Tilz/ Topics/Advocacy%20case%20study%20-%20Debt% 20relief%20Uganda.pdf

Gilson L, Russell S and Buse K (1995) 'The political economy of user fees with targeting: Developing equitable health financing policy', *Journal of International Development* 7: 369-401.

Gilson L (1997) 'The lessons of user fee experience in Africa', *Health Policy and Planning* 12(4): 273-285.

Gilson L and McIntyre D (2005) 'Removing user fees for primary care in Africa: The need for careful action', *British Medical Journal* 331: 762-765.

Global Health Watch (2005) *Global health watch, 2005*, Global Health Watch, Cape Town.

Govt of Malawi, Ministry of Health and Population (MoHP) (2002) 'SWAps: Today, tomorrow, together', *Final report of the SWAp design mission*, Govt of Malawi, Lilongwe.
– (2005) *Annual report of the work of the Malawi health sector for the year July 2004-June 2005*, Ministry of Health, Lilongwe.

Hillman D (2006) 'Speech to the leading group's meeting on innovative financing mechanisms: Fighting hunger and poverty through pilot projects', *Brasilia*, 6 July 2006, Stamp Out Poverty, London, downloaded at http://www.tobintax. org.uk/?lid=10376

Hongoro C and Chandiwana S (1994) 'Effects of user fees on health care in Zimbabwe', mimeo, Blair Laboratory and Zimbabwe Ministry of Health and Child Welfare, Harare.

Hutton G (2004) *Charting the path to the World Bank's 'No blanket policy on user fees'*, DfID Health Systems Resource Centre, London, accessed Dec 2006 at http://www. dfidheal thrc.org/publications/health_sector_financing/04Hut01.pdf.

Hussein A and Mujinja P (1997) 'Impact of user charges on government health facilities in Tanzania', *East African Medical Journal* 74: 751-757.

Jakab M and Krishnan C (2004) 'Review of the strengths and weaknesses of community financing', in Preker A and Carrin G (eds) *Health financing for poor people: Resource mobilisation and risk sharing*, World Bank, Washington DC.

Kamuzora P and Gilson L (2006) 'Factors influencing implementation of the community health fund in Tanzania', *Health Policy and Planning* 22: 95–102.

Kipp W, Kamugisha J, Jacobs P, Burnham G and Rubaale T (2001) 'User fees, health staff incentives and service utilisation in Kabarole district, Uganda', *Bulletin of the World Health Organisation* 79: 1032-1037, WHO, Geneva.

Kutzin J (1998) 'Health insurance for the formal sector in Africa: "Yes, but…"', in Beattie A, Doherty J, Gilson L, Lambo E and Shaw P (eds) *Sustainable health care financing in southern Africa*, World Bank, Washington DC.

Lennock J (1994) *Paying for health: Poverty and structural adjustment in Zimbabwe*, Oxfam, Oxford.

Lewis M (2005) 'Addressing the challenge of HIV/AIDS: Macroeconomic, fiscal and institutional issues', *Working paper* 58, Centre for Global Development, Washington DC.

Mackintosh M and Koivusalo M (2005) *Commercialisation of health care: Global and local dynamics and policy responses*, Palgrave Macmillan, Basingstoke.

Makinen M, Waters H, Rauch M, Almagambetova N, Bitran R, Gilson L, McIntyre D, Pannarunothai S, Prieto A, Ubilla G and Ram S (2000) 'Inequalities in health care use and expenditures: Empirical data from eight developing countries and countries in transition', *Bulletin of the World Health Organisation* 78: 55-65.

Mann G, Squire SB, Nhlema B, Luhanga T, Salaniponi FML, Kemp J (2002) 'Expanding DOTS? Time for cost-effective diagnostic strategies for the poorest in Malawi', *Late breaker session, 33rd World Conference on Lung Health of the International Union Against Tuberculosis and Lung Disease, Montreal Canada 6-10 October 2002*, International Union Against TB and Lung Disease, Montreal.

Manzi F, Kida F, Mbuyita S, Palmer N and Gilson L (2004) *Exploring the influence of workplace trust over health worker performance; Preliminary national overview report: Tanzania*, Health

Economics and Financing Programme, London School of Hygiene and Tropical Medicine, London, at www.lshtm.ac.uk/ hpu/hefp, www.wits.ac.za/chp

McCoy D and Gilson L (1997) 'Improving and monitoring the equity of health care provision: A discussion of the selection of indicators', mimeo, South Africa.

McIntyre D, Muirhead D, Gilson L, Govender D, Mbatsha S, Goudge S, Wadee H and Ntutela P (2001) 'Geographic patterns of deprivation and health inequities in South Africa: Informing public resource allocation strategies', *EQUINET policy paper* 10, EQUINET, Harare.

McIntyre D, Gilson L and Mutyambizi V (2005) 'Promoting equitable health care financing in the African context: Current challenges and future prospects', *EQUINET discussion paper* 27, EQUINET, Harare.

McIntyre D, McLeod H, Thiede M (2005b) 'Comments on the National Treasury discussion document on the proposed tax reforms relating to medical scheme contributions and medical expenses', mimeo (21 Sept), Health Economics Unit and Department of Public Health and Family Medicine, University of Cape Town, Cape Town.

McIntyre D (2007) *Learning from experience, health care financing in low and middle income countries*, Global Forum for Health Research, Geneva (in press).

McPake B, Hanson K and Mills A (1992) 'Implementing the Bamako Initiative in Africa: A review and five case studies', *Public Health and Policy Publication* 8, Department of Public Health and Policy, London School of Hygiene and Tropical Medicine, London.

Ministry of Health and Social Services, Namibia and WHO (2005) 'Equity in health care in Namibia: Towards a needs-based allocation formula', *EQUINET discussion paper* 26, MoHSS (Namibia), WHO, EQUINET, Harare.

Mudyarabikwa O (2000) 'An examination of public sector subsidies to the private health sector: A Zimbabwe case study', *EQUINET policy paper* 8, EQUINET, Harare.

Mubyazi G and Hutton G (2003) 'Understanding mechanisms for integrating community priorities in health planning, resource allocation and service delivery: Results of a literature review', *EQUINET discussion paper* 13, EQUINET, Harare.

Mwabu G, Mwanzia J and Liambila W (1995) 'User charges in government health facilities in Kenya: Effect on attendance and revenue', *Health Policy and Planning* 10: 164-170.

National Treasury (2005) 'Discussion document on the proposed tax reforms relating to medical scheme contributions and medical expenses', Govt of South Africa, Pretoria.

OECD DAC (2006) *Aid statistics* accessed Nov 2006 at: http://www.oecd.org/ department/0,2688,en_2649_ 34447_1_1_1_1_1,00.html

OPM/ODI (2003) *General budget support evaluability study*, DfID, Evaluation report EV643 Vol 1, London.

Pearson M (2005) 'Abolishing user fees in Africa? It depends…', *Technical approach paper*, HLSP Institute, London, downloaded 2 March 2007 at www.hlspinstitute.org/files/project /83490/abolishing_user_fees.pdf

Rusike I (2007) 'CWGH memo on the parliamentary consultations for the National Health insurance scheme in Zimbabwe, Harare', CWGH, Harare.

Save the Children UK (2005) 'The cost of coping with illness', *East and Central Africa briefing*, SCF, London.

Schneider P and Diop F (2004) 'Community-based health insurance in Rwanda', in Preker A and Carrin G (eds) *Health financing for poor people: Resource mobilisation and risk sharing*, World Bank, Washington DC.

Semali I and Minja G (2005) 'Deprivation and the equitable allocation of health care resources to decentralised districts in Tanzania', *EQUINET discussion paper* 33, EQUINET, Harare.

South African Reserve Bank (1970-2003) *Annual reports of the South African Reserve Bank*, Govt of South Africa, Pretoria.

Swedish International Development Cooperation Agency (SIDA) (2003) *Mapping of sector-wide approaches in health*, Institute for Health Sector Development, London, at http://www.hlspinstitute.org/files/project/15377/IHSD mapping.pdf

Uganda Debt Network (UDN) (2004) *The poverty reduction strategy papers and resource allocation to the health sector in Uganda*, UDN, Kampala.

UNAIDS (2004) *Report on the global AIDS epidemic*, UNAIDS, Geneva.

UN Committee on Economic, Social and Cultural Rights (2000) *The right to the highest attainable standard of health: CESCR general comment 14*, OUNCHR, Geneva, at http://www.unhchr.ch/tbs/doc.nsf/ (symbol)/E.C.12.2000.4.En? OpenDocument

UNDP (2002) 'Financing the development goals: An analysis of Tanzania, Cameroon, Malawi, Uganda and Philippines', *UNDP summary report*, UNDP, New York, at http://www.undp.org/ffd/MDGfinal.pdf.
– (2005) *Human development report 2005*, OUP, New York, at http://hdr.undp.org/reports/view_reports. cfm?type=1 June 2 2007

Verheul E and Rowson M (2002) 'Where is health?' *Tropical Medicine and International Health* 7(5): 391-394.

Waddington C and Enyimayew K (1989) 'A price to pay: The impact of user charges in Ashanti-Akim district, Ghana', *International Journal of Health Planning and Management* 4: 17-47.
– (1990) 'A price to pay, part 2: The impact of user charges in the Volta Region of Ghana', *International Journal of Health Planning and Management* 5: 287-312.

Walford V (2002) *Health in poverty reduction strategy papers: An introduction and early experience*, DFID Health Systems Resource Centre, London.

Wang'ombe J (1997) 'Health sector reform policies on cost recovery, the sub-Saharan Africa experience in the 1990s', unpublished paper.

Willis C and Leighton C (1995) 'Protecting the poor: The role of means testing', *Health Policy and Planning* 10: 241-256.

Witter S (2005) *An unnecessary evil? User fees for health care in low-income countries: User fee removal must be accompanied by long-term donor support*, Save the Children, Connecticut, at http://www.savethechildren.org.uk/scuk_cache/scuk/cache/cmsattach/3027_An%20Unnecessary%20Evil.pdf

World Bank (2002, 2005) *World development indicators database 2002 and 2005*, World Bank, Washington, accessed 2 June 2007 at http://devdata.worldbank.org/wdi2005/index2.htm
– (2006) *World development indicators database*, World Bank, Washington, accessed 2 June 2007 at http://devdata.worldbank.org/wdi2006/ contents/Section4.htm
– (2006h) *The costs of attaining the Millennium Development Goals*, World Bank, Washington DC, available at http://www.world bank.org/html/extdr/mdgassessment. pdf#search=%22 costing%20of%20the%20MDGs%22)

WHO (2000) *World health report 2000: Health systems: Improving performance*, WHO, Geneva, available at http://www.who.int/whr/2000/en/
– (2004) *World health report 2004: Changing history,* WHO, Geneva, available at http://www.who.int/whr/2004/en/
– (2006) *Core health indicators database 2006*, WHO, Geneva, accessed November 2006 at: http://www.who.int/whosis/en/
– (2006b) *International migration of health personnel: A challenge for health systems in developing countries*, report by the secretariat to the 59th World Health Assembly, WHO, Geneva.

WHO Commission on Macroeconomics and Health (2004) *Investing in health: A summary of the findings of the WHO Commission on Macroeconomics and Health*, WHO, Geneva accessed June 2007 at http://www.who.int/macrohealth /infocentre/advocacy/ en/investinginhealth02052003.pdf

WHO Regional Office for Africa and Eastern Mediterranean (2004) *Mid-term progress report on Abuja declaration for malaria control*, WHO, Geneva, downloaded 10 March 2007 from www.afro.who. int/malaria/publications/Abuja ProgressReport2004.pdf

Yates R (June 2006) *International experiences in removing user fees for health services: Implications for Mozambique*, DfID Health Resource Centre, London.

Zigora T, Chihanga S, Makahamadze R, Hongoro C, Ropi T (1996) 'An evaluation of the abolition of user fees at rural health centres and rural hospitals,' unpublished paper, Blair Research Laboratory, Ministry of Health, Zimbabwe, Harare.

SECTION
5

Valuing
AND RECLAIMING INVESTMENTS IN
HEALTH
WORKERS

KEY ISSUES

Without health workers there can be no health system. East and southern African countries are suffering from an unprecedented shortage of health workers. Significant numbers have migrated to other countries. Within countries, many have found employment in urban hospitals and the private sector, leading to rural shortfalls. Delivering equitable health systems calls for immediate and forward-looking measures to train and retain health workers and ensure they can work effectively, especially within district and primary health care systems.

The first, immediate steps are often financial, to address real wage declines and improve real earnings. These new salary scales are best backed by a mix of incentives that address health workers' concerns, including opportunities for professional development, meaningful career paths and training loans as well as improved working, living and social conditions. Health workers need incentives that address their social needs, such as transport, housing, children's education, electricity, community support and access to health care, including antiretrovirals. These measures have already been shown to improve the retention of health workers and improve their performance. They need to be financed and supported by strategic management, information and monitoring systems, together with mechanisms for co-operation across sectors and for constant dialogue with health workers.

This resource demand is confronted by the loss to the public sector of the investments made in training through out-migration to high income countries. The resource flows are significant and have a real impact on state obligations to health and health care. They thus need to be managed through enforceable and transparent international agreements, with provisions for compensatory investments for east and southern African countries to produce, value and retain their health workers.

Valuing health workers

Without health workers there is no health system. As pointed out in Section 3, health workers provide the services, transmit the knowledge and values and build the social relations that exist in health systems. The globalisation described in Section 2 has led to significant advances in technology and knowledge, so that the technology now exists to prevent and treat all the major health problems we experience in the region. Yet, as the experience with antiretroviral roll out described in Section 3 highlights, unless health workers are available and willing, financial and other resources for health care cannot flow to those who need them. As indicated in Sections 3 and 4, the measures we take to improve health systems depend on health workers for their implementation.

Yet many health systems in the region do not have enough health workers to implement essential services. Many health workers feel undervalued and frustrated working in under-resourced health services with weakening returns for their own families' wellbeing or security. Some have responded by moving to better-resourced services in non-governmental organisations or the private sector, or to higher income countries in and beyond the region. This adds to the outflow of social resources from poor communities and countries in the region. It further increases economic and social differentials, including access to health care:

> '*Other than work-related frustrations I do get satisfaction. Ja, mostly when you interpret it – it is a calling. With me, reward for doing this job is not only monetary. You know, making a humble contribution to people's lives – that makes it different. It makes our job satisfying. But again there is that element of dissatisfaction, ja well that aspect – I mean we are human we need to have a better lifestyle. So when the money is not there and mostly when you compare with other professions, it can become frustrating.*'

South African health care worker, Gilson *et al.*, 2004

One of the effects of the market reforms in health described in Section 3 was to make health workers less visible as actors and more subject to cost efficiency targets as they are considered to be just a part of the health sector's resources. The fall in real wages of public sector health workers in many countries and the scant attention to their professional or family conditions or their views, as change was introduced, left many feeling under-valued and demoralised. Many health workers left the public sector health services and many with experience and skills left the region, adding to the resource outflows.

Strengthening national health systems cannot be done without valuing and 'reclaiming' our health workers. This section explores our options for doing this.

Strengthening national health systems cannot be done without valuing and 'reclaiming' our health workers.

Adequate health workers with relevant training

Health worker, local government, community meeting, Zimbabwe
Source: Rusike, 2006

Any discussion on adequacy of health workers needs to include the critical cadres who support community health, primary health care and the inter-sectoral work that has an impact on health outcomes. Yet information on these cadres in the region is often limited, with most studies focusing on doctors and nurses. We recognise this limitation in the evidence and try to include the voices and images of a wide spectrum of health workers.

There are wide variations in the numbers and concentration of health workers in the region. For example, there are over 50 fold differences in the number of doctors and pharmacists per 100,000 people and 30 fold differences in the number of nurses (see figure 5.1). Significant absolute shortages exist, with Lesotho, Madagascar, Malawi, Mozambique, Tanzania, Uganda and Zimbabwe having the worst ratios of health workers per 100,000 people (see table 5.1). Behind these aggregated figures are large differences within countries between public and private health care sectors, so even those that seem to have more adequate numbers of health workers have poor ratios in the public sector.

Table 5.1 Health workers per 100,000 population, 2004*

Country	Physicians	Nurses	Midwives	Dentists	Pharmacists	Public and environmental health workers	Health management & support workers
Angola	8	115	4	0	0	10	0
Botswana	40	265	0	2	19	0	46
DRC	11	53	0	0	2	0	28
Kenya	14	114	0	4	10	20	6
Lesotho	5	62	0	1	3	3	1
Madagascar	29	32	0	2	1	1	34
Malawi	2	59	0	0	0	0	0
Mauritius	106	369	0	19	116	19	165
Mozambique	3	21	12	1	3	3	50
Namibia	30	306	0	6	14	12	387
South Africa	77	408	0	13	28	6	62
Swaziland	16	630	0	3	6	10	35
Tanzania	2	37	0	1	1	5	2
Uganda	8	61	12	1	3	4	24
Zambia	12	174	27	4	10	9	99
Zimbabwe	16	72	0	2	7	14	4
AFRO region 2002	21.7	117.2[a]		3.5	6.3	4.9	41.1
United Kingdom	2300	1212	63	101	51	25	2120

* Except Angola 1997, Lesotho 2003, Tanzania 2002, UK 1997 ; [a]nurses and midwives figure combined for the AFRO region

Source: WHO, 2005; 2006a; WHO AFRO, 2007

Figure 5.1 Number of doctors, nurses per 100,000 population in east and southern African countries, 2004

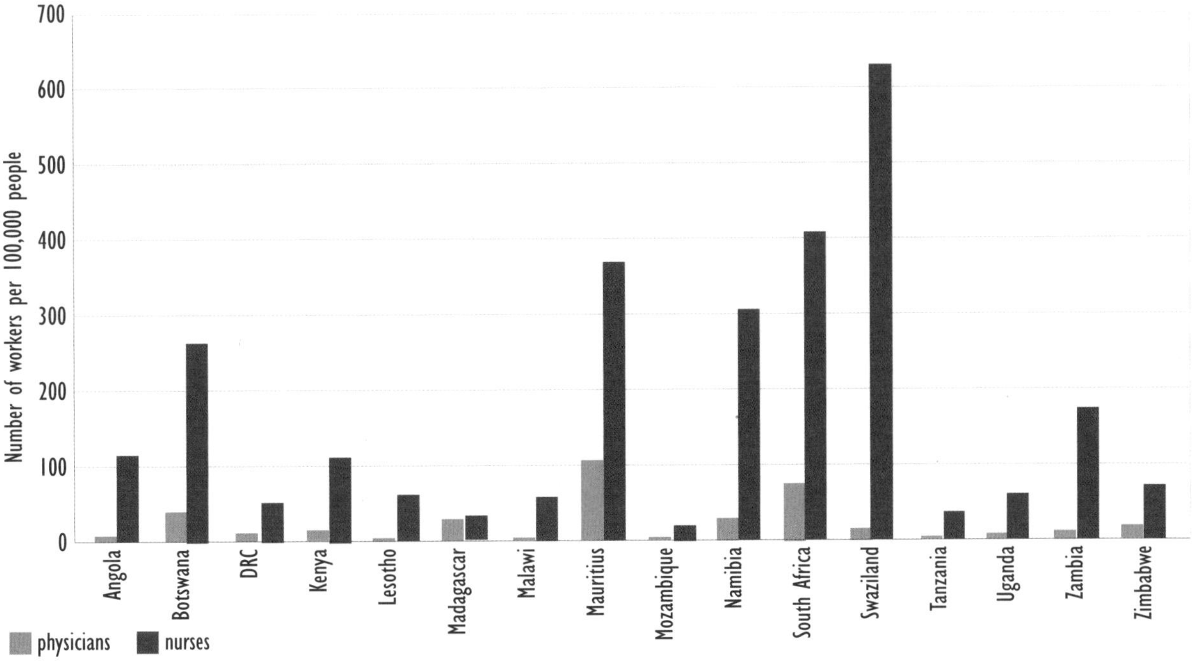

physicians   nurses

Source: WHO, 2005

Only five countries in the region meet the 'Health for all' standard of a minimum of one doctor per 5,000 people – South Africa, Namibia, Madagascar, Mauritius and Botswana. Five do not even reach half this level (WHO, 2005; UNDP, 2005). No east and southern African countries have met the WHO cited threshold of 2.5 doctors, nurses and midwives per 1,000 people which is needed to reach levels of assisted deliveries of 80 per cent (WHO, 2006a). Ten countries had levels of key personnel below one per 1,000 and of attended births of below 61 per cent. In contrast, the United Kingdom, recipient of much health worker migration from the region, has up to 1,000 fold differences in the density of some categories of health workers, a density of nearly 12 key workers per 1,000 and near universal access to attendance by a skilled person at birth (see tables 5.1 and 5.2).

Even these yet unreached norms may underestimate the real demand for health workers in the context of the high burdens of disease and the demands of antiretroviral treatment roll out. Almost all countries in the region have identified health worker shortages as a key factor limiting antiretroviral roll out. The relationship shown in table 5.3 on page 147 suggests that countries with high HIV prevalence levels and lower health worker levels have achieved lower antiretroviral roll out than others.

AIDS has exacerbated the shortfalls. In Swaziland, half of the 7 per cent net loss of health workers per year is due to HIV and AIDS (Commission of the EC, 2005). In Malawi and Zambia, five to six fold increases in health worker illness and death rates were reported in the past decade, with increased levels of health worker absenteeism linked to illness, attendance of funerals and nursing sick family members.

Table 5.2 Health worker adequacy and health outcomes, 2004

Country	Total doctors, nurses and midwives/1000 2004*	% Births attended by skilled health personnel 1991-2004	Total personnel /1000 <1 or total % attended births <61%
Angola	0.42	47.1	
Botswana	1.02	94.2	
DRC	0.21	60.7	
Kenya	0.43	41.6	
Lesotho	0.22	55.4	
Madagascar	0.20	51.3	
Malawi	0.20	60.5	
Mauritius	1.58	98.5	
Mozambique	0.12	47.7	
Namibia	1.12	75.5	
South Africa	1.62	84.4	
Swaziland	2.15	70.0	
Tanzania	0.13	46.3	
Uganda	0.27	39.0	
Zambia	0.71	43.4	
Zimbabwe	0.29	72.5	
WHO standard	2.5	80.0	
United Kingdom	11.92	99.0	

* Except Angola (1997); Lesotho (2003); Tanzania (2002)

Source: WHO, 2005; WHO, 2006a; UNDP, 2005

The World Bank and NEPAD estimate that Africa will need US$500 million in 2006, rising to US$6 billion per year by 2011.

The shortfall is massive and responding to it goes beyond short-term project funding.

Workers report overload due to the increased burden of care on remaining workers from these losses and concern about contracting the disease at work (Padarath *et al.*, 2003; SAMWU and UWC, 2006).

'*My exposure to HIV positive clients sometimes makes me uneasy ... it is not easy to do an HIV test ... and although I use protection (at work) I do feel uneasy. I am now having doubts about my own status.*'

'*An HIV positive patient once made a comment that he will prick us with the needle that we were injecting him with. There is no security inside so our lives are in danger. The patient knew that he could infect us if he pricked us with the needle.*'

'*My partner is very uneasy about the work I do. He is scared of the potential infection. My family will suffer if I'm infected because I am not in full-time employment.*'

Primary care health workers, South Africa, SAMWU and UWC, 2006

There has been some assessment of the cost of closing the gap and ensuring an adequate health workforce. The World Bank and NEPAD estimate that Africa will need US$500 million in 2006, rising to US$6 billion per year by 2011. These funds are estimated to meet the costs of an additional one million health workers, providing the incentives for them to work in rural or remote areas, covering the cost of introducing a better skill mix and more effective support for community workers, as well as the cost of training and maintaining this workforce (Commission of the EC, 2005).

The shortfall is massive and responding to it goes beyond short-term project funding. The need to mobilise significant resources to address this shortfall has led to a re-examination of public-sector expenditure limits set by the International Monetary Fund and ministries of finance. While not explicitly set for health workers, budget ceilings on the wage bill (such as in the poverty reduction and growth facility programme) have discouraged increased spending on wages and external funding for wages. This has led to short-term measures to address shortfalls and overcome these limits, like meeting allowances and non-state vertical projects, undermining a more systematic response to a growing health worker crisis (Wemos, 2006).

Meanwhile new initiatives have emerged to meet the substantial gap in health workers. For example, the US$272 million six-year emergency human resources programme for Malawi has received budget support from the Government of Malawi, the Department for International Development and the Global Fund for AIDS, Tuberculosis and Malaria, overcoming donor reluctance to put money into recurrent spending and encouraging others to do the same (Palmer, 2006).

This level of funding and the focus on recurrent spending has been facilitated by a shift in approach towards longer-term commitments, putting funds into budget support and pooling resources across different donors.

While addressing shortfalls clearly demands large funds directed to national programmes, it is important that these initiatives do not overshadow or give poor recognition to the categories of health workers that sustain the primary health care system, including paraprofessional health workers, traditional healers and community health workers.

The absence of accessible evidence on the numbers and distribution of these workers signals their lack of visibility in the health system. Tanzania's medical licentiates, Zimbabwe's primary health care nurses and Malawi's medical assistants fill skills gaps and have taken on widening roles at the primary care levels of health systems. Other health care workers are implementing tasks previously carried out by doctors. For example, Zambia amended its laws that prohibited nurses from prescribing medication and carrying out invasive procedures. Similarly, in Botswana, nurses have the authority to prescribe medication when a doctor is not present. Tanzania's 'medical licentiates' receive training in basic health sciences, obstetrics and surgery, and practise in district hospitals. In Malawi, health surveillance assistants, with just six weeks of training, have become the largest and most widely spread group of health workers. In Uganda, traditional healers play a key role in HIV prevention and counselling. Community health workers have taken on many roles, supporting primary health care, community home-based care, treatment follow-up like directly observed treatment, reproductive health, youth health and a range of other interventions for specific needs or social groups. Community health workers have the potential to improve service outreach, enhance uptake of services, increase community health literacy and enhance communication between health workers and communities (Lehman *et al.*, 2003).

Table 5.3 Health worker adequacy and antiretroviral treatment outcomes, 2004/05

	% adults with HIV 2003	Total doctors, nurses and midwives/1000 2004*	% total in need receiving ART 2005
Angola	3.9	0.42	6
Botswana	37.3	1.02	85
DRC	4.2	0.21	4
Kenya	6.7	0.43	24
Lesotho	28.9	0.22	14
Madagascar	1.7	0.20	0
Malawi	14.2	0.20	20
Mauritius	n.a	1.58	n.a
Mozambique	12.2	0.12	9
Namibia	21.3	1.12	71
South Africa	21.5	1.62	21
Swaziland	38.8	2.15	31
Tanzania	8.8	0.13	7
Uganda	4.1	0.27	51
Zambia	16.5	0.71	27
Zimbabwe	24.6	0.29	8

Source: WHO, 2005; UN, 2004; WHO, 2006a

While addressing shortfalls clearly demands large funds directed to national programmes, it is important that these initiatives do not overshadow or give poor recognition to the categories of health workers that sustain the primary health care system, including paraprofessional health workers, traditional healers and community health workers.

Do International Monetary Fund budget rules threaten funding for health workers?

Since the controversy first arose in Uganda, in May 2002, the International Monetary Fund has stated that it would never actually insist that countries reject grants for health care. But it also qualified its statements by saying, for example, 'there is a level at which the management of aid flows and their impact on the economy, needs to be monitored', or 'very occasionally, there are ceilings that affect total government employment'.

In Uganda, the finance minister insisted that the country could not accept a US$52 million grant from the Global Fund for AIDS, Tuberculosis and Malaria because doing so would exceed the established health budget for 2002. The International Monetary Fund, he said, would not tolerate such a move as exceeding budgeted expenditures encourages inflation or an unsupportable rise in the value of the national currency. It was a catch-22: to accept the Global Fund for AIDS, Tuberculosis and Malaria grant, Uganda would have to cut an identical amount from its existing health budget but the programme requires that its funds supplement, rather than substitute, budgeted national funds. The International Monetary Fund's resistance to increased spending comes largely from its insistence on low inflation rates. While economists debate on how much inflation a country can tolerate without threatening growth, many, including some at the World Bank, say that a growing economy can sustain an inflation rate of up to 20 per cent (others say 40 per cent). The International Monetary Fund almost always requires that countries maintain an inflation rate of 5 per cent or less in order to stay 'on-track' with their programmes.

Ugandan activists learned of this situation at a time when United States treasury secretary, Paul O'Neill, and the rock star, Bono, were touring Africa and were due to stop in Kampala. The activists secured a detailed letter from the prominent United States economist, Jeffrey Sachs, denouncing the International Monetary Fund's alleged prescriptions, which was read at public forums. O'Neill termed the International Monetary Fund's concerns 'bogus' and 'baloney', and raised the issue with President Yoweri Museveni. The International Monetary Fund representative in Kampala at the time declined to comment. In December 2003, the Ugandan finance ministry finally broke the stalemate by accepting the first US$18 million of the grant.

In response to critics of its policies, the International Monetary Fund says that ways can be found to accept funds without creating inflation risks. However, it has yet to issue firm guidelines. Health and treatment activists have in the meantime called on finance institutions to encourage flexibility in budget ceilings in health, education and other sectors central to human development, as well as to urge that countries implement a moratorium on any restrictions on recruitment, salary and benefits in these sectors to adequately respond to social demands, such as those of the HIV and AIDS epidemic.

Ambrose, 2004

But they may also, if poorly resourced and supported, take on unfair burdens, both for themselves and for the poor households and individuals they work with (AU, 2006; Padarath *et al.*, 2003).

If new resources for health workers are to improve household health, they need to reach and have impact on health workers at community, primary care and district hospital levels. The negative impacts of health worker and health system shortfalls are most strongly felt by poor households who largely depend on this level of services for care. Hence, for example, while there is a general relationship between inadequate numbers of health workers and poor attendance of births by qualified personnel in east and southern African countries, poor households are two to five times more likely to experience this than wealthy households (see table 5.4).

The differentials in health care, described in Section 1, are affected by the unequal distribution of health workers between public and private health sectors, urban and rural areas and across different levels of the health system. As we found in Section 1, aggregate national wealth does not always improve this situation and can worsen it where economic inequality is high. The inequitable distribution of health personnel between public and private sectors is more intense the more developed the private sector. In South Africa, where the private sector consumes 58 per cent of total health expenditure, private health services capture 73 per cent of general practitioners, catering for less than 20 per cent of the population (Padarath *et al.*, 2003). Within the public sector, health personnel – especially those with higher skills – are more likely to be found

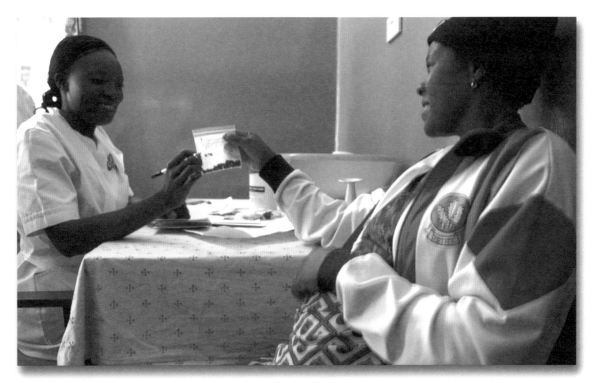

Health worker- client communication, health centre, Malawi
Source: B Goddard

Health information systems in east and southern African countries would thus need to record and report on the distribution of health workers between public and private sectors, across geographical areas and between levels of services to ensure equity in efforts to achieve adequacy of numbers.

in urban rather than rural areas and in 'richer' rather than 'poorer' local authorities, especially when the differences between these areas are marked (McIntyre *et al.*, 1995) (see table 5.5).

Health information systems in east and southern African countries thus need to record and report on the distribution of health workers between public and private sectors, across geographical areas and between levels of services to ensure equity in efforts to achieve adequacy of numbers.

Table 5.4 Distribution of health workers: % births attended by skilled health personnel by income quintile in selected east and southern African countries, 2003

	Births attended by health personnel (%) bottom quintile	Births attended by health personnel (%) top quintile	Ratio top: bottom quintile
Kenya	23.2	79.6	3.4
Madagascar	29.6	88.5	3.0
Malawi	43	83	1.9
Mozambique	18.1	82.1	4.5
Namibia	55.4	97.1	1.8
South Africa	67.8	98.1	1.4
Tanzania	28.9	82.8	2.9
Uganda	19.7	77.3	3.9
Zambia	19.7	91.1	4.6
Zimbabwe	56.7	93.5	1.6

Source: WHO, 2005

Table 5.5 Distribution of the health workforce, 2004 (excluding Tanzania: 2002)

Country	Physicians		Nurses		Dentists		Pharmacists		Midwives		Radiographers	
	Rural	Urban	Rural	Urban	Rural	Urban	Rural	Urban	Rural	Urban	Rural	Urban
DRC	1865	3962	18425	10364	33	126	360	840	1350	726	67	123
Madagascar							0	175			0	39
Malawi											0	30
Mauritius	562	741	2313	2125	73	94	102	184	94	72	58	61
Namibia							0				88	233
Swaziland	6	165	1935	2655	0	17		46	559	1679	4	26
Tanzania	456	366	8608	2121	98	49	55	56	2257	306	143	
Uganda	864	1345	12192	2613	54	63	9	206	3117	1047	66	98
Zambia					54	215					60	192

Source: WHO, 2007; *Global Health Atlas* database, http://globalatlas.who.int/globalatlas/DataQuery/, accessed 8 March 2007

An outflow of health workers

The inequality in the distribution of health workers is being widened by an increasing outflow of health workers, from public to private health systems, from services close to communities to high level referral services and from low to high income countries. There is a global conveyor belt of health workers moving from lower to higher income settings (see figure 5.2), with significant losses now taking place from the east and southern African region to New Zealand, Australia, Canada, the United States and the United Kingdom (Padarath *et al.*, 2003). These outflows are mirrored by inflows into high income countries (see figure 5.3).

Public Services International seized the occasion of International Workers' Day to call for fair globalisation and to defend high quality public services. The General Secretary, Hans Engelberts said:

> '*Globalisation has so far failed to deliver tangible benefits for working women and men and it is usually the lowest paid who have paid the highest price. A fair globalisation means committed and adequate investment in vital public services such as health, water, sanitation, electricity and education, where the contributions of workers are properly recognised and recompensed. It is through the proper funding and provision of these services that we will achieve more just and inclusive societies. Policies which drive countries, particularly developing countries, to restructure, outsource and privatise their public services only serve to perpetuate poverty and underline inequalities.*'

May day message, Public Services International, 2007

There seems to be a global conveyor belt of health workers moving from lower to higher income settings.

Figure 5.2 Pattern of movement and migration of health personnel

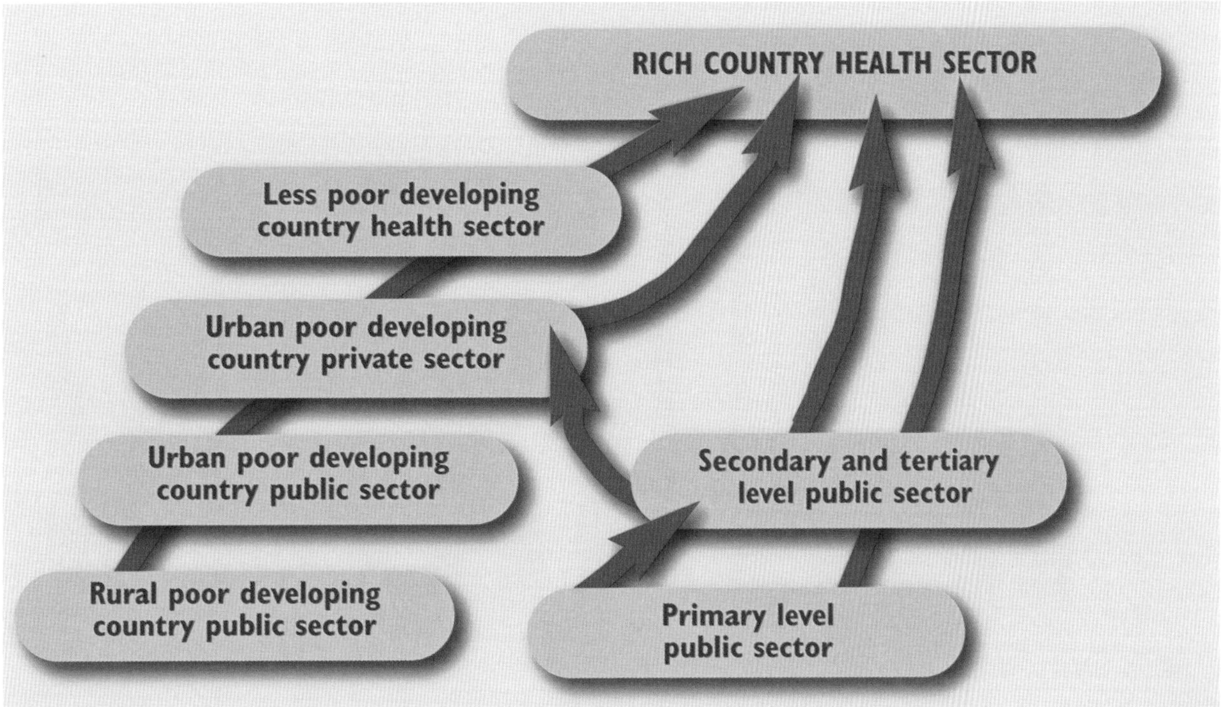

Source: EQUINET steering committee, 2004

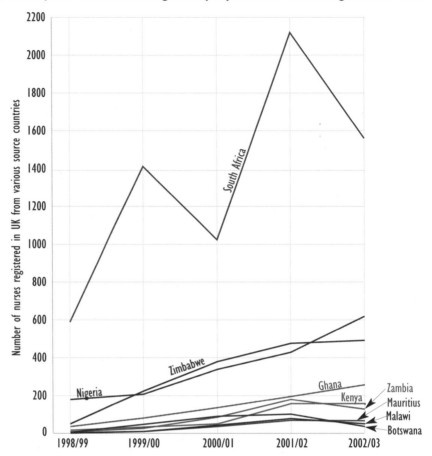

Figure 5.3 African-trained nurses registered per year in the United Kingdom, 1998–2003

Adapted from: Bach, 2003, citing Nursing and Midwifery Council, London

Figure 5.4 International and United Kingdom sources of new nurse registration, 1989-2003

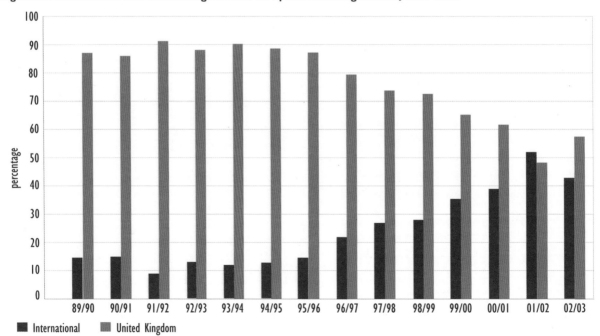

■ International   ▥ United Kingdom

Generated from UKCC/NMC data, Source: Buchan and Dovlo, 2004

For recruiting countries, obtaining health workers from Africa makes economic sense. The cost of training a general practitioner in the SADC region is estimated at around US$60,000, compared to US$184,000 to train a professional in the United States. The savings from recruitment are about US$120,000 per doctor for recruiting countries (EQUINET and HST, 2004; Marchal and Kegels, 2003). There is an equity gain for receiving countries, as foreign health workers often fill less desirable posts and settle in rural, under-served, high need, deprived areas. Not surprisingly, therefore, international recruitment has grown relative to local sources (see figure 5.4).

For undervalued health workers, migration can also make economic sense, although the factors driving migration are more complex (see table 5.6).

'Why work in a place where no one cares about you and your profession?'

South African pharmacist, Dambisya, 2005

Pay differentials are certainly an important pull factor, with significant differences between source and destination countries (see figure 5.5).

While wage differentials send signals of economic gain for health workers, there are many hidden costs. Migrating health workers may do basic, menial tasks with limited or no opportunity to use their skills and expertise. Salaries may not be commensurate with those of local health workers and many emigrants do not qualify for social assistance or social security, or for employee benefits such as contributions to pension schemes. Migrants may experience workplace racism and the loss of personal and social networks.

Figure 5.5 Ratio of nurse wages (purchasing power parity US$), destination to source country

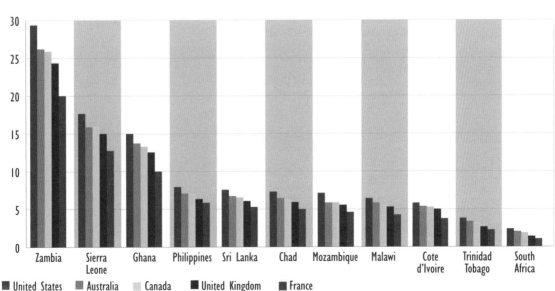

Source: Vujicic *et al.*, 2004

Table 5.6 Factors influencing migration from east and southern Africa

Within recruiting countries	Within east and southern African countries
PULL FACTORS draw inward migration	**PUSH FACTORS** drive outward migration
• inadequate trained health personnel in high income countries and rising demand for chronic care • higher rates of pay (see, for example, figure 5.8) • improved working conditions, work safety • education and career development opportunities • improved child schooling • political and social security	• pay levels • poor job satisfaction • weak professional recognition • poor health service resources • frustration with responses to health worker issues • perceived unfair policies • perceived work related risks • lack of career development opportunities • civil conflict and safety concerns • lack of economic security • poor housing and quality education for children • cost of living, taxation levels • gender violence and discrimination
STAY FACTORS weaken migrant return	**STICK FACTORS** increase health worker retention
• risk of disruption to children's education • reluctance to disrupt new lifestyle patterns • promising career paths • lack of return incentives or knowledge of job opportunities	• high morale among and recognition of health workers • rewards, fringe benefits and incentives • support for a career path • family kinship, social, cultural and patriotic ties. • costs of re-qualification and relocation • time-consuming and costly immigration procedures • fear of the unknown

Source: EQUINET and HST, 2004; lipinge *et al.*, 2006

Many health workers would prefer not to leave home.

Many health workers would prefer not to leave home:

> *'The Public Services International participatory research on migration and women health workers conducted in 2003–2004 showed the effects of structural reforms on women health workers as they struggle with heavy workloads, low and inequitable wages, violence in the workplace, inadequate resources and the responsibility of caring for their families. For these reasons, many women health workers have migrated or are considering migrating to work in the developed countries. However, when asked about their choices, a majority of the workers replied that they would prefer to stay in their home countries if they could earn a living wage.'*

Policy statement Public Services International, 2005a

The costs and benefits for families and communities are the least understood or quantified dimension.

The costs and benefits for families and communities are the least understood or quantified dimension. On the one hand, the returns in remittances play a significant role in family and national inflows. For countries, as shown in Section 2, this is outweighed by losses of African capital and savings to foreign banks. Families may gain some additional security by having a foreign migrant, but lose the direct labour and social contribution of that member. Public sectors lose training investments, health systems lose experience and supervision, and in some cases the losses undermine the functioning of whole units. While some countries globally have exploited this export market of health workers, this strategy needs to be questioned in a region where no country has even the most basic levels of health worker adequacy, particularly for the lowest income communities. Managing migration in this context must be linked to strategies that seek to value and retain health workers.

Widening shortfalls and growing outflows of health workers, most marked for low income communities, are increasingly being labelled as a crisis. Like other crises, such as famine, this has been developing systematically through decades of public sector employment freezes, real wage declines and out-migration. It has been felt in the lowest income, more marginal communities for some time but more recently it has become a matter for attention at higher levels, for example, through the African Union 'Year for development of human resources with special focus on health workers' in 2004, the New Economic Partnership for African Development (NEPAD), the Ministers of Health in East, Central and Southern Africa group (ECSA) and even more recently, at global level, in the Global Health Worker Alliance and WHO high-level taskforce on health workers.

Addressing this issue calls for a two-pronged approach. Like the issue of food sovereignty discussed in Section 2, one approach is for east and southern African countries to invest in measures that value and support local systems, providing incentives for health workers to stay in the health system. A second approach is to challenge and address the global and national factors that undermine local systems. We will discuss both aspects.

©M Ndholvu and TARSC, 2007

The health worker crisis in Zambia

The current human resources crisis in Zambia was brought into focus by the mid-term review report of the National Health Strategic Plan (2001-2005) in 2004, which stated:

> 'On the human resource front, the stage is now close to being a disaster. Warning signs have been present for some years, and even the casual observer at the local level can immediately see the gravity of what is happening…. Health care is a labour-intensive industry and cannot be delivered only through action plans, physical facilities or supplies. Without addressing this issue, we fear that most, if not all, of the essential indicators can be expected to deteriorate, to a point where the public health sector would be in danger of collapse.'

The review outlined the various aspects of the crisis:

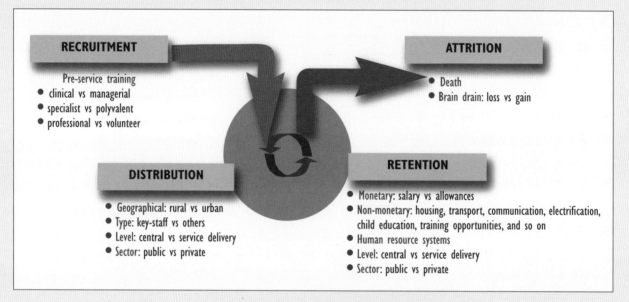

It pointed to numerous signs of the severe shortage of health personnel:

- Many health facilities are understaffed.
- Numerous rural health centres have no professional staff at all.
- 50 per cent of rural health centres have only one qualified staff member.
- Service delivery in hospitals is affected, with many level three hospitals understaffed and dozens of patients being attended to by one nurse.
- Public expenditure ceilings have led to a limitation on recruitment.

Koot and Martineau, 2005

Valuing and retaining health workers

Intervening in the crisis may not start with following the trail of migrating health workers. It may rather begin with giving focus to the health workers remaining in many levels of the system. These workers form the core of a functioning health system, but are also exhausted, overworked, face difficult working conditions, fear the risk of HIV and other infections, are unable to access treatment and encounter obstacles in accessing housing and education.

> '*How does one care for someone when we do not care about ourselves? Health care workers have kept silent for so long. Do you know what silence is? Silence is the absence of sound. Sound is when you make an impression and from us as nurses there is no sound or impression. That is why the government can make legislation without asking the health workers. The message of silence – it is 'unagreed', but everyone accepts it as a YES. I appeal to everyone to consider your silence because if you don't want to say yes, raise your voice and say NO!*'

Industrial Health Research Group, 2006

To take action, some governments have set up new institutional mechanisms giving themselves the flexibility to address health worker issues within the often stringent civil service rules. Zambia, for example, created autonomous health boards, not bound by civil service rules, with the flexibility to hire personnel on contract rather than as civil servants (Koot and Martineau, 2005). Zimbabwe recently set up a Health Services Board to separate health worker employment from the direct control of the public services commission (Health Reporter, 2004).

The first, immediate steps are often financial – we need to address real wage declines and improve real earnings. Formal improvements through salary increases, top-ups and allowances replace (or sometimes complement) more informal measures health workers have taken to mitigate falling real wages. Research in Malawi found that such informal measures included additional locum, part-time and overtime work, treating private patients during official work hours, consultancies, selling medicines and adding income from workshop per diems (Muula and Maseko, 2005). In the last decade, countries in the region have introduced or allowed a range of financial incentives for health workers to improve incomes, including some less planned, informal incentives (see table 5.7).

Some measures, like dual practice, have created new problems. In practice, the measure can be difficult to regulate and resources may leak from public to private sector work.

However, more significantly, all of these financial measures call for stable macro-economic conditions to retain value. With annual inflation in east and southern Africa ranging in 2003 from 1 per cent (Namibia) to 263 per cent (Zimbabwe)(a range that has since widened), inflation erodes financial incentives in the very environments where they are most needed.

The first, immediate steps are often financial – we need to address real wage declines and improve real earnings.

Table 5.7 Financial incentives for health workers in east and southern African countries

COUNTRY	FINANCIAL INCENTIVES
Angola	Unplanned: Under-the-table payments Planned: Direct exposure subsidy, overtime pay, evening and night shift subsidy
Botswana	Reasonable salary, overtime pay (higher rates for nurses than doctors)
DRC	Unplanned: Dual employment, under-the-table payments Planned: Efficient payments, performance-based bonus, increased overtime pay
Kenya	Dual practice, extraneous allowances, risk allowances, salary adjustments
Lesotho	Accelerated increment for rural workers, overtime and night duty allowances, mountain allowance, housing subsidy, top-up pay for church hospital workers
Madagascar	No data available.
Malawi	Salary top-ups, professional allowances, retirement packages (earlier for church hospitals; more generous for government), housing allowances, car allowances, subsidised utilities, access to loans, dual practice, church hospital assistance with school fees, medical expenses, housing
Mauritius	Reasonable salary, disturbance allowance for Rodrigues and outer islands, higher pay from savings
Mozambique	Dual employment, under-the-table payments, medical assistance fund, salary top-ups, housing and fuel subsidies, per diems, extra-hours contracts
Namibia	Reasonable salary, end of service benefits, housing schemes, medical aid, car ownership schemes
South Africa	Salary increase, scarce skills and rural allowances, limited dual practice, sponsorship for education, affordable medical insurance Proposed: New remuneration structure for health workers
Swaziland	60 per cent pay rise for human resources for health, car and housing allowances
Tanzania	Differential salary structure for human resources for health compared to other civil servants, dual practice, Selective Accelerated Salary Enhancement Scheme (SASE), Mkapa Fellows programme for training in HIV and AIDS care, stipend and end-of-service bonus Proposed: Rural incentives
Uganda	Enhanced salaries, lunch allowances, dual practice, under-the table payments, sponsorship for further training
Zambia	Rural doctors: good salary, housing subsidy, hardship allowance, children's fees, end-of-contract bonus, access to loans, salary top-ups — medical school staff, bonus for best performing and best improved health centre in one district (pilot study) Planned: Extending rural incentives to other health workers
Zimbabwe	Salary review for all health professionals, call allowances — better rates in rural than urban areas, dual practice, part-time work in non-health sector, assistance with school fees and housing allowances

Sources: Dambiswa, 2007; Department of Labour, 1996; EQUINET, HST and TARSC, 2006

Thus while they have short-term value in boosting health worker confidence, they need to be supplemented by measures to address wider health worker concerns.

For many health workers, a range of other factors affects their desire to remain within the national, public sector health system (Dambiswa, 2005; Iipinge *et al.*, 2006). Retaining health workers means paying attention to a wider range of factors than pay. Some non-financial incentives being introduced into health systems in the east and southern African region are shown in table 5.8.

While it is not possible to prescribe the ideal mix of non-financial incentives, countries have selected from a mix of measures covering:

While it is not possible to prescribe the ideal mix of non - financial incentives, countries have selected from a mix of measures, including professional development, improved working conditions and access to health care.

- professional development and meaningful career paths, including training loans;

- improved working conditions;

- improved living and social conditions and incentives to address social needs such as transport, housing, child education, electricity, community support; and

- access to health care for health workers, including access to antiretroviral treatment.

Tackling these health worker issues and introducing change in the health system is not simply a matter of finances or technical design. It calls for management and communications skills, and draws on sectors other than the health sector.

Tackling these health worker issues and introducing change in the health system is not simply a matter of finances or technical design. It calls for management and communications skills, and draws on sectors other than the health sector.

The government co-ordination required to introduce the incentives and systems for retention need high level political support. Recent actions to fast-track recruitment in Tanzania have only been possible as a result of high-level agreements between health, finance and public sector management officials. Similarly, the recent introduction of the scarce skills and rural allowances programme in South Africa was only possible because of agreement between officials of the health, treasury and public service management departments, as well as with representatives of health professionals (Gilson and Erasmus, 2005).

Lusaka health workers using participatory methods to review effectiveness of a change process
Source: Lusaka District Health Board, Equity Gauge Zambia, 2006: 20

Table 5.8 Non-financial incentives for health workers in east and southern African countries

COUNTRY	NON-FINANCIAL INCENTIVES
Angola	Functional health information system; expansion and upgrading of facilities
Botswana	Performance-based incentives, health worker planning with management information system, upgrading of facilities, higher training opportunities; workplace HIV programme
DRC	Continuing professional development, monitoring and evaluation, supervision, improved communication
Kenya	Strengthened management, HIV and AIDS workplace programme, psycho-social support groups, speedy recruitment of staff
Lesotho	Accelerated grade policy, continuing professional development programme, higher promotion prospects for rural health workers, bonding Proposed: Improvement in facilities and equipment, IT support, staff housing, staff security, staff transport, employee support centres, sabbatical leave, formal job regrading, improved career management, better posting policy, streamlined human resource management policies and procedures, human resource information system
Madagascar	Celebration of community health workers achievements
Malawi	HIV Policies in the workplace, training opportunities, improved workplace conditions, staff rotation, better human resource management and supplies through sector-wide approaches, churches offer transport for visits and shopping, free housing, free medical care (private rooms), bonding for training
Mauritius	Improved workplace, continuing professional development programme, decentralisation of operational management.
Mozambique	50 per cent bonus in calculation of years of service for rural staff, use of service cars, free housing, free food, human resource management system, DREAM initiative with free AIDS treatment, better communication. Proposed: bicycles, motor cycles, tea/coffee, greater staff rotation, television and internet access, solar panels where there is no electricity, performance appraisal
Namibia	Job security, career paths, training opportunities, performance appraisal
South Africa	Improved working conditions and infrastructure, performance appraisal system, career progression, community service, bonding, certificate of need, recreational facilities, better planning and management, medical care, private sector allows short postings abroad.
Swaziland	Private sector: lower workload, many training opportunities, supervision, good facilities Government (plans): better accommodation, childcare facilities, provision of antiretrovirals and AIDS services to health workers
Tanzania	Open performance appraisal and management, housing, performance-based contract, Mkapa Fellows programme for skills enhancement, alumni association membership
Uganda	Higher training opportunities, promotions, management, increased research capacity, decentralisation, HIV and AIDS treatment and care
Zambia	AIDS treatment, better infrastructure, training opportunities, performance-based contracts, staff transport, accommodation, electrification, support for nurse tutor training, trophy and plaque awards
Zimbabwe	Bonding, training opportunities, performance management system, recruit more human resources for health to reduce workload, community — improvements in housing and working environment

Sources: Dambiswa, 2007; Department of Labour, 1996; EQUINET, TARSC and HST, 2006

The Zambia health worker retention scheme

The Zambia health worker retention scheme provides: a contract of three years with district authorities with support for basic professional conditions (theatre, X-ray department, laboratory and so on.); a housing plan eligible for a maximum one-off €2,500 subsidy; a monthly hardship allowance depending on remoteness of the district – D (€250 per month) or C (€200 per month); education for up to four children paid on full cost recovery basis and access to a loan of up to 90 per cent of the value of the three year contract (between €6,480 and €8,100) towards the purchase of a vehicle or a house mortgage. Also provided is an end-of-contract incentive of between €1,800 and €2,250. Personnel in this scheme are given priority in selection for postgraduate training. These benefits are dependent on satisfactory performance assessment. This has been approved by cabinet as an official pilot scheme within the public service reform programme and by the co-operating partners within the 'Harmonisation in practice' initiative. The scheme has contracted 66 doctors for rural areas, mainly redistributing doctors from tertiary hospitals to rural hospitals. Doctors are reported to be more enthusiastic about their work. Some challenges have been noted. Preparation needs more attention, and administration and performance management also need to be improved.

Other initiatives are being explored, including:

* sponsored and bonded health workers;
* recruitment of clinical care experts at the provincial level;
* construction of staff housing; and
* training of nurse tutors, curricula review and general strengthening of training institutions.

Koot and Martineau, 2005

Some new measures, such as restricting practice in better staffed areas, may be contested by strong professional and private sector lobbies. Cautious of negative responses, countries may introduce a sequence of short-term policy measures, sometimes with less effective impact. Like antiretroviral treatment roll out, this is a field in which countries in the region are having to learn through the implementation process. This makes all the tools of learning while doing important:

* building networks between practitioners and health workers across the region to exchange and share experience;
* gathering relevant and timely evidence to support policy and practice;
* analysing how different options for practice support long-term policy directions towards universal national health systems; and
* choosing those options that maximise positive outcomes.

These approaches all rely on reasonably accurate and available information. Information systems focusing on health workers are still weak and remain a vital area for investment. The paucity of regional information on health workers other than doctors and nurses is evident and brings the completeness of information systems into question. As figure 5.6 on page 164 shows, there is a large difference between data recorded in east and southern Africa sending countries (in this case South Africa) and data in receiving countries, with much lower rates of emigration recorded in the former (Stilwell *et al.*, 2003).

Management practices send signals to health workers about whether they are cared for and recognised, and many health workers feel uncared for and unrecognised. Management capacities are often strongest in the richest, urban areas that are able to motivate effectively, with clearly structured plans and budgets for additional resources. In order to promote equity in decentralised systems, increased central government support of management capacities is essential, particularly in historically disadvantaged areas (Makan *et al.*, 1997). This includes supervision guidelines, job descriptions and induction guidelines, health management information systems and support for negotiation and leadership skills.

On a country–by-country basis, auditing and action on the systems for introducing and managing change are as essential as the incentives themselves.

Institutional changes to support retention strategies in Malawi

Malawi human resources for health strategies are supported by strengthened policy and systems across the health sector, through:

- a human resources for health strategic framework and plan, encompassing all plans and interventions related to human resources for health in the private and public sectors;

- review of existing recruitment and deployment policies, strategies and practices;

- a national recruitment and deployment policy and plan;

- review of the human resources for health function at all levels across the health sector (Human Resource Management Section D, Ministry of Health directorates, regulatory bodies, Health Services Council, treasury, and so on);

- strengthened information systems at all levels to adequately and accurately inform human resources for health policy, planning and practice; and

- regular analysis and use of data to inform human resources for health policy and strategic and operational decision making.

EQUINET, TARSC and HST, 2006

Introducing these changes also demands meaningful participation by professional organisations and unions to support the leadership, communication and institutional trust needed for change.

> 'I just wish our employer would consult us more as health workers because we do have a say in these issues as they affect us directly. They should consult us before decision-making so that they could know our opinions, feelings and views before deciding on the things that should be done. If they did this I would trust my employer more.'

South African nurse, Gilson et al., 2004

Some regard strong labour relations and union or employer bargaining councils as an obstacle to change; others view them as essential in negotiating change. Beyond the institutional changes to give governments greater flexibility in responding to health worker issues, deeper institutional processes re-orient health workers, rebuild trust between health workers and authorities, and encourage collective forms of work organisation and supportive management practices. The processes and expertise of labour market institutions present potential assets for these processes, not obstacles.

Reclaiming resources from health worker migration

> 'The migration of skilled health sector workers reflects the global inequity in the investment and distribution of scarce human resources. The failure of many rich countries to develop their own human resources for health has led them to resort to large-scale international recruitment to address their health staffing needs. At the same time, failed reforms and decreased spending in public health in both home and host countries have led to the departure of health care workers to find other employment, or to work abroad.'

Public Services International, 2005b

While the major task is for east and southern African countries to organise the resources and systems to value and retain health workers, this is undermined by the lost experience and resources due to out-migration. This is not simply an issue for the region; it involves recruiting countries and the wider global community.

Responses to the losses include various 'ethical recruitment codes' being negotiated, several of which apply in the east and southern African region. While these recognise the right of freedom of movement and the demand to protect the rights of migrant workers, they also recognise the need to protect countries with vulnerable health systems. Generally, the codes focus on and seek to limit active recruitment or to subject it to bilateral agreements.

Codes, such as those listed on page 165, set out intention and carry some political weight, but experience problems regarding monitoring and enforceability.

Introducing these changes also demands meaningful participation by professional organisations and unions to support the leadership, communication and institutional trust needed for change.

Codes set out intention and carry some political weight but experience problems regarding monitoring and enforceability.

While welcomed, they are often voluntary, have limited effect and can, at worst, allow practices to continue under a blanket of goodwill, especially where monitoring, verification and enforcement to enhance compliance are weak. Evidence suggests that recruitment of nurses to the United Kingdom increased in the early years after the code was introduced and only recently fell with measures above and beyond the code, like increased local training of health workers (Pagget and Padarath, 2007).

The outflow is not only beyond the region. Within the region, the migration of skilled people to South Africa from other SADC countries in the early 1990s raised concerns about a regional brain drain and prompted a SADC policy to limit regional recruitment of health personnel in higher income SADC countries. In 1999, 78 per cent of rural doctors in South Africa were non-South Africans, mainly from Kenya, Malawi and Zimbabwe (Martineau *et al.*, 2002; ILO, 2006). South Africa set a 'moratorium on the registration of all foreign doctors' with the South African Health Professional Council in 1996. A 'South African policy on recruitment and employment of foreign health professionals' in April 2006 (DOH, 2006) forbade individual applications, including those generated through passive recruitment:

> '*4.7 Recruitment of individual applicants from identified developing countries, in particular from another SADC country, will not be endorsed by the Department;*
>
> *4.8 Foreign applicants are employed in terms of the prerogative of the Employer and may not migrate from one employer to another (public/private) or between provinces. Migration to urban areas, with less than three years of "rural" service, will not be supported.'*

Figure 5.6 Data from sending and receiving countries of health worker migration

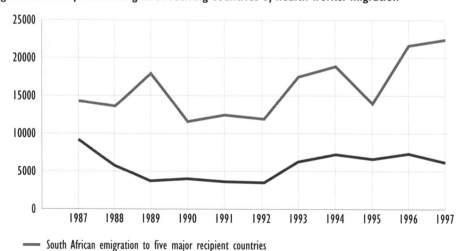

— South African emigration to five major recipient countries
— South African emigration to five major recipient countries (South African statistics)

Source: Statistics South Africa (Tourism and Migration): Tourism and Migration, Pretoria http://www.statssa.gov.za/default1.asp Last accessed 22/8/03, 2003 in Stilwell *et al.*, 2003

An overview of international codes of practice and agreements in east and southern Africa

The United Kingdom Code of Practice on Ethical International Recruitment of Health Personnel, 1999 (revised in 2004) precludes the active recruitment of health care professionals from developing countries, unless there is a government-to-government agreement to support recruitment activities. It applies to the United Kingdom National Health Service and independent (private) sector agencies. It has no legal force.

The Commonwealth Code of Practice for the International Recruitment of Health Workers, 2003 covers the 54 Commonwealth countries and discourages the targeted recruitment of health workers from countries which are themselves experiencing shortages. It refers to the need for workers to have completed their obligations in the source countries before migrating, for recruiters to 'consider ways in which they could provide assistance to source countries and for source countries to develop retention strategies for workers'. Certain phrases on compensating source countries for worker losses proved to go a step too far and Australia, Canada and the United Kingdom declined to sign the code.

The 2004 World Health Assembly resolution 57.19 calls for member states to develop more effective human resources policies that address issues of retention, planning and management, salaries and incentive schemes, and bilateral agreements for exchange programmes. It tasks WHO to support this with information systems for monitoring human resources issues, research and an international instrument.

The International Council of Nurses, representing 124 nursing associations, including many in Africa, developed a position statement on ethical nurse recruitment in 2001. While recognising the right of individual nurses to migrate, the statement emphasises the adverse effects of international migration of nurses on health care quality in some source countries. It lists key principles for ethical nurse recruitment, focusing on: credible nursing regulation; access to full employment; family-friendly environments and re-insertion programmes in receiving countries; freedom of movement; freedom from discrimination; good faith contracting; equal pay for work of equal value; and ethical regulation of recruitment.

The 2005 General Assembly of the World Federation of Public Health Association proposed a position statement on ethical restrictions on international recruitment of health professionals from low-income countries and calls for source countries to try to mitigate push factors, including through adequate and regular payment, professional development opportunities, sabbatical time, career pathways and opportunities for research.

The World Conference of Family Doctors Code of Practice for the International Recruitment of Health Care Professionals, 2002 covers largely the same ground as the International Council of Nurses, Public Services International and Commonwealth statements and codes and suggests that countries only recruit and advertise from another country when a bilateral agreement exists.

Arguably, enabling some migration within the region is preferable to closing these options, if it leads to losses beyond the region. Other countries in the region have managed migration agreements. For example, Namibia has an agreement with Kenya and Cuba to employ specific categories of health workers – nurses from Kenya and Cuba, and doctors from Cuba. However it is still unclear how these agreements link to national strategies to ensure adequacy and retention, and closing this loop would be important.

At international level, the policies are less clear. The weak impact of ethical codes makes these a useful signal of policy intent but not effective for managing costs and benefits. Countries in the region have had long-standing agreements with several governments, church organisations and other non-state organisations to obtain health workers, such as doctors from Cuba and China, faith-based organisation personnel from Europe and Iran, and non-governmental organisation personnel from Europe and the United States. Increasingly countries are entering into multilateral agreements, such as the European Union economic partnership agreement described in Section 2, that provide a means to address these issues:

> '*Bilateral and multilateral agreements are considered by some to be preferable to the 'code of practice route', since they ensure a more predictable and transparent process for both countries, shift the cost of migration from the individual migrant to the final client, can incorporate a variety of provisions and could create a 'genuine partnership between countries which could tip the terms of trade more in favour of the source country'.*'
> Bach, 2003:24

The World Conference of Family Doctors suggests the following areas for bilateral agreements:

- how this recruitment will be done;
- the benefits to each country;
- the nature and degree of compensation that should be paid to contribute to the support and training of health workers in their country of origin;
- the steps required to ensure that any recruitment by agencies or government is conducted and monitored according to this code of practice;
- the inclusion of health workers recruited from abroad under the receiving country's employment laws;
- the provision of full and accurate information to potential recruits regarding the nature of the job, selection procedures and their contractual rights and obligations;
- the support, further education, training and continuing professional development available to recruited health workers that is equivalent to that provided to other health workers;
- the support and encouragement of nationals to return to work in their country of origin (WONCA, 2002).

Such agreements would need to incorporate the issue of lost public sector investment in training health personnel in east and southern Africa. SADC health ministers in June 2001 noted that the 'active and vigorous recruitment' of their health professionals could be seen as looting from these countries and is similar to that experienced during colonisation when all resources, including minerals, were looted to industrialised countries'. The statement also pointed out that the pattern of movement of skilled people 'further entrenches inequitable wealth and resources' (Gilson and Erasmus, 2005:4).

Ministers of health from the region continue to assert that high income countries recruiting health workers trained in African public sector systems constitutes an unfair and perverse subsidy from poor to rich country health systems that needs to be addressed.

Ministers of health from east and southern African countries continue to assert that high income countries recruiting health workers trained in African public sector systems constitutes an unfair and perverse subsidy from poor to rich country health systems that needs to be addressed.

East, Central and Southern African Health Community

The 42nd Regional health ministers' conference 6–11 February 2006 Resolutions of the 42nd Regional Health Minister's Conference RHMC/42/R4 Human Resources for Health

- Noting that several recommendations made during previous regional health ministers' conferences continue to be pertinent human resources issues that need full implementation and periodic evaluation;
- Acknowledging that the HIV and AIDS pandemic adversely impacts on human resource and quality health care;
- Recognising that adequate human resources are critical for the effective implementation of HIV and AIDS interventions;
- Recognising that out-migration of scarce health professionals from the east, central and southern African region is a growing problem which continues to deplete the existing health care workforce;
- Recognising that without accurate, current data for human resource policies, planning and management, meaningful development in the region is difficult:

The 42nd regional health ministers' conference urges member states to:

- develop national systems of continuing professional development that promote on-the-job and team-based training;
- develop a system for tracking continuing professional development;
- develop and strengthen innovative mechanisms for staff recruitment based on norms that are regularly reviewed;
- adopt a common position on compensation for health workers recruited by developed countries;
- adopt a common position on ethical recruitment of health workers;
- develop financial and non-financial strategies to encourage retention of health professionals.

Addressing this concern through bilateral and multilateral agreements is not simply a matter of equity. These agreements can address real costs of recruitment, encourage investment in local training and, if linked to investments that value and retain health workers, will reduce migration as an escape from hostile conditions.

There is growing policy pressure for this redistributive investment in health systems. The 2004 World Health Assembly resolution called for member states to establish mechanisms to mitigate the adverse impact on developing countries of the loss of health personnel through migration but did not make direct proposals for investment funds. After pressure from African countries, the 2006 59th World Health Assembly articulated the principle of investing in the training of health workers (Tayob, 2006). It is time to shift the question from whether to make these investments to how to make these investments.

...there are new opportunities and approaches to address costs of health worker migration in international agreements. The provision of budget support for expanding and retaining health workers signals that external funders have moved away from a blanket disapproval of recurrent spending and have found measures to manage the risks.

As noted earlier, there are new opportunities and approaches to address this issue in international agreements. The provision of budget support for expanding and retaining health workers, like that in Malawi, signals that external funders have moved away from a blanket disapproval of recurrent spending and have found measures to manage the risks. The energy of the regional and global community needs to focus on mobilising, organising and applying substantial public resources to invest in health workers. For east and southern African countries, this situation provides further rationale for controlling the wider outflows through debt and other means. These resources are vital to support and intensify the measures that the region has begun to take to value, orient and retain health workers. Without the health workers, there is no health system.

REFERENCES

African Union (2006) 'Best practice case studies on HIV/AIDS, tuberculosis and malaria', *Special Summit of African Union on HIV/AIDS, Tuberculosis and Malaria, 2-4 May 2006, Abuja, Nigeria*, AU, Abuja.

Ambrose S (2004) 'IMF budget rules threaten health funding: Grants from Global Fund for AIDS, Tuberculosis and Malaria in danger', *Economic Justice News Online* 7(3), '50 years is enough', Washington DC, downloaded 2 March 2007 at http://www.50years.org/cms/ejn/story/171

Bach S (2003) *International migration of health workers: Labour and social issues*, International Labour Organisation, Geneva.

Buchan J and Dovlo D (2004) 'International recruitment of health workers to the UK: A report for DfID', DfID Health Systems Resource Centre, London, at http://www.dfid healthrc.org/Shared/publications/reports/int_rec/int-rec-main.pdf

Commonwealth Secretariat (2003a) *Commonwealth Code of Practice for the International Recruitment of Health Workers*, Commonwealth, London.
– (2003b) *Companion document to the Commonwealth Code of Practice for the International Recruitment of Health Workers*, Commonwealth, London.

Commission of the European Communities (2005) 'EU strategy for action on the crisis in human resources for health in developing countries', communication from the Commission to the Council and the European Parliament, EU, Luxembourg.

Dambiswa Y (2005) 'The distribution of pharmacists trained at the University of the North, South Africa', *EQUINET discussion paper* 31, EQUINET, Harare.
–(2007) 'A review of non-financial incentives for health worker retention in east and southern Africa', *EQUINET discussion paper* 44, EQUINET, Harare.

Dept of Health, South Africa (2006) *Policy on recruitment and employment of foreign health professionals in the Republic of South Africa, 1 April 2006*, Govt of South Africa, Pretoria.

Dept of Health, United Kingdom (2002) *Guidance on international nursing recruitment: Delivering the NHS plan: Next steps on investment, next steps on reform*, Govt of UK, London.
– (2004) *Code of Practice for the International Recruitment of Healthcare Professionals*, Govt of UK, London, at www.dh.gov.uk/publications

Dept of Labour, Namibia (1996) *Labour Act No. 2*, Govt of Nambia, Windhoek.

East, Central and Southern African Health Community (2006) 'Resolutions of the 42nd Regional Health Minister's Conference', *42nd Regional Health Minister's Conference 6-11 February 2006*, Human Resources for Health, ECSA, Arusha.

EQUINET steering committee (2004) 'Reclaiming the state: Advancing people's health, challenging injustice', *EQUINET policy paper* 15, EQUINET, Harare.

EQUINET, TARSC and Health Systems Trust (2004) 'Equity in the distribution of health personnel', *Regional research review meeting report, Johannesburg, South Africa, 15-17 April 2004*, EQUINET, Harare.
– (2006) 'Report of a regional planning meeting on equity in health workers, Lusaka, Zambia, 3 April 2006', *EQUINET meeting report*, EQUINET, Harare.

Gilson L, Khumalo G, Erasmus E, Mbatsha S, McIntyre D (2004) 'Exploring the influence of workplace trust over health worker performance', *Preliminary national overview report: South Africa*, Health economics and financing programme, London School of Hygiene and Tropical Medicine, London, available at www.lshtm.ac.uk/hpu/hefp, www.wits.ac.za/chp

Gilson L and Erasmus E (2005) 'Supporting the retention of health resources for health: SADC policy context', *EQUINET discussion paper* 26, EQUINET, Harare.

Health Professions Council, Dept of Health, South Africa (1995) 'Moratorium on the registration of all foreign doctors', Govt of South Africa, Pretoria, at http://saqa.org.za/doh/docs/pr/1995/pr1025.html

Health reporter (2004) 'Gazetting of Health Services Bill hailed', *The Herald*, 22 Nov, Harare.

Iipinge S, van der Westhuizen L, Hofnie K, Pendukeni M (2006) 'Perceptions of health workers about conditions of service: A Namibian case study', *EQUINET discussion paper* 35, EQUINET, Harare.

Industrial Health Research Group (2006) 'Raising our voice, breaking our silence: Health workers' experiences and needs around occupational health services in Cape Town, South Africa', *EQUINET PRA project report*, EQUINET, Harare.

International Council of Nurses (2001) *Ethical nurse recruitment position statement*, ICN, Geneva.

International Labour Organisation (ILO) (2006) *Migrant health workers: Is one country's gain another's pain?*, ILO, Geneva, downloaded 20 Sept 2006 at http://www.ilo.org/public/english/bureau/inf/features/03/healthworkers.htm

Koot J and Martineau T (2005) 'Mid-term review: Zambian health workers retention scheme 2003-2004', Royal Netherlands Govt/Govt of Zambia, Lusaka.

Lehmann U, Friedman I, Sanders D (2003) 'Review of the utilisation and effectiveness of community-based health workers in Africa', *Joint Learning Initiative paper* 4-1, Human Resources for Health Development, Geneva.

Lusaka District Health Board, Equity Gauge Zambia (2006) 'Strengthening community–health centre partnership and accountability in Zambia', *EQUINET PRA report*, EQUINET, Harare.

Makan B, Morar R, McIntyre D (1997) *District health systems development in the Eastern Cape province: District financing and financial management capacity*, District Financing in Support of Equity, Univ. of Cape Town, Health Economics Unit, Cape Town.

Marchal B and Kegels G (2003) 'Health workforce imbalances in times of globalisation: Brain drain or professional mobility?', *International Journal of Health Planning and Management* 18 (supp 1):89-101.

Martineau T, Decker K, Bundred P (2002) 'Levelling the playing field for developing country health systems', *Briefing note on international migration of health professionals*, Liverpool School of Tropical Medicine, Liverpool, at www.liv.ac.uk/lstm/hsrhome.html

McIntyre D, Bloom G, Doherty J, Brijlal P (1995) *Health expenditure and finance in South Africa*, Health Systems Trust and World Bank, Durban.

Muula A and Maseko F (2005) 'Survival and retention strategies for Malawian health professionals', *EQUINET discussion paper* 32, EQUINET, Harare.

Padarath A, Chamberlain C, McCoy D, Ntuli A, Rowson M and Loewenson R (2003) 'Health personnel in southern Africa: Confronting maldistribution and brain drain', *EQUINET discussion paper* 3, EQUINET, Harare.

Pagget C, Padarath A (2007) 'A review of codes and protocols in relation to the migration of health workers in east and southern Africa', *EQUINET discussion paper* 42, EQUINET, Harare.

Palmer D (2006) 'Tackling Malawi's human resources crisis', *Reproductive Health Matters* 14(27):27-39.

Public Services International (2005a) *Policy statement on international migration with particular reference to health services*, PSI, Ferney-Voltaire Cedex, France, available at http://www.world-psi.org/
– (2005b) *PSI statement on defending women health workers' rights and equity in the global healthcare workforce*, PSI, Ferney-Voltaire Cedex, France, at http://www.world-psi.org
– (2007) *May Day press release*, PSI, Ferney-Voltaire Cedex, France, at http://www.world-psi.org/Template. cfm?Section=Home&CONTENTID=17257&TEMPLATE=/ContentManagement/ContentDisplay.cfm

South African Municipal Workers Union (SAMWU) and School of Public Health, Univ. of the Western Cape (2006) 'Issues facing primary care health workers in delivering HIV and AIDS related treatment and care in South Africa', *EQUINET discussion paper* 36, EQUINET, Harare.

Statistics South Africa (2003) *Tourism and migration*, Govt of South Africa, Pretoria, accessed 22 August 2003 at http://www.statssa.gov.za/default1.asp

Stilwell B, Diallo K, Zurn P, Dal Poz M, Adams O, Buchan J (2003) 'Developing evidence-based ethical policies on the migration of health workers: Conceptual and practical challenges', *Human Resources for Health* 1(1):8.

Tayob R (2006) 'Editorial: Developing country trade and health issues demand attention at the 59th World Health Assembly', *EQUINET Newsletter* 65 (1 July 2006), at http://www.equinetafrica.org/newsletter/index. php?issue=65.

UNDP (2005) *Human development report 2005: International co-operation at a crossroads: Aid, trade and security in an unequal world*, UNDP, New York.

United Nations (2004) *Millennium Development Goals database*, UN, New York.

Vujicic M, Zurn P, Diallo P, Adams O and Dal Poz M (2004) 'The role of wages in slowing the migration of health care professionals from developing countries', *Human Resources for Health* 2(3): 3, WHO, Geneva.

Wemos (2006) *IMF macroeconomic policies and health sector budgets*, WEMOS, Amsterdam, at www.wemos.nl/Documents/wemos_synthesis_report.pdf

World Federation of Public Health Associations (2005) 'Ethical restrictions on international recruitment of health professionals from low-income countries', *Proposal by the American Public Health Association at the General Assembly of the WFPHA, May 16, 2005*, World Federation of Public Health Associations, Washington DC.

World Health Assembly (2004) *International migration of health personnel: A challenge for health systems in developing countries*, WHO, Geneva.

World Health Organisation (WHO) (2005) *World health report 2005: Make every mother and child count*, WHO, Geneva.
– (2006a) *World health report 2006: Working for health*, WHO, Geneva.
– (2007) *WHO Global health atlas database*, WHO, Geneva, accessed 8 March 8, 2007 at http://www.who.int/globalatlas/DataQuery/default.asp

WHO AFRO (2007) *Country health profiles*, WHO AFRO, Brazzaville, at www.afro.who.int/home/countryprofiles.html

World Organisation of National Colleges, Academies and Academic Associations of General Practitioners/Family Physicians (WONCA) (2002) *The Melbourne manifesto: A code of practice for the international recruitment of health care professionals*, WONCA, Victoria, at www.srpc.ca/librarydocs/Melbourn.htm.

SECTION
6

ORGANISING
PEOPLE
CENTRED
health systems

KEY ISSUES

Our concept of equity includes people (individually and as groups) having the power to direct resources to their health needs – particularly people with the greatest health needs. This collective capability means people can assert their own needs and interests, influence the allocation of societal resources towards those needs and challenge the distribution of power and resources that block their development.

Health systems that address equity thus need to overcome barriers to people's involvement in accessing, using and deciding on their services. Barriers arise when administrative systems and processes and health worker attitudes disempower people. Health systems overcome barriers through the way services are organised, financed, provided and reached by communities; through the orientation of health workers; through the process of communication; and through the mechanisms they provide for dialogue between and interaction with communities. When health systems are organised to involve and empower people, as 'people-centred health systems', they can create powerful constituencies to protect public interests in health.

Reclaiming the resources for health calls for a state that is able to claim the space to protect and advance public interests in the global environment, a more robust form of participatory democracy within the national environment and a more collectively organised and informed society.

Achieving a redistribution of the resources for health in the face of powerful competing forces demands a strong alliance of public interests in health. There are many examples in east and southern Africa of the health gains that occur when state and civil society, parliament, state and health workers and other public–public interests co-operate. These examples show how alliances of public interests can protect public health in global negotiations and can lever a more equitable and effective distribution of resources in relation to health needs.

Empowering communities for health

The previous sections describe how health systems can organise to meet health needs against underlying counter-currents that lead to outflows of resources from households and the region. As discussed in Section 3, when health systems do this they are not only in a better position to deliver relevant comprehensive health services, they also send powerful signals about the social values of the people who shape and work within the system and the role of society in health.

The disparities described in Section 1 and the market reforms in health care described in Section 2 not only leave people vulnerable to untreated ill health but also marginalise communities who cannot afford or access the health system. This undermines their right to health, creating individual struggles over basic entitlements and disrupting social cohesion and integration. In contrast, the primary health care approach to universal health systems, described in Section 3, backed by fair financing measures and health workers who are valued, as described in Sections 4 and 5, send a powerful message of social solidarity and foster social inclusion.

Equity is not simply about organising services and resources for a passive population. If people themselves are not organised to use and defend their services, the services will be poorly exploited and can be easily withdrawn, even when they are vital to health.

Equity also includes the power and ability people (and social groups) have to direct resources to their health needs, particularly for those with the worst health.

> Equity also includes the power and ability people (and social groups) have to direct resources to their health needs, particularly for those with the worst health.

This understanding of equity recognises that social disadvantage and powerlessness underlies the social stratification that generates health inequity (London, 2004; Marmot, 2006), as well as the improvements in health that are possible when people are able to strengthen their social networking, organisation and influence (Wallerstein and Duran, 2006).

Community participation and social empowerment are often talked about in health systems. However, as discussed in this section, unless social power is clearly understood, organised towards health and supported by people-centred health systems, the actions we take to participate in health may make little real difference to the resources for health. On the other hand, health systems organised around social participation and empowerment create powerful constituencies to protect public interests in health.

By 'empowerment' we refer to the collective capability of people to assert their own needs and interests, to influence the allocation of resources towards their needs and to challenge the distribution of power and resources and the actions that block their development.

> By 'empowerment' we refer to the collective capability of people to assert their own needs and interests, to influence the allocation of resources towards their needs and to challenge the distribution of power and resources and the actions that block their development.

The inequalities and challenges described in the previous sections of this analysis, and the policies and programmes we outline to deal with these inequalities, demand strong, redistributive states that act in the public interest. In Section 2, for example, we discussed how governments need the power, authority and democratic legitimacy to confront strong global and corporate forces. Taking strong public interest positions is not, however, equivalent to more authoritarian politics nationally. Communities want robust states but not states that seek to dominate. Hence when structural adjustment programmes were introduced in a 'top-down' manner, with the position 'there is no alternative', citizen–state relations were damaged, not only by citizens being marginalised and impoverished due to weakening state services, but also by the loss of confidence in an authoritarian state that did not listen to local views (Olukoshi, 1998; Mkandawire, 2006). In contrast, states acting with society have been able to achieve significant advances in health.

Control of breast milk substitutes in Zimbabwe

At independence in 1980, Zimbabwe had inherited high levels of malnutrition among children under the age of five years. The ministry recognised that one important factor affecting nutrition was breastfeeding patterns and that a factor affecting this was the role of the manufacturers of infant formula in promoting the use of their products. The *1994 Zimbabwe demographic health survey* found, for example, that exclusive breastfeeding was being practised on average for only two weeks longer in rural areas than in urban areas.

In 1981, Zimbabwe adopted the WHO International Code on the Marketing of Breast milk Substitutes that aimed to protect infant health by stopping the promotion of breast milk substitutes and bottle-fed complementary foods. As an entry point to implementing the code, government carried out a study on health workers' knowledge levels and bottle feeding practices as well as the role of baby milk companies in promoting their products. The study raised awareness among health workers who reported that one in ten mothers were using infant formula and breast milk and that the use of infant formula was increasing. The major baby food company at the time, Food Specialities Private Limited – generally known by its brand name, Nestlé – had 'medical delegates' who frequently visited health institutions, spoke with staff and the public, including pregnant women and mothers, and demonstrated the use of formula with the help of a nurse. This gave professional legitimacy to the use of infant formula. Samples of baby food products were also left at the health units visited. While company delegates insisted these were for research and training purposes, they were often used by health staff and others for infant feeding.

In 1982 the Ministry of Health issued a Circular Minute No. 80 of 1982 which forbade health staff from receiving free samples, gratuities, hospitality, calendars or advertising materials from companies that promoted breast milk substitutes. Health workers were also trained to promote breastfeeding. A 1984 primary health care evaluation found that this had an important effect on stopping these practices. Parliament was also involved in this process, incorporating the Code on the Marketing of Breast Milk Substitutes into the Public Health Act in 1985, followed by the drafting of regulations on the

The example of control of breast milk substitutes in Zimbabwe below highlights the potential for public health progress when states are backed by global policies and work with health workers, civil society and parliaments to encourage, regulate and enforce responsible corporate practice in health.

Losing social confidence and action for health deprives health systems of one of the region's most abundant and powerful assets – its people. Despite the high levels of poverty, people in the region have high levels of social capabilities, literacy (see figure 6.1) and strong social networks.

code. The Public Health (Breast milk and Substitutes and Infant Nutrition) Regulations, 1998, Statutory Instrument 46 of 1998 took over ten years to be instituted. This was a result of the need for extensive advocacy and education for all stakeholders, including health workers, civil society and industry, with an inter-ministerial committee, that included representatives from baby food manufacturers, managing the process of developing the regulations, creating mutual understanding and ensuring transparency.

Bringing industry into the process and clarifying the scope of the regulations through information briefs avoided obstacles. While the regulations did not stop the sale of infant formula and other infant food products, they prevented the marketing of breast milk substitutes in a way that interfered with breast feeding. The regulations prohibited donating free samples to mothers and required labelling in all three national languages on the importance, benefits and superiority of breast milk to substitutes, clearly stating the adverse effects on breastfeeding of bottle feeding. In amendments the regulations also recognised the circumstances where breastfeeding substitutes may be necessary, such as for cases of multiple births or destitute orphans. The code caters for all infants regardless of their HIV status and while it acknowledges that mothers with HIV may choose not to breastfeed, it emphasises that parents have a right to make informed choices regarding infant feeding based on scientific and factual information and not commercial pressure.

An infants nutrition committee involving all stakeholders, including the representatives of the baby milk manufacturers, monitors implementation compliance. In 2006, 25 code monitors were trained and compliance has improved, with a challenge noted of imported baby food items not meeting standards set in the regulations.

While no study has been undertaken to directly evaluate the outcome, the *1999 Zimbabwe demographic health survey* finding that the duration of exclusive breastfeeding had more than doubled (1.3 months) compared with the 1994 levels (0.5 months), suggests the positive effect of the law and wider efforts made in promoting breast milk.

Chanetsa, 2007

Figure 6.1 Adult literacy and adult female literacy in east and southern African countries, 2004

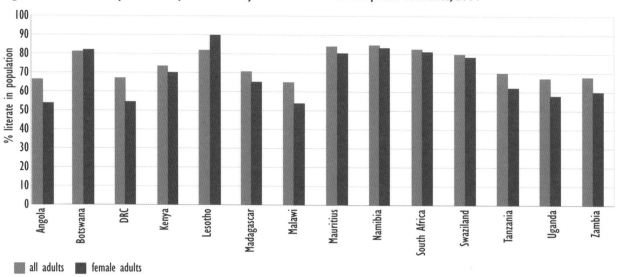

Note: Zimbabwe and Mozambique data not available.

Source: World Bank, 2005

These assets represent a critical resource to build on and strengthen the 'public sphere' at local, national and regional level. It means reclaiming the public space and resources for citizens, community-based organisations and social movements to contribute and be heard, and providing meaningful space and resources for their relationships with the state and valuing their voices over commercial interests in health.

World Social Forum 2007
Source: I Rusike

Supporting empowerment in health systems

While social empowerment is not simply a matter for health, the health system has significant potential to support and benefit from it.

In Section 3 we described the core obligations to health and the universal health systems and primary health care approaches that are important to meet these and to support social action in health. The primary health care approach is centred on the role and participation of communities in reaching people more effectively and stimulating a sense of individual and community responsibility for preserving and improving health. Primary health care facilitates:

> '...*processes by which individuals and families assume responsibility for their own health and welfare and for those of the community, and develop the capacity to contribute to their and the community's development... They come to know their own situation better and are motivated to solve their common problems. These enable them to become agents of their own development instead of passive beneficiaries of development aid.*'
>
> 1978 International Conference on Primary Health Care at Alma Ata, Statement, WHO, 1978b

The synergy and co-operation with communities are organised at the interface between communities and workers in the health system. The health system facilitates or disables this depending on:

- the way services are organised, financed, provided and reached by communities;
- the orientation of health workers and the process of communication; and
- the mechanisms and resources provided for dialogue between and interaction with the health system.

The features of health systems that enable participation have been discussed in previous sections. Section 3 discussed and exemplified the universal provision of quality accessible health facilities to community level based on primary health care. The community health interventions that these systems support are more fully described across a range of reports (Baez and Barron, 2006; Loewenson, 2003; Gilson *et al.*, 2007). In Section 4 we pointed to the removal of cost barriers to services, such as user fees, and the devolution of meaningful budgets to lower levels of the health system to facilitate and support social roles. In Section 5 we outlined the importance of staffing health services adequately and supporting community health workers in prevention, health promotion, primary health care and home-based care roles, particularly in under-served rural and urban areas. Across all sections we highlighted the importance of organising health interventions to deliberately and formally acknowledge and resource community roles. Hence, for example, adequate funds must be set aside to train representatives for joint health service–community committees, to finance communications and outreach work at primary level and to organise and support community roles in health.

While social empowerment is not simply a matter for health, the health system has significant potential to support and benefit from it.

Health systems facilitate links with communities through how they are organised and funded, through the orientation of health workers and through the mechanisms and resources provided for dialogue with and action by communities.

Investment in communications, skills and knowledge transfer and social roles in health systems is vital for the performance of health services, and should be earmarked and ensured at all levels.

Recognising this, in recent years EQUINET has through the institutions in the network implemented work to strengthen skills for participatory reflection and action in health.

Investment in communications, skills and knowledge transfer and social roles in health systems is vital for the performance of health services, and should be earmarked and ensured at all levels.

A synergy between the community and primary health care can make an important contribution to improvements in health, especially in the more marginalised communities. This is identified in Section 1, and exemplified through the role of immunisation outreach, treatment literacy and directly observed treatment strategies in the treatment and care for tuberculosis and other key health interventions (see the contribution of directly observed treatment strategies to tuberculosis control in table 6.1).

The orientation of health workers and communication between health workers and communities have proved central in building more people-centred health systems. Despite this, investment in communication is often poor and training for health workers may not include skills in facilitating and supporting dialogue. Yet experience in the region shows that when this investment is made, the partnerships between health workers and communities improve, to the benefit of both.

Recognising this, in recent years EQUINET has, through the institutions in the network, implemented work to strengthen skills for participatory reflection and action in health.

Table 6.1 Tuberculosis control in east and southern African countries, 2003

	% TB cases detected under DOTS	% TB cases cured under DOTS
Angola	100	74
Botswana	68	71
DRC	63	78
Kenya	46	79
Lesotho	70	52
Madagascar	77	74
Malawi	35	72
Mauritius	28	92
Mozambique	45	78
Namibia	86	62
South Africa	100	68
Swaziland	35	47
Tanzania	43	80
Uganda	44	60
Zambia	65	83
Zimbabwe	42	67

Sources: WHO, 2004; UNDP, 2005

Child participation, community health meeting, Tanzania
Source: M Masaiganah

Using participatory methods in community–health worker partnerships in Zambia

The need for community partnership and participation in the provision of equitable and people-centred health systems has been recognised in Zambia through the most recent health reforms initiated in the early 1990s with a vision 'to provide equity of access to cost-effective quality health care as close to the family as possible'. The strategies for these reforms centre on the principles of leadership, accountability, partnerships and sustainability (affordability) at all levels of the health system.

Neighbourhood health committees were developed to enhance accountability and community participation in planning, budgeting and implementing health activities. Although most communities have been involved in the planning and budgeting of health activities on an annual basis, the evidence showed that health centres did not incorporate or implement these community plans to any great extent. Communities were not well informed of the available resources or their disbursement and use at health centre and community levels, leading to tensions and misunderstandings between health workers and the local communities they served. In 2006 a pilot participatory reflection and action (PRA) approach, drawing from an EQUINET supported training programme and the Zambia Equity Gauge, was implemented with two district health management teams in Zambia, one urban (Lusaka) and the other rural (Chama).

The intervention yielded positive changes in health providers' attitudes towards the community members and the partnership between them in planning, resource allocation and implementation. Communication and information exchange were identified as the most important contributors to partnership.

On the other hand community members were able to participate with more confidence in the health centres' activities, particularly in information gathering and sharing for planning and activity implementation. Participatory reflection and action approaches were found effective in improving communication and interaction between community members and health providers and attaining a people-centred health system in a resource-limited setting, such as Zambia.

Equity Gauge (Zambia) and Lusaka Health Board, 2006

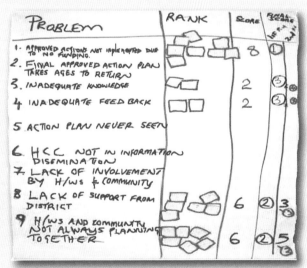

Participatory reflection by community and health workers in a district in Zambia
Source: Mbwili, 2006

This approach is based on the understanding that most real learning and change takes place when a community becomes dissatisfied with aspects of their lives and wants to change some things.

When this happens, a facilitator can assist the process of change by providing a situation where health workers and community members:

- reflect critically about what they are doing, drawing on their experiences and knowledge;
- look for patterns to help analyse their experiences;
- identify and obtain any new information or skills they may need; and
- plan for action.

This process is like a spiral. Often the first plan of action will solve some aspects of the problem but will not go deeply enough to deal with the root causes of the problem. By setting a regular cycle of reflection and action, communities can learn from their successes and continue to find better solutions to their difficulties, thus moving closer each time to achieving positive change in their lives. Across almost all cases, using participatory reflection and action approaches has strengthened dialogue and mutual understanding between communities, health workers and authorities, while also strengthening partnerships in acting on shared identified health needs:

> '...the participatory reflection and action approach has really made me a changed person because I used to say that it [planning] is done only by the managers and not anybody else.'

Health worker, Lusaka, cited in Lusaka Health Board and Equity Gauge (Zambia), 2006

The experience has also indicated the importance of using these approaches within community-based activities during the training of health workers, to embed community and primary health care orientation at that stage. Working with communities, participatory reflection and action approaches can change health worker attitudes towards community knowledge and roles, and vice versa, to the benefit of both:

> 'The most important lesson I learned was that no matter how much you try to put yourself in the shoes of others, you cannot really feel like them. I am saying this because when we came up with our own health needs, the community also came up with wonderful different health needs. So I learned that if we were implementing partners and have to implement these health needs of ours, without consulting the community, we could have been wrong. So it is really important that community members always be involved when something about the community needs to be done.'

University of Namibia and the Ontevrede community, 2006

The spiral model — 1 start with people's own experience; 2 look for patterns; 3 add new information and theory; 4 practise skills, strategise and plan for action; 5 apply in action

Addressing equity thus means re-looking at health systems: overcoming long-standing blocks in administrative systems, health worker attitudes and health system processes that disempower participation.

Addressing equity thus means re-examining health systems: overcoming long-standing blocks in administrative systems, health worker attitudes and system processes that disempower participation (Kalumba, 1997).

Much attention is often given to structures and activities set up to promote participation in health systems (Baez and Barron, 2006). This section argues that these are important, but not sufficient.

Structures need to be backed by resources directed to the level of health systems where this interaction with the public takes place and by providing earmarked, sustained resources for social roles in health.

While the discussion in Section 4 explored how community financing and community-based health insurance has been used to mobilise resources for health systems from communities, equally important discussion needs to take place within health systems on how these resources are allocated to support public roles in health. Budgets often include some allocations to stakeholder boards and mechanisms for consultation within services. However, these funds are often inadequate for meaningful levels of communication, technical work or outreach. This undermines the role of these mechanisms, or leaves vital social components of health systems to be funded by international agencies. Countries have set up community health funds for specific budget support of health activities within communities but these are also often dependent on external funding. Even parliamentary committees in the region have limited resources for their role in health in some countries in the region, as discussed later.

The structures set up to promote community involvement also need to use participatory processes that draw on and use local experience and that provide opportunities for collective reflection, analysis and decision making on actions.

As noted earlier, health workers often need further support and orientation to enable such processes.

The global and national conditions discussed in Section 2 directly affect the opportunities for these forms of empowerment. The growth in information through the internet, telecommunications and the media appears to offer significant new means for people to assert their own needs and interests but often people living below poverty levels do not access even a radio. Despite the commitments to the rights and goals outlined in Section 3, the reality of global, national and local interests, mechanisms and environments can present challenges to the distribution of power and resources, particularly when the institutional systems for decision making do not fairly represent poor people or low-income countries. Section 2 describes how wider policies and systems at global and national level are often well organised to protect wealth, including corporate wealth, marginalising poor communities.

Health systems are deeply affected by these wider environments. However, obligations to protect health rights set out in laws and conventions and their goal to improve health gives health systems the mandate and the opportunity to challenge conditions that undermine health, including those conditions that lead to social exclusion and disempowerment.

Structures need to be backed by resources directed to the level of health systems where this interaction with the public takes place and by providing earmarked, sustained resources for social roles in health.

The structures set up to promote community involvement also need to use participatory processes that draw on and use local experience and that provide opportunities for collective reflection, analysis and decision making on actions.

Participatory methods for community–health worker interaction in Namibia

Using participatory reflection and action approaches in Ontevrede, an informal settlement in Namibia, the University of Namibia explored community and health worker priorities and the actions that could be taken on these health issues.

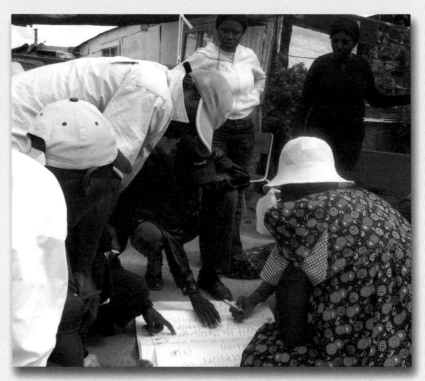

Community members discuss health actions, Ontevrede, Namibia
Source: Hofnie, 2006

Community members felt it was an eye opener for the community to stand up and initiate their own plans or something that could be complemented by others. One of the community leaders said the following:

> 'We were actually sleeping. I think change is needed in our situation. As community leaders, we did not know what to do and how to direct the community. But now we have learned a lot. For us, this exercise was an eye opener. It has become clear to us that we can plan according to our needs and also go and convince other people in good faith. Now we can write letters to the municipality to propose things we want to do and come into negotiations on the whole issue of our situation, not only the toilets, because we are suffering for too long. Our children are also growing now under these circumstances. This plan we came up with the other day is a very important one for all of us who were present, and particularly for us as leaders. We will call a meeting to discuss it with the whole community.'

University of Namibia and the Ontevrede community, 2006

Mechanisms for people-centred health systems

Beyond the design of financing strategies and services, the formal organisation of planning, decision making and authority within the health system can facilitate or impede empowerment, the redistribution of resources and the organisation of primary health care oriented approaches and social action.

There has been a decade or more of debate and policy reform around ways to govern and manage health systems, particularly around 'decentralisation' in the governance of health systems. Different experiences of these formal mechanisms in the region are exemplified in table 6.2. It is not possible to firmly identify which organisational form has been most successful in enabling social roles in health or enhancing equity in health systems. Other factors appear to influence these outcomes, including the wider socio-political context, health worker capabilities, organisational culture, the adequacy of resources and how they are allocated, the population health orientation of health systems and the organisation of services.

Table 6.2 Forms of decentralisation in selected east and southern African countries

Form	Description	Examples from the region
DECONCENTRATION	• Administrative responsibilities transferred to locally-based offices of central government ministry in the health system. • Accountable to higher levels of government.	Zambia, Malawi: deconcentration to district health management teams. Mozambique: deconcentration to provincial offices (Harbeson, 2001).
DEVOLUTION	• Political authority transferred to statutory agency or local government municipality. Health functions of the whole public system decentralised to local government. • Able to generate revenue due to statutory status. • Accountable to electorate.	South Africa: some health functions devolved to local government. In practice not fully independent. Malawi: Intentions still in process, need constitutional amendments (UNCDF and UNDP, 2001). Mozambique: Some functions, for example, environment and cemeteries (Libombo, 2003).
DELEGATION	• Managerial responsibilities transferred to a semi-autonomous organisation, for example, parastatal or board. • Aim to free central government from day-to-day management function. • Accountable to central government.	Zambia and Kenya: creation of hospital boards to manage hospitals and district boards to oversee districts on behalf of government (Oyaya and Rifkin, 2003; UNCDF and UNDP, 2001).
PRIVATISATION	• Transfer government functions to a private (profit or non-profit) entity. • Accountable to government and consumers services.	Kenya: transferred provision of curative care to private sector but functioning poorly due to lack of regulations and weak oversight (Oyaya and Rifkin, 2003). Limited in east and southern Africa. Has mainly been voluntary organisations and missions providing services on behalf of government.

Source: Baez and Barron, 2006 from models developed by Mills, 1994; Gilson et al., 1994; Gilson and Travis, 1997

Effectiveness of district health boards in Zambia

In 1992 the government of Zambia facilitated community involvement in health care delivery through legislation establishing district health boards and neighbourhood health committees.

District health boards look after community health interests by approving district health plans which reflect community needs, ensuring equitable allocation of resources and ensuring accountability of the health care system to the community. The boards approve all health development plans in the district and the reports on these plans, including initiatives to mobilise financial and other resources for health locally. Such plans are expected to start from the neighbourhood health committees. They monitor and evaluate progress of all health-related activities and report to the Central Board of Health. They ensure the sound use of resources, oversee human resources and promote good working environments. The district health boards promote intersectoral co-operation and support community involvement through community-based volunteer health workers and neighbourhood health committees.

A cross-sectional survey in two provinces of Zambia found, however, that despite legal provision and policy intention to cover these roles, information flow between the community and district health boards was weak, links were informal or non-functional and meetings were held irregularly. The district health boards lacked involvement and consultation with the community. Some social groups, like women, were poorly represented and did not know how to become involved. Procedural issues were unclear to members – what they were expected to do, how to remove non-functional board members from office or how to challenge decisions of technical experts in the district health management team. Little guidance was provided on their roles from government and few resources made available to support their activities. Community members were not aware of the district health boards and their functions and had little outreach to neighbourhood health committees. Plans submitted from neighbourhood health committees could be changed at higher levels without feedback to the community and communities had weak capabilities in developing plans and funding proposals.

The survey team proposed options to ensure that district health board member selection included women, that board members were trained to understand and perform their roles and that information flow to and from district health boards and neighbourhood health committees was improved. They also propose that district health boards be monitored formally and at community level to assess and support their effective functioning.

Macwan'gi and Ngwengwe, 2004

Decentralising authority within the health system cannot be simply equated with having stronger partnerships between health services and communities, nor can it be assumed that such partnerships are used to enhance equity in the performance of health systems. For the governance of health systems to play a role in reclaiming the resources for health, attention has to be given to the level of communication and joint planning taking place and the tools used to organise this communication to direct resources towards health needs.

Experiences from Zambia suggest that 'representative' mechanisms cannot be assumed to represent communities, especially vulnerable groups. These mechanisms really involve and 'talk to' only a portion of the population – often a third or less of communities. Specific and explicit additional investments are needed to avoid representation becoming stultified and to reach groups more widely, especially those groups that are already marginalised.

There are many features of health systems documented that undermine participation. Top-down policy formulation, weak information flow and user charges that place barriers to access can alienate community members (Baez and Barron, 2006; EQUINET/ TARSC/ CHESSORE, 2005b; TARSC, EQUINET, WHO Afro, 2000). Health workers have been reported to feel that community members have poor knowledge or weak competencies on health issues (Macwan'gi and Ngwengwe, 2004; University of Namibia and Ontevrede, 2006). Health workers and authorities may be reluctant to 'give up' their power or control over health systems. They may use bureaucratic and hierarchical ways of working that make it difficult for communities to interact, and health workers may themselves get few formal rewards and face potential political risks for doing so (Ngulube *et al*, 2004). A Zambia study of the context for participatory mechanisms found that health managers often cascade decisions from national to lower levels in an authoritarian way, using governance structures primarily to rubber stamp decisions, irrespective of local priorities. Community inputs, while received, were often perceived as less useful (Ngulube *et al.*, 2005).

There are also various examples documented of how health systems have put in place processes or mechanisms to facilitate social roles, draw social input or encourage social action. Some of these are described in table 6.3 on page 186. These often work better when processes are also taking place within communities to prepare and organise them for these roles.

Information exchange is vital in the interaction between health systems and communities. Yet often evidence used in planning is inaccessible to communities and difficult to understand. The local health information system is often not analysed locally to support local planning. Some health systems make this an important area of job performance for health workers. In South Africa, for example, the primary health care supervisors' job description includes the use and discussion of information at clinic and sub-district level to improve services and programmes. Later, an additional task was added – to attend clinic committee meetings to share

Decentralising authority within the health system cannot be simply equated with having stronger partnerships between health services and communities, nor can it be assumed that such partnerships are used to enhance equity in the performance of health systems. For the governance of health systems to play a role in reclaiming the resources for health, attention has to be given to the level of communication and joint planning taking place and the tools used to organise this communication to direct resources towards health needs.

There are also various examples documented of how health systems have put in place processes or mechanisms to facilitate social roles, draw social input or encourage social action. These often work better when processes are also taking place within communities to prepare and organise them for these roles.

Table 6.3 Health systems strategies to facilitate and enable social empowerment

Actions within health systems and services	Actions within civil society and communities
Provide statutory rights to information such as right to information laws.	Raise the visibility of previously ignored health issues, through campaigns, monitoring, community research.
Organise processes that bring professionals into supportive roles with communities such as through joint health campaigns, through PRA processes, and reward health these worker roles.	Provide special mechanisms to engage marginal groups through consultative mechanisms, participatory appraisals, drama, increased resident involvement in local planning.
Formalise in law or guidelines, recognise, resource and provide tools for joint community–health service committees at sub-district or clinic level to involve communities and manage local processes.	Include community information and preferences in planning: such as through participatory budget planning, community giving evidence to parliamentary committees and popularising policy debates.
Build skills and leadership within health workforces and local authorities to work with communities.	Support the development of capacities in communities to engage with bureaucracies and authorities.
Ensure partnerships between health services and communities are governed by clear agreements, uninterrupted financing and are monitored and evaluated.	Encourage and advocate for political leadership to support participatory processes.
Apply participatory processes in areas of resource allocation. Provide forums that review budgets and mechanisms for drawing public input on budget reviews.	Draw attention to needs and inequities in resource allocation; propose alternative budget allocation priorities, for example, youth, child and gender 'friendly' budgets.
Make information and planning systems accessible to public monitoring. Organise planning around evidence that is accessible to communities and use of funding benchmarks linked to specific health goals to facilitate public understanding and accountability.	Organise community methods for monitoring the performance of health systems against social priorities, such as report cards on client satisfaction, price monitoring surveys and community surveys that gather evidence on health and service performance.

Sources: Savigny et al., 2004; Goetz et al., 2001; Wallerstein and Duran, 2006; Baez and Barron, 2006; Loewenson et al., 2004; Ngulube et al., 2005; Macwangi et al., 2004.

...where mechanisms for communication between health workers and communities are supported with training and resources by civil society organisations and the state, and receive health worker and primary health care system support, they can make real improvements in health outcomes.

the information and the progress with committee members, in order to enhance community participation through empowerment with information (Baez and Barron, 2006). The Tanzania Essential Health Interventions project, described opposite, provides an example of how district level information supporting local planning produces marked improvements in health outcomes, with a fall in under five child mortality by over 40 per cent in the five years following the introduction of evidence-based planning (Savigny et al., 2004).

While the Tanzania Essential Health Interventions project case study uses technical information, there are many examples of health workers at primary health care level using simpler forms of information to encourage accountability to communities on how local resources are used.

Can such local initiatives be made more widespread and more systematic within our health systems?

These initiatives take leadership – from communities and health workers – but they also demand resources and recognition. Systems designed around cost efficiency do not see the value of such inputs yet. As the Zimbabwe case study on health centre committees shows, where mechanisms for communication between health workers and communities are supported with training and resources by civil society organisations and the state, and receive health worker and primary health care system support, they can make real improvements in health outcomes.

The Tanzania Essential Health Interventions project

The Tanzania Essential Health Interventions project's research into three distinct areas – health systems, health behaviour and health impacts – provided critical insights that aided health care reforms in Rufiji and Morogoro. One of the most striking findings of the inquiries into health-seeking behaviours, for example, was that most deaths (close to 80 per cent) occurred at home rather than at a health facility. This statistic underscored earlier doubts about the use of attendance and cause-of-death statistics – compiled by the government on the basis of health facility data only – as an aid for planning health budgets. Surely, this form of planning could not be reliable since it was based on only 20 per cent of deaths. Since demographic surveillance system information, by contrast, captures all deaths – those that occur in health facilities, in households and elsewhere – it can be counted upon to give a more accurate and complete portrait of the burden of disease as experienced by the community.

Another surprising revelation arising from research into health-seeking behaviour was that the people who had sought modern health care prior to their deaths greatly outnumbered those who had not. For malaria, 78.7 per cent used modern care, only 9.4 per cent used traditional care and 11.9 per cent used no care at all. These figures prove that the death rates in Rufiji and Morogoro were not primarily an outgrowth of a preference for traditional healers over modern health care (as some observers had speculated) but were more reasonably seen as related to problems of access, delay or the apparent inability of modern health facilities to prevent these patients from dying.

Formative research into the health systems planning process confirmed that planning was not being conducted as a response to the burden of disease, but instead was driven by a wide range of factors, including donor agencies' agendas, bureaucratic inertia and simple guess-work.

Tanzania Essential Health Interventions Project, 2004

M Ndhlovu, Source: TARSC

Reviews of experience in and beyond east and southern Africa suggest that these approaches work best where there is more sustained contact between communities and service providers, where communities are locally organised and physically concentrated, and where there are clear incentives to collective action (Goetz *et al.*, 2001; Gilson *et al.*, 2007; Loewenson, 2007). They are also more effective where there are adequate resources and staff in the health system. These resources need to be directed at the level of interface with civil society, in information flows and

Mtaa dispensary health information system, Kwale, Kenya

The key figure in developing and operating the health management information system at Mtaa was a volunteer and a district health committee member. She had been trained as a nurse-aid and then attended the training course for district health committee members and became particularly interested in what was said about health management information systems. She started collecting data for the Mtaa dispensary and writing it up on a blackboard and on charts, using information taken from the registers completed by the nurse-in-charge.

At the end of each month, she notes how many patients have been treated for different health problems and writes the figures for the top five diseases up on the board. She also gets the figures for growth monitoring and immunisation from the health action days implemented by the dispensary and the villages. For the main health activities the Mtaa district health committee sets targets and the board shows whether the dispensary is achieving this target every month.

The information is used in the district health committee meetings and is available to the public to see what the committee is doing about their health problems. As she says:

> *The people know how many patients have been seen and the amount of money collected, and what we did with it.'*

After two years, there were encouraging indicators that, not only at Mtaa but across all six dispensaries, there was a positive impact: use for preventive care increased by 54 per cent and curative care by 15 per cent. None of the dispensaries was without drugs for even a single day.

Kwale Health System Strengthening Project (KHSSP), 2005
as cited in Baez and Barron, 2006

in communication within and between different levels of the health system, where commercialisation of services does not place cost and other barriers to access and where donor demands are not given priority over local inputs (Baez and Barron, 2006; EQUINET, TARSC, CHESSORE, 2005b; TARSC, EQUINET, WHO Afro 2000, Loewenson, 2007). They require time and sensitivity to local socio-cultural conditions as well as stable socio-political conditions.

Health centre committees in Zimbabwe

Public sector clinics are the primary source of health care for communities in Zimbabwe but are not well resourced in terms of basic supplies and staffing. Health centre committees appear from a study to be associated with improved health resources at clinic level and improved performance of primary health care services. In the study, clinics with health centre committees had on average more outreach and primary care staff, more immunisation outreach, better drug availability at clinics and improved community knowledge of health and available health services than those without.

The study indicated that areas with health centre committees performed better on primary health care statistics (environmental health technicians visits, oral rehydration solution use) than those without and that there was improved contact between health services and the community. Many of the areas of improved performance related to the primary health care system where communities can exert pressure, rather than to the medical care services. Communities and health centre committees agreed that communication is the most limiting factor in improving health centre committee performance. The study found that health centre committees themselves receive no resource support for this role and are poorly equipped with information.

The study suggests an association between health centre committees and improved health outcomes, even in the highly under-resourced situation of poor communities and poorly resourced clinics. Despite this, weak formal recognition, ambiguity in roles and inadequate resources or training for their role were found in all study sites, and the attitude and responsiveness of the health authorities and strength of community leaders varied across the districts studied. Formalising health centre committee roles and authority, strengthening communication with district health personnel, training in key areas of committee functions and providing some resources for communication and outreach, could consolidate and widen positive gains in health. A functioning primary health care system also seems to be a vital contributor to positive outcomes.

Loewenson, 2004

© M Ndhlovu and TARSC 2007

Social action for public interests

Primary health care flourishes where social action supports it and social action is sustained where primary health care is strong. If this virtuous cycle is to grow it needs a wider context of norms and institutions that support social justice and collective rights, together with recognition that these are best implemented through the actions of those most affected.

Primary health care flourishes where social action supports it and social action is sustained where primary health care is strong. If this virtuous cycle is to grow it needs a wider context of norms and institutions that support social justice and collective rights, together with recognition that these are best implemented through the actions of those most affected.

In Section 3, we presented the international and national rights, norms and obligations that allow states to defend public interests in relation to health. Some, such as the SADC Social Charter, arise from engagement between civil society (in this case trade unions) and the state. For these norms to translate into real improvements in health at community level, especially for disadvantaged communities, experience from the region suggests that these rights need to be coupled with community engagement, so that they are used to build and are advanced through social action (London, 2004).

Civil society has played an important role in this process. Civil society organisations have diverse experience, skills, expertise and knowledge and have used these to monitor health outcomes and health system performance, reported on these outcomes, and raised awareness among community groups and health workers on health needs and to argue for health resources (Kamupira and London, 2005). Civil society has monitored resource allocations, tracked budget expenditures, costs of health inputs and access to treatment, engaging and petitioning the state and parliament on the findings. Equity is at the heart of many of these actions, as civil society seeks to make health needs visible, argue for a fairer share of resources for these needs and, beyond this, organise communities to make claims over these resources, arising from their rights to health.

Community Working Group on Health members at a health meeting, Zimbabwe
Source: CWGH, 2005

People's Health Movement

The right to health care campaign

The People's Health Movement is a global social movement for health. The movement recognised the urgent need to address the global health system crisis characterised by:

- weakening public health systems;
- privatisation and promotion of private insurance;
- failure to implement comprehensive primary health care;
- unresponsive, fragmented and often donor-driven health programmes; and
- a shortage of health care personnel.

All these factors were seen to lead to the denial of quality health care for a large proportion of the world's population.

The People's Health Movement initiated a global right to health care campaign, developed in collaboration with various networks, coalitions and organisations sharing a similar perspective. This campaign documents violations of health rights, presents country level assessments of the right to health care and advocates for fulfillment of commitments to the right to health care at the national, regional and global levels.

The People's Health Movement perspective is 'right to health – health for all'. The right to health includes rights to a range of social determinants of health (for example, clean water, food security and nutrition, education, housing, clean and safe environments) as well as, importantly, the right to health care.

People's Health Movement, 2007

Civil society supporting rights to health in Malawi

The Local Initiatives for Health project in Malawi has used a community scorecard to put the rights-based approach into action. A participatory rights-based methodology supported rural communities in identifying priority health issues and using their scorecard on these issues to build dialogue between themselves and the providers. Social mapping was used to identify vulnerable groups in communities and link them to health service providers and other social support systems. Through this, communities were able to promote non-discrimination in drug dispensing, in the overall treatment of patients and in the provision of supplementary feeding and clinical care.

Kalumba cited in EQUINET, 2004

This action can connect local needs to national or even global resources, and raise claims from local to global level.

> 'The economic partnership agreement between the European Commission and African countries will impact on households who are surviving on small-scale farming. Chicken imported from Europe is cheaper than chicken produced locally. In Chad and Cameroon we grow rice but the rice imported from India is cheaper. So local farming suffers. We think we should give a chance to Africa. We are now signing petitions, where we collect millions of signatures and take them to our head of state, so he may have a reason not to sign the agreement and will see that our populations are against this process. So far we have succeeded in collecting four million signatures at the grassroots level.'
>
> ACORD Cameroon in an interview with I Rusike, World Social Forum, 2007

Civil society organisations in east and southern Africa have supported this virtuous cycle between primary health care and social action by:

- organising evidence and giving voice to low-income community issues;

- raising the visibility of the health conditions of poor communities;

- facilitating service outreach and use by informing and organising communities;

- supporting services to respond to community values and cultural norms;

- promoting transparency and accountability of services to low-income communities; and

- making services more responsive to the perceptions of poor people (Loewenson, 2003).

These positive features, observed in some studies, are not uniform to all civil society organisation interventions. Civil society organisations have internal weaknesses that impede their work in poor communities. They have, for example, complex internal politics; unclear legal authority; unstable funding; donor dependency; and weak mechanisms for monitoring and scaling up work. Civil society organisation leadership is often reported to be dominated by men and higher-income groups, who act to secure their own self-interest and may be unwilling to confront state or funding bureaucracies in the interests of poor people. These internal weaknesses diminish civil society organisations' willingness or capacity to engage with or challenge the state to address the needs of the poor and undermine their ability to reach the poorest groups, serve their agenda or strengthen advocacy of their interests (Loewenson, 2003). Not all the obstacles confronting pro-poor civil society organisation interventions are internal. These organisations may meet resistance from corporate and state interests, authoritarian styles of business and government, and poorly developed media and communications systems.

Single issue campaigns, while powerful, can split vision, efforts and resources. Yet major networks of civil society in east and southern Africa identified a unified aspiration for equity and social justice through people-led and people-centred health systems, outlined on page 194.

These actions within civil society resonate with those of other institutions in east and southern Africa that have the potential and power to organise social action for public interests in health.

Parliaments have, for example, contributed to policy space and public debate in support of health equity through their representative, legislative and oversight roles, including budget supervision.

Parliaments have a role in ensuring that ratified international treaties that promote health are implemented through domestic laws (such as TRIPS flexibilities and the Convention on the Elimination of All Forms of Discrimination against Women) and that those with potential negative impacts (such as GATS) are not signed or ratified. These roles have been used in east and southern Africa to protect or advance equity-oriented public policy, promote health system reforms or prioritise allocations to specific areas of health systems. Parliamentary processes offer the opportunity for public input even in polarised political environments (Chebundo, 2006).

> Parliaments have, for example, contributed to policy space and public debate in support of health equity through their representative, legislative and oversight roles, including budget supervision.

For example:

- In Kenya, civil society, medicine distributors, government and some public health conscious members of parliament challenged areas of the intellectual property law that did not give adequate authority to government to procure essential drugs at reasonable cost (HAI Africa, 2006).

- In South Africa and Zimbabwe, equity-oriented budget monitoring has both raised attention to areas of health system performance that need to be strengthened through increased resource allocation, and prioritised equity-oriented areas of health spending under conditions of scarcity (Chebundo, 2006; Ngomane and Ntuli, 2006).

- In South Africa, portfolio committees on health and finance, legislators from each provincial parliament and from the National Association of Local Government were supported by a technical partner (Health Systems Trust) to: develop a stronger understanding of equity issues in health and health care in South Africa; to understand trade-offs involved; develop and review indicators of equitable resource allocation; and to analyse policy and legislative proposals. Visits linked budgets to system weaknesses and health workers' views:

    'Parliamentarians contributed towards ensuring that the need to redress inequity was kept high on the public agenda' (Ngomane and Ntuli, 2006:11).

Resolutions of the Health Civil Society Network, October 2005

We are united, together with health civil society in the region, around the core principles and values of:

- the fundamental right to health and life;
- equity and social justice;
- people-led and people-centred health systems;
- public over commercial interests in health (health before profits);
- people-led and grassroots-driven regional integration.

To take these values forward we are reclaiming the state in health and have identified the five priorities listed below:

1 Building a national people's health system

- We are struggling to build integrated health systems underpinned by the principles of equity that address our lives, not just our illnesses and that keep us healthy.
- We will link, network and foster strategic alliances with partners, inside and outside the health sector, to develop a unified voice.

2 Organising people's power for health

- We are organising people's power to amplify our voice, claim our right to health and control our resources for health.

3 Having adequate fairly-treated health workers

- Our health systems need adequate, well-trained and fairly-distributed health workers at all levels of our systems, in places where people need them most.
- Health workers in the public sector need to be motivated through decent conditions, training, incentives, living wages and safe work environments, in a way that promotes gender equity.

4 Sufficient and equitable funding of our health systems

- We demand sustained increased investments in the public sector in health. We expect our governments to meet their Abuja commitment to allocate at least 15 per cent of government spending to health.
- We demand an end to African wealth unfairly flowing out of the continent so that we have the resources for our health.
- We demand an end to unfair charges for poor people for health.

5 Global solidarity for economic and trade justice

- We expect our parliamentarians to ensure our countries have the independence and sovereignty to protect our right to health.
- We remind those who go to the World Trade Organisation that: 'No deal is better than a bad deal.'

Health Civil Society Network in East, Central and Southern Africa, 2005

- In Kenya the African Population Health Research Centre used evidence on differentials in access to reproductive health services and health outcomes to lever parliamentary support in repositioning family planning and reproductive health in health priorities. Parliamentarians were able to 'negotiate' a line item in the budget for family planning and reproductive health that gave them the basis to mobilise support for the resources, monitoring performance and increasing resource allocation to this area through a specific coalition of members of parliament (Mugisha, 2006).

- Tanzania's parliament has, through a coalition of parliamentary committees, taken a number of positions and initiatives to promote poverty reduction. These include the expansion of basic primary education, focusing on poverty reduction in budget oversight and participating in 'community scorecards' and 'citizen report cards' to give participatory field assessments of service delivery and policy results in key areas identified for action in national strategies. These actions have been facilitated by strong, experienced committee chairs, a clear policy focus and consensus-building around key goals (Draman and Langdon, 2005; Eberlei and Henn, 2003).

These examples are among many that demonstrate the potential impact of parliamentary roles on the design and performance of health systems. A review of parliamentary experience suggests that equity-oriented outcomes are most likely to happen when national policy is oriented towards equity, when parliamentary reforms have opened the policy space and means for parliamentary action, and where parliamentarians actively visit constituencies and interact directly with health workers and communities (Ngomane and Ntuli, 2006; Chebundo, 2006; Mataure, 2003; Musuka and Chingombe, 2006).

Regional networks have played a supporting role (Musuka, 2005; Chebundo, 2006), including the SADC Parliamentary Forum, the East African Assembly, the East African Legislative Assembly, the Commonwealth Parliamentary Association and the Association of Parliamentary Committees on Health in East and Southern Africa. The latter, formed by parliamentarians and clerks from parliamentary committees on health in east and southern Africa in 2005, has begun to exchange experience and share technical inputs in health (Chebundo, 2006).

There have been constraints. For example, parliaments may only become involved in budget processes at a late stage when it may be difficult to reorient measures towards more equitable options. Parliamentarians sometimes feel unprepared for this work and the committees often change membership in five-year intervals or less.

Parliamentary input to health budgets in Zimbabwe

Before 2000, Zimbabwe's budget was crafted exclusively by the executive without input from parliament and civil society. Public involvement was limited to budget briefings and parliament's role was limited to debating the budget as presented. The fifth Parliament of Zimbabwe, beginning in 2000, implemented parliamentary reforms to change the course of parliamentary processes. This changed parliament's legislative functions, oversight role over executive programmes and policy implementation, representational approaches and its budgetary process. The committee system, where one committee works with one sector ministry, was introduced.

Following this, a re-engineered budget process was introduced. Around March/April each year, the portfolio committees call for budget meetings with the relevant ministry officials and stakeholders from civil society, business, local authorities and professional groups for the sectors. These meetings provide the opportunity for the committee and the stakeholders to indicate to the ministry what they consider to be the priority areas for inclusion in the budget. In the health sector, an 'all-stakeholder', full-day budget consultative meeting is organised at the beginning of the budget formulation stage. Stakeholders present both oral and written submissions of their envisaged priority areas to the ministry and the committee. The consultations are supported by technical input.

Through this process the committee has:

- shifted from simply calling for increased allocations from treasury to focusing on prioritising targets and considering equity implications;
- compared health allocations against set equity goals and benchmarks set by both national policies and international standards; and
- tracked quarterly spending and compared spending to priorities in resource allocation.

After consultations the committee contributes ideas to the ministry team who drafts their bids, with inputs from its various departments. In August/September the committee requests the ministry to provide its consolidated draft bids and holds further all-stakeholder consultation to see whether priority areas are reflected in the bids. The Ministry of Health and Child Welfare then sends its bids to treasury, with detailed justification, and waits for its share when the national budget is presented to parliament. The parliamentary committee on health also prepares its findings and recommendations for presentation of a composite report from all portfolio committees to parliament.

This experience has shown that health resources can best be influenced through collective input and strong representation during the early priority setting stage with the respective ministries, rather that at the late stage of treasury presentation. The process has had some impact in Zimbabwe, with the preventive budget share rising from 9 per cent to 12 per cent in 2006, a stand-alone budget for mental health and an increasing share of the national budget going to health.

Chebundo, 2006

The fundamentals of policy orientation emerge upstream from party ideologies and constitutional frameworks (Sekgoma *et al.*, 2006). Resource constraints and the inaccessibility of some areas may bias the opportunity people have to engage parliaments towards higher-income urban groups. Electoral systems based on proportional representation may make individual members of parliament unwilling to criticise government policies even where they see problems for health equity at constituency level.

Reclaiming the resources for health thus calls for both a more robust, effective state in the global environment and a more robust form of participatory democracy in the national environment.

This section highlights both the potential for the practical experiences in working towards this and the local, national and global impediments to achieving it. It emphasises that organising participatory democracy at local and national level is not a resource-intensive exercise – it can be done and has been done with limited resources. It has more to do with how power is organised, shared and used.

One impediment identified and a key area for action to address the scale of the public health challenge in the region, is the current fragmentation of public interests in health. At the same time, this section has many examples of health gains that occur when state, civil society, parliament, health workers and other public interests co-operate. This suggests there are much wider health gains to be made in systematically organising and strengthening the wider collective alliance of public interests across state, government and society.

In the final section, drawing together the major findings of this analysis, we discuss the commitments and actions that such an alliance of public interests in health in and beyond the region can pursue to advance health and health equity in east and southern Africa.

Reclaiming the resources for health thus calls for both a more robust, effective state in the global environment and a more robust form of participatory democracy in the national environment.

One impediment identified and a key area for action to address the scale of the public health challenge in the region, is the current fragmentation of public interests in health. At the same time, this section has many examples of health gains that occur when state, civil society, parliament, health workers and other public interests co-operate. This suggests there are much wider health gains to be made in systematically organising and strengthening the wider collective alliance of public interests across state, government and society.

REFERENCES

Baez C and Barron P (2006) 'Community voice and role in district health systems in east and southern Africa: A literature review', *EQUINET discussion paper* 39, EQUINET, Harare.

Chanetsa J (May 2007) 'Control of breast milk substitutes in Zimbabwe', *Case study report* produced for EQUINET, Harare.

Chebundo B (2006) 'Parliaments in the re-engineered budget process in health: Case study', unpublished paper, Harare.
– (2006b) 'Regional networking of parliamentary committees on health, SEAPACOH case study', unpublished paper, Harare.

Draman R and Langdon S (2005) 'PRSPs in Africa: Parliaments and economic policy performance', *Project on Democracy and the Rule of Law*, mimeo, State and Democracy Division, Deutsche Gesellschaft fur Technische Zusammanarbeit, Eschborn.

Eberlei W and Henn H (2003) *Parliaments in sub-Saharan Africa: Actors in poverty reduction?*, Division 42, State and Democracy, Planning and Development Dept, Section Economic Affairs, PRSP/Africa Department, Deutsche Gesellschaft fur Technische Zusammenarbeit, Eschborn.

EQUINET (2004) 'Reclaiming the state: Advancing people's health, challenging injustice', *Meeting report of the Regional Conference on Equity in Health, Durban, South Africa, June 2004*, EQUINET, Harare.

Equity Gauge (Zambia) and Lusaka Health Board (2006) 'Strengthening community–health centre partnership and accountability in Zambia', *EQUINET PRA project report*, EQUINET, Harare.

EQUINET, TARSC and CHESSORE (2005b) 'Strengthening community voice and agency in health', *EQUINET meeting report, Zambia*, EQUINET, Harare.

Gilson L, Kilima P and Tanner M (1994) 'Local government decentralisation and the health sector in Tanzania', *Public Administration and Development* 14: 451-477.

Gilson L and Travis P (1997) 'Health system decentralisation in Africa: An overview of experiences in eight countries', *WHO Regional Seminar on Decentralisation, Bamako, January 1997*, WHO, Geneva.

Gilson L, Doherty J, Loewenson R, Francis V (2007) *Final report of the Knowledge Network on Health Systems WHO Commission on the Social Determinants of Health*, WHO CSDH, Geneva.

Goetz AM, Gaventa J and Jenkins R (2001) 'Bringing citizen voice and client focus into service delivery', *IDS working paper* 138, Institute of Development Studies, Brighton.

Harbeson L (2001) 'Rebuilding local capacities in Mozambique: The national health system and civil society', *Civil society and political renaissance*, Kumarian Press, Bloomfield, available at http://www.idrc.ca/en/ev-87954-201-1-DO_TOPIC.html.

Health Action International (HAI) Africa (2006) *Health Action International Africa Network Update 4*, July/Aug 2006, HAI Africa, Nairobi.

Health Civil Society in East and Southern Africa Network (2005) 'Resolutions of the Health Civil Society in Southern and East Africa meeting, 13 October 2005,' presented at the *Southern African Social Forum, Harare, 13 October 2005*, EQUINET, Harare.
– (2005b) 'Health civil society in east and southern Africa: Towards a unified agenda and action for people's health, equity and justice', *EQUINET meeting report*, EQUINET, Harare.

Kalumba K (1997) 'Towards an equity-oriented policy of decentralisation in health systems under conditions of turbulence: The case of Zambia', *WHO discussion paper* 6, World Health Organisation, Zambia.

Kamupira M and London L (2005) 'Human rights commitments relevant to health made by states in southern Africa: Implications for health equity', *EQUINET discussion paper* 25, EQUINET, Harare.

Libombo A (2003) 'Health systems development and reproductive health, experience of Mozambique', speech at *Making the Link: Sexual-Reproductive Health and Health Systems Conference, 9–11 September*, Univ. of Leeds, Leeds.

Loewenson R (2003) *Civil society – state interactions in national health systems: Annotated bibliography on civil society and health*, WHO/TARSC, accessed 2 June 2007 at http://www.tarsc.org/WHOCSI/
– (2007) 'Building voice and agency in health: public action within health systems', in Bennett S, Gilson L and Mills A (eds), *Health, economic development and household poverty*, Routledge, London.

Loewenson R, Rusike I and Zulu M (2004) 'Assessing the impact of health centre committees on health system performance and health resource allocation', *EQUINET discussion paper* 18, TARSC, CWGH and EQUINET, Harare.

London L (2004) 'Can human rights tools serve as a tool for equity?', *EQUINET policy paper* 14, School of Public Health and Family Medicine, Univ. of Cape Town, South Africa and EQUINET, Harare.

Macwan'gi M and Ngwengwe A (2004) 'Effectiveness of district health boards in interceding for the community', *EQUINET discussion paper* 19, EQUINET and Univ. of Zambia, Harare.

Marmot M (2006) 'Health in an unequal world', the *Lancet* 368 (9552): 2081-2094.

Mataure M (2003) 'Parliamentary functions and reforms and their application in promoting health equity in southern Africa', *EQUINET discussion paper* 16, Public Affairs and Parliamentary Support Trust and EQUINET, Harare.

Mills A (1994) 'Decentralisation and accountability in the health sector from an international perspective: What are the choices?', *Public Administration and Development* 14: 281–292, accessed 15 August 2006 at http://www.wits.ac.za/whp/rightsandreforms/docs/Africa.pdf

Mkandawire T (2006) 'Disempowering new democracies and the persistence of poverty', *Democracy, Governance and Human Rights programme paper* 21, UNRISD, Geneva.

Mugisha F (2006) *The Nairobi Equity Gauge work with parliaments: Case study*, African Population Health Research Centre, Nairobi.

Musuka G (2005) 'Descriptive study of debates on health equity matters in the Zimbabwean National Legislative Assembly', unpublished research paper, TARSC, EQUINET, Harare.

Musuka G and Chingombe I (2006) 'The role of parliamentary committees on health in east and southern Africa in building equitable, people-centred national health systems', unpublished paper, Centre for Health Policy and EQUINET, Harare.

Ngomane T and Ntuli A (2006) 'Parliamentary roles in equitable health budgets: Case study', unpublished paper, South Africa.

Ngulube TJ, Mdhluli L, Gondwe K and Njobvu C (2004) 'Governance, participatory mechanisms and structures in Zambia's health system: An assessment of the impact of health centre committees on equity in health and health care', *EQUINET discussion paper* 21, CHESSORE, EQUINET, Harare.

Ngulube TJ, Mdhluli L and Gondwe K (2005) 'Planning and budgeting for primary health care in Zambia: A policy analysis', *EQUINET discussion paper* 29, CHESSORE, EQUINET, Harare.

Olukoshi A (1998) *The elusive Prince of Denmark: Structural adjustment and the crisis of governance in Africa*, Nordiska Afrikainstitutet, Uppsala.

Oyaya CO and Rifkin SB (2003) 'Health sector reforms in Kenya: An examination of district level planning', *Health Policy* 64: 113, 127.

People's Health Movement (2007) *Right to health care campaign*, PHM, Cairo, available at http://www.phmovement.org/en/campaigns/righttohealth

Rusike I (2007) 'Interview with ACORD Cameroon', unpublished, World Social Forum, Nairobi, Kenya.

Savigny D, Kasale H, Conrad M and Reid G (2004) 'Fixing health systems', *In Focus*, IDRC, Ottawa, available at http://www.idrc.ca/in_focus

SADC heads of state (August 2003) *SADC Social Charter*, Dar es Salaam.

Sekgoma B, Afuba MD, Eba PM (2006) *Handbook on gender, human rights and HIV and AIDS*, SADC PF, Gaborone.

Tanzania Essential Health Interventions Project (2004) *Tanzania Essential Health Interventions Project*, IDRC, Ottawa.

TARSC, EQUINET, WHO Afro (2000) 'Public participation in health systems' *Regional meeting report, Pangolin Lodge, Harare, 17-19 May 2000*, EQUINET with WHO Afro, Harare.

United Nations Capital Development Fund (UNCDF) and UNDP (2001) 'Malawi concept paper: Empowerment through governance and development management as a strategy towards poverty alleviation', *Malawi on the move: The re-orientation of UNDP and UNCDF/UNDP support to the Malawi decentralisation process (2002-2006)*, UNDP, New York.

UNDP (2005) *Human development report: International cooperation at a crossroads: Aid, trade and security in an unequal world*, UNDP, New York, available at http://hdr.undp.org/reports/global/2005/

Univerity of Namibia and Ontevrede Community (2006) 'Creating nurse student awareness on community knowledge on health in Ontevrede (unsatisfied) informal settlement, Namibia', *EQUINET PRA report*, EQUINET, Harare.

Wallerstein NB and Duran B (2006) 'Using community-based participatory research to address health disparities', *Health Promotion Practice* 7:312.

World Bank (2005) *World development indicators database, 2005*, World Bank, Washington, accessed 2 June 2007 at http://devdata.worldbank.org/wdi2005/index2.htm

WHO (1978) *Primary health care*, joint report of the Director General of the WHO and the Executive Director of UNICEF, WHO, Geneva.
– (1978b) 'Declaration of Alma-Ata', *International Conference on Primary Health Care, Alma-Ata, USSR, 6-12 September 1978*, WHO, Geneva.
– (2004) '3 by 5' progress report, WHO, Geneva.

Taking action
TO RECLAIM THE RESOURCES
FOR HEALTH

SECTION

7

KEY ISSUES

The first six sections of the analysis frame the issues that affect equity in health in east and southern Africa, present and analyse evidence on these issues and propose strategies for acting on them.

This section consolidates this analysis. It summarises the policy measures and actions that would advance equity to enable poor households and communities to claim a fairer share of national resources, for east and southern African countries to claim a more just return from the global economy and for redistributive health systems to claim a larger share of national resources. There is growing opportunity for a win-win resolution between measures that reduce a drain of resources from east and southern African economies, and national measures that redistribute these resources for wider economic and social gain. We propose ways for public leadership and social action to facilitate this.

These equity values and measures need to be championed. Towards this, as EQUINET, we have identified indicators that reflect progress in four key dimensions of equity, drawn from our analysis. We argue for these to be monitored and reported on to assess progress in implementing commitments and as inputs for strategic reviews of the policies, investments and processes used to advance health and to build universal and equitable health systems.

This section outlines the debates and knowledge gaps arising in the analysis and invites contribution to these. EQUINET, as a network of institutions within the region, remains committed to generating knowledge, facilitating dialogue and analysis, and supporting practice to deliver on equity goals.

Commitments and actions to advance equity in health

We opened this analysis of health equity in east and southern Africa with two stories. The first was the story of Mr Banda, a 41 year old man living in a rural community in the region, infected with HIV and suffering from tuberculosis for a second time, despite having been treated once. He had exhausted his physical and personal resources to access health services. The barriers Mr Banda faces arise from the same poverty and social conditions that re-expose him to illness, even after treatment. The second story, from Uganda, demonstrated the improvements in health and wellbeing that occur in the region when these barriers are overcome.

These stories demonstrate that there are alternatives and thus choices. We have experience of ways in which our societies and health systems have redistributed resources, improved the incomes and quality of life of disadvantaged communities and brought effective health care close to communities – and in so doing, improved health. We present some examples of these experiences across the sections of the analysis. These actions take place at all levels – globally, nationally and within local communities. While Mr Banda's situation is evident at local level, local responses are affected by policies and actions at national and global level.

The evidence in this analysis points to three ways in which 'reclaiming' the resources for health can improve health equity for:

- poor people to claim a fairer share of national resources;
- a more just return for east and southern African countries from the global economy; and
- a larger share of global and national resources to be invested in redistributive health systems.

Claiming a fairer share of national resources for poor households and people...

Our region is rich in natural wealth but high in household poverty. The resources for healthier, longer and better quality lives, and for more effective, comprehensive health systems, exist within the region.

Yet the analysis in Section 1 shows that the region continues to experience a high prevalence of HIV and AIDS related mortality, tuberculosis, malaria and other communicable and non-communicable diseases, as well as illness and mortality related to reproductive roles. This health profile reflects the living, working and community conditions associated with high and, in some cases, rising levels of poverty, including: food insecurity; poor access to safe water, sanitation, energy, transport and shelter; weakened social networks and gender and social violence. The AIDS epidemic has exacted a high toll on health in the region. Tragically, countries that made greater social gains before the AIDS epidemic, particularly in health and education, have suffered greater losses after.

Within countries in the region and across communities, groups with different levels of income, assets, rural or urban residence, mother's education and other socio-economic conditions have different health outcomes. They also have different levels of access to health care. While access to health care has improved in the region over the past two decades, relative disadvantage in access by income, place of residence and maternal education persist.

The evidence shown in Section 1 indicates that these differentials have not been reduced by aggregate national gross domestic product growth and that, in some cases, they have even widened. It appears that inequalities in wealth, assets, in the returns to employment and in social factors like education, affect how much households benefit from growth in the national economy and are able to translate this into improved wellbeing. Poor opportunities for health continue to be passed across generations through this vicious cycle. What is most problematic for health is that this appears to have been intensifying since 1995, adding new challenges to historical legacies.

Unless we can break the cycle and improve the benefits that households with previous disadvantage obtain from growth, most households will continue to lack the basic resources for health.

Our first indicator of a sustainable basis for improved health in the region is, therefore, for disadvantaged individuals and households to access a larger share of national resources.

Our first indicator of a sustainable basis for improved health in the region is, therefore, for disadvantaged individuals and households to access a larger share of national resources.

We would measure this change not only through indicators of poverty and income distribution but, more importantly, through the extent to which disadvantaged social groups and households can access national resources. From the factors related to health, this calls for measures that widen the distribution of control over assets and wealth (such as land, housing and production capital), the economic and social returns people get from employment (improving the ratio between wages and profits), and the access disadvantaged people, especially women, have to health and education services.

Breaking a vicious cycle of economic and social inequality is not simple. All countries in the region have expressed a commitment to it. Two important policy dimensions affect delivery on this, however, that we discuss later:

- The first, identified in Sections 1 and 2, relates to how countries in the region engage with a process of globalisation that is associated with widening inequalities globally, with Africa in a highly disadvantaged position.
- The second, identified in Sections 3 to 5, relates to the options that countries have, particularly within health systems, to redistribute resources nationally.

Claiming a just return from the global economy for east and southern African countries ...

With a doubling of income gaps between the richest and poorest people in the world in the last four decades and significant global inequalities in wealth, countries in east and southern Africa face a strategic challenge in engaging in this highly unequal global economy.

The challenge that we particularly point to is the outflow of material, financial and social resources from the region, with relatively poor returns to national economies. This is depleting the resources for health. In the private sector, net inflows in the 1970s shifted to substantial outflows after the 1990s, reflecting losses in falling terms of trade, through capital and financial market outflows, in reduced foreign direct investments for production and in falling domestic savings. This is amplified by public and social losses through debt payments and the outflow of human and natural resources.

The trends and policy perceptions described indicate that after nearly three decades of liberalisation and export-oriented economic policy, the view that increased integration into the current global economy invariably brings progress can be contested.

The two examples explored in the analysis, access to food and access to medicines, both fundamental to health, show that without a more strategic engagement, the unfettered exercise of global trade and finance measures undermines nutrition and health care in the most vulnerable communities, increases household poverty and reduces public resources for health.

The call for a fairer form of globalisation and a more just return to Africa from the global economy is not a new one. It is voiced in various forums and commissions, including in the United Nations. This analysis adds further evidence for that call. We understand that this is not simply a matter for the benevolence of powerful nations. We suggest options for east and southern African countries to intervene as states, domestically, and to engage, collectively, to negotiate and claim a more just return for African resources from the global economy. We observe that these same strategies of active state intervention, subsidy, public investment and regulation, used by wealthy countries to promote their own industrial development and services, need to be available within the global economy for east and southern Africa countries to address their development needs.

...these same strategies of active state intervention, subsidy, public investment and regulation, used by wealthy countries to promote their own industrial development and services, need to be available within the global economy for east and southern Africa countries to address their development needs.

Some of the options for this, raised in Sections 2 to 5, include:

- improved disclosure of financial flows, controlling capital flight and profit or dividend outflows and taxing currency transfers;

- debt cancellation;

- using tariffs and subsidies and canvassing for investments to develop, protect and diversify infant industries and smallholder agricultural production;

- negotiating foreign direct investment that adds value to natural resources and stimulates local industry;

- widening population access to land, water, forests, fishing areas and other productive resources through genuine redistribution;

- meeting the SADC commitment to a budgetary allocation of 'at least 10 per cent of national budgetary resources' to agriculture and rural development within five years, preferentially allocated to smallholder and women's production, and stimulating local market links, especially for smallholder and women producers;

- resisting the commercialisation and privatisation of public goods, including health care, water and other essential services, and not making irreversible commitments under the General Agreement on Trade in Services to liberalise these services;

- enacting and using Trade-related Intellectual Property Rights (TRIPS) flexibilities in full for access to medicines, including through regional co-operation to procure, compulsorily license and stimulate local production of pharmaceuticals and other medical technology;

- ensuring that trade agreements explicitly recognise and include clauses to protect health, support capacities for this, compensate for public revenues lost, involve health officials in negotiations and include health impact assessments where relevant;

- avoiding commitments to liberalise health services and providing for full use of TRIPS flexibilities; and

- negotiating, through bilateral agreements, for investment in public sector training and retention incentives for health workers to address the out-migration of skilled health workers from Africa.

These measures draw support from regional co-operation and south-south networks.

The analysis points to the loss of public confidence in states and their loss of legitimacy that occur when the benefits of globalisation are felt by a diminishing group of people, with wider social decline. This happened under the World Bank and International Monetary Fund sponsored structural adjustment reforms. The political leadership that negotiates improved returns from the global economy is thus also called upon to distribute the returns from this more fairly to the wider population.

There is growing opportunity for a win-win balance between measures that reduce a drain of resources from east and southern Africa economies, and national measures that redistribute these resources for wider economic and social gain. Efforts to widen access to prevention, treatment and care for HIV and AIDS, as outlined in Section 3, demand full use of TRIPS flexibilities. Increased public sector financing for health to strengthen district health systems that are free at point of care, as outlined in Section 4, provides clear pathways for equitable use of funds released from debt cancellation. Measures to produce, value and retain health workers at the levels of the health system they are most needed, as outlined in Section 5, provide an effective channel for bilateral funds that compensate for perverse subsidies from out-migration.

> The political leadership that negotiates improved returns from the global economy is thus also called upon to distribute the returns from this more fairly to the wider population.

Claiming a larger share of national and global resources for redistributive health systems ...

There are many ways east and southern African countries can deliver on their long-standing commitment to overcome unfair differences in health and allocate more resources to those with greater health needs. In Section 3 we show, for example, how measures to improve access to land and production inputs for smallholder and women producers are associated with improved nutrition. In Section 1 we show the importance of women's education for a range of health outcomes. Most of these measures lie outside the health sector.

Health systems can, however, make a difference in these areas by providing leadership, shaping wider social norms and values, providing public health motivation and working across sectors in a shared approach.

> We describe, in Section 3, the comprehensive, primary health care oriented, people-centred and publicly-led health systems that have been found to improve health, particularly for the most disadvantaged people with greatest health needs. These systems are based on the universal right to health and founded on policy values of universality and equity. They are advanced and protected against challenge by political and public health leadership and public alliances.

The primary health care strategy orients the whole health system towards promoting health and preventing ill health as the first line of action and towards providing relevant, accessible care – areas of health intervention that are often lost when systems are driven by more specialised responses to disease. The multiple challenges to health experienced in the poorest communities call for comprehensive approaches, integrated within levels of care closest to these communities.

East and southern African countries made considerable progress in health through health care systems based on primary health care. Resource scarcities, rather than public health effectiveness, drive more selective, vertically-organised approaches, with reduced investment in the systems to support these approaches. Yet lessons learned from the roll out of prevention and treatment for HIV and AIDS, described in Section 3, indicate that the most equitable and sustainable way to achieve goals for treatment and prevention is through universal, comprehensive, people-centred health systems, particularly at district level.

> While many sectors contribute to health, the analysis presents evidence of the important contribution that health systems have continued to make to overcoming differentials in health, even in the face of wider challenges from economic inequality, poverty and AIDS.

While many sectors contribute to health, the analysis presents evidence of the important contribution that health systems have continued to make to overcoming differentials in health, even in the face of wider challenges from economic inequality, poverty and AIDS.

The persistence of disadvantage in access to health care by income, place of residence and maternal education, however, weakens this contribution. It means, unacceptably, that those with highest health needs have poorer health care access, when the opposite should apply.

In Sections 3 to 6, we identify some reasons why this is happening:

- the higher share of spending on health goes to the highest income groups in the population so they capture the greater share of public spending on health;
- people lack the power to overcome the barriers that arise to their use of health services at different stages, particularly as poverty and inequalities in wealth widen;
- the investment in and integration of comprehensive primary health care in Africa is declining;
- decentralisation reforms have not successfully supported primary health care approaches;
- urban, higher level hospitals, less used by poor communities, continue to receive a greater and, in some cases, increasing share of resources; and
- private for-profit and commercialised health services have grown and user charges have risen.

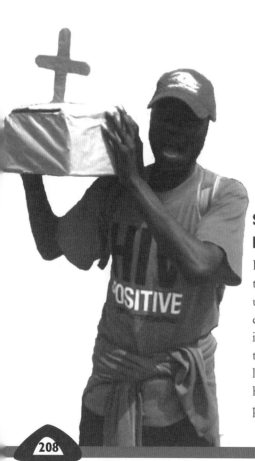

Strong, rights-based, accountable and equity-oriented public leadership in health ...

Public policy choices can, however, address these problems. We argue that this calls for public leadership in health systems to define strategies for universality and equity and to lever the role of all sectors – including external funders – towards national health goals. Leadership needs to invest in and support the community and social roles in health, managing the pressures for commercialisation and linking short-term resources to long-term health system plans, to ensure adequate investment in primary health care and district health systems. This demands a strengthened public sector in health.

As we present in Section 4, the current average spending of US$29 per capita on health in the region is well below the US$60 per capita WHO estimates as essential for a functional health system – or even the US$34 per capita estimated by the Macroeconomic Commission on Health to cover the most basic interventions for major public health burdens.

> To start with, governments are called on to increase their own financing to health to reach at least the 15 per cent commitment made in Abuja, excluding external financing.
>
> We argue, however, for 'Abuja PLUS' – that is for government commitments to health to be matched by international delivery on debt cancellation, releasing the resources currently going to debt servicing to be used to develop health systems.
>
> We also argue for a significantly greater share of this government spending to be allocated to district health services. An indicative target to aim towards would be 50 per cent of government spending to district health services (up to and including level 1 hospital services), of which half (25 per cent of total) should be on primary level health care.

We argue for 'Abuja PLUS' – that is for government commitments to health to be matched by international delivery on debt cancellation, releasing the resources currently going to debt servicing to be used to develop health systems. We also argue for a significantly greater share of this government spending to be allocated to district health services.

Public leadership calls for a stronger and more sustained assertion of public interest in health, with regulation of commercial interests that are harmful to health, and resistance to privatisation and commercialisation of services essential for health.

The major elements of health systems cannot be organised through the market. Health is a universal human right, calling for a foundation of rights and obligations to protect people's health.

The major elements of health systems cannot be organised through the market. Health is a universal human right, calling for a foundation of rights and obligations to protect people's health.

As we detail in Section 3, this demands that countries ratify regional and international conventions, such as the African Charter on Human and Peoples' Rights (1986), the SADC Social Charter and the International Covenant on Economic, Social and Cultural Rights (1976). Countries can integrate these conventions into national law and provide for obligations in the constitution to protect the health and health care of the population, specifically of vulnerable groups, like children.

The analysis draws attention to ways to progressively translate these rights into real entitlements. We also argue that this will not happen without a strong alliance of public interests in health through state and civil society, parliament, health workers and other public interests.

Across the analysis we present examples from the region of the health gains that occur when such alliances of public interests protect and advance public health, whether in global negotiations, in levering a more equitable and effective distribution of resources for and within health systems or in enhancing use of health systems. This calls for an enabling state and particularly one that facilitates a more robust form of participatory democracy in the national environment.

There are many ways to exercise this leadership and organise health systems to overcome inequalities in health. In this analysis we have focused on three that we consider important at this stage: how fairly we finance health systems; how we organise, value and retain our health workers; and the role we give to people and social action.

Guaranteeing universal access through fair financing ...

No one who needs health services should be denied access due to inability to pay and the costs of health care should not threaten livelihoods. Within the context of poverty and inequality in east and southern Africa, this means that those with greater ability to pay should contribute a higher proportion of their income than those with lower incomes, and those with higher levels of health need should get a greater share of health resources.

A number of measures are proposed in Section 4 to achieve this:

- a steady increase in progressive tax funding as the core to universal coverage;
- clear measures to bring various forms of health insurance within a strategic plan for universal coverage;
- tax and regulatory measures to improve efficiency and equity in the private health sector;
- use of all funds collected to improve equitable access to defined entitlements to comprehensive, primary health care oriented health services, planned for and monitored to ensure that entitlements equate to real access; and
- equity measures in resource allocation of national budgets, with increased allocations to district and primary health care systems.

One of the areas of increased spending is on health workers. Without health workers there is no health system. There is a massive shortfall in health workers in east and southern Africa, with losses due to AIDS, significant outflows in health worker migration and many health workers found in urban hospitals and private services. There seems to be a global conveyor belt of health workers moving from lower to higher income settings and out-migration, whose costs to communities or health systems are still poorly understood or quantified. Yet, many health workers would prefer not to leave home.

Investments that value and retain health workers...

Delivering equitable health systems calls for immediate and longer-term measures to train and retain and ensure effective and motivated work from health workers, especially those within the public sector district and primary health care systems.

Drawing on the region's experience, the strategies for this include:

- immediate financial measures, to address real wage declines and improve real earnings, particularly for public sector health workers;

- a mix of non-financial incentives that address continuous professional development, working, living and social conditions and needs, including safe work and access to antiretrovirals;

- additional resources to finance all forms of incentives needed;

- investment in and improvement of strategic management capacities and systems and in information and monitoring systems;

- dialogue with health workers to improve communication and trust between themselves and both their employing institutions and the communities they serve; and

- bilateral agreements providing compensatory investments to east and southern African countries for perverse subsidies due to out-migration, directed to measures to produce, value and retain health workers.

Participatory health systems, empowering social action for health ...

Implementing and defending these features of health systems is not simply a matter for technocrats, health workers or state officials. Our concept of equity includes the power and ability people (and social groups) have to direct resources to their health needs, particularly for those with worst health. This refers to people's collective ability to assert their own needs and interests, influence the allocation of societal resources towards their needs, and challenge the distribution of power and resources that block their development.

The market reforms in health care described in Section 2 and the disparities described in Section 1 do not only leave people vulnerable to untreated ill health, they also marginalise communities who cannot afford or access the health system. They create individual struggles over basic entitlements and disrupt social cohesion and integration. In contrast, the primary health care approach to universal health systems, described in Section 3, backed by fair financing measures and health workers who are valued, as described in Sections 4 and 5, send a powerful message of social solidarity and foster social inclusion.

Hence the call for a robust state to resist encroachments on health and defend public interests in global engagements. This is not equated with an authoritarian state that does not listen to local views, particularly if we are to tap one of the region's most abundant and powerful assets – its people.

Our concept of equity includes the power and ability people (and social groups) have to direct resources to their health needs, particularly for those with worst health. This refers to people's collective ability to assert their own needs and interests, influence the allocation of societal resources towards their needs, and challenge the distribution of power and resources that block their development.

While health systems have a huge potential to empower people, stimulate social action and create powerful constituencies to advance public interests in health, as we describe in Sections 3 to 6, they do not always do so.

To more effectively engage these social potentials, drawing from examples in the region, we propose that health systems:

- formally recognise in law and institutional practice the community role in health systems;

- budget and provide adequate resources for the mechanisms and processes for direct public participation in health, including the communications, training, forums and outreach processes;

- orient, train and reward health workers and community leaders who can facilitate and use participatory processes to plan and implement health actions, informed by policy guidance;

- establish mechanisms to monitor commitments and plans and ensure accountability, including community and civil society mechanisms; and

- encourage civil society organisation support for community capacities and roles in health.

Reclaiming the resources for health thus calls for: a state that is able to advance public interests in the global environment; a robust, systematic form of participatory democracy within the national environment; and a more collectively organised and informed society.

These measures are within our means to achieve in the region but demand concerted action.

Progress and targets in reclaiming the resources for health

The contested decades of structural adjustment have shown us that public interests need to be vigorously championed, monitored and reported on if we are to advance health in the face of challenge. Yet the most marginalised people and households are often the most silent in communicating their views and experience.

In Section 5 we quoted a primary care health worker:

'*Health care workers have kept silent for so long. Do you know what is silence? Silence is the absence of sound. Sound is when you make an impression and from us as nurses there is no sound or impression. That is why the government can make legislation without asking the health workers. The message of silence – it is 'unagreed', but everyone accepts it as a YES. I appeal to everyone to consider your silence because if you don't want to say yes, raise your voice and say NO.*'

Source: Interdisciplinary Industrial Health Research Group,, 2006

How much greater is the silence of rural communities, vulnerable children and unemployed women who lack the formal mechanisms to articulate their concerns? For this reason, for example, we have relied not only on published evidence for this analysis but also on reported experience, a diversity of views and images from the region.

Silence is not an option in a world of competing interests.

To champion those values, principles and systems that we have identified as central to reclaiming the resources for health, we have identified selected targets and indicators, discussed in our analysis, that reflect our progress in key dimensions of equity. We propose that governments, parliaments and civil society within countries and across the east and southern African region monitor and report on these quantitative and qualitative targets and indicators to assess how well we are doing in implementing our commitments.

> '...4. The strategy proposes strengthening of health systems with the goal of reducing disease burden through improved resources, systems, policies and management.
>
> This will contribute to equity through a system that reaches the poor and those most in need of health care. Investment in health will impact on poverty reduction and overall economic development.'

Africa health strategy: 2007–2015, Third Session of the AU Conference of Ministers of Health, Johannesburg, 9–13 April 2007; CAMH/MIN/5(III)

We recognise that targets poorly reflect diverse contexts and approaches to reach shared goals. Yet their power to inspire and galvanise action is without question. We also recognise that a short list of indicators may poorly reflect the scope of issues and work relevant to health equity outlined in this analysis. Yet we need manageable signals from concrete evidence to understand how well we are delivering on the political and policy commitments to equitable and universal health systems cited in the analysis. These not only inform public alliances around desired outcomes but, as a community of actors, inform planning and review of the key processes, investments and policy decisions that we make to contribute to those outcomes. They can thus usefully be integrated, quantified and linked to concrete strategies and timeframes within national strategies and plans, parliamentary budgeting and oversight, civil society advocacy and in engaging with international partners.

MARKERS OF PROGRESS

Advancing equity in health

1 Formal recognition and social expression of equity and universal rights to health and health care included, with specific provisions for vulnerable groups, in the constitution and national law;

2 Achieving United Nations goals of universal access to prevention of mother to child transmission, condoms and antiretroviral treatment by 2010;

3 Eliminating income and urban/rural differentials in access to immunisation, attendance by a skilled person at birth and access to prevention of mother to child transmission within east and southern African countries;

4 Eliminating income and urban/rural differentials in maternal mortality, child mortality, and under 5 year stunting within east and southern African countries;

5 Eliminating differentials in maternal mortality, child mortality and under 5 year nutrition (weight for age) between countries in the region; and

6 Achieving the Millennium Development Goal of reducing by half the number of people living on US$1 per day by 2015.

 MARKERS OF PROGRESS

Household access to the national resources for health

7 Achieving universal primary and secondary education in women;

8 Achieving the Millennium Development Goal of reducing by half the proportion of people without sustainable access to safe drinking water by 2015;

9 Reducing the Gini coefficient in all east and southern African countries to at least 0.4 (the lowest current coefficient in east and southern Africa);

10 Increasing the ratio of wages to profits;

12 Abolishing user fees from health systems;

13 Overcoming the barriers that disadvantaged communities identify that they face in accessing and using health and essential services; and

14 Meeting standards of adequate provision of health workers and of vital and essential drugs at primary and district levels of health systems.

MARKERS OF PROGRESS ━━━━━━━━▶

Resourcing redistributive health systems

15 Achieving the Abuja commitment of 15 per cent government spending on health – excluding external funding;

16 Achieving the WHO target of US$60 per capita spending on health systems;

17 Increasing progressive tax funding to health to a significantly larger share, with a reducing share of out-of-pocket financing in health;

18 Establishing a plan and strategy for harmonising the various health financing schemes into one framework for universal coverage;

19 Establishing a clear set of comprehensive health care entitlements for the population;

20 Allocating at least 50 per cent of government spending on health to district health systems (including level 1 hospitals) and 25 per cent of government spending on primary health care;

21 Implementing a mix of non-financial incentives agreed with health workers organisations, including access to antiretroviral treatment; and

22 Formally recognising in law and earmarking budgets for training, communication and mechanisms for direct public participation in all levels of the health system.

 MARKERS OF PROGRESS ━━━━━━━━▶

A more just return for east and southern African countries from the global economy

23 Debt cancellation;

24 Reducing the global Gini coefficient across countries to at least 0.4 (halving the current coefficient);

25 Allocating at least 10 per cent of budget resources to agriculture, with a majority share used for investments in and subsidies for smallholder and women producers;

26 No new health service commitments in the General Agreement on Trade in Services (GATS) and inclusion of all TRIPS flexibilities in national laws;

27 Inclusion of health officials in trade negotiations and inclusion of explicit clauses and measures to protect health in all relevant trade agreements; and

28 Establishing bilateral and multilateral agreements to fund health worker training and retention measures, especially involving recipient countries of health worker migration from east and southern Africa.

A review of progress on these indicators provides a stimulus for exchange of experience and promising practice within the region.

A review of progress on these indicators provides a stimulus for exchange of experience and promising practice within the region. The process enhances the accountability of public and private sectors and external funders for these outcomes and ensures that our policy measures, such as budget processes, usefully contribute to these outcomes.

While the indicators are selected for their availability in existing data sources, discussing progress along these parameters would usefully reveal how well our information and management systems are able to provide timely and publicly accessible information on key dimensions of equity. This may act as a stimulus and strengthen systems to generate and review this type of information, including through the participatory engagement of communities.

These targets and indicators relate to global, continental and regional commitments, to national policies and processes and to community level perspectives and experience. We see them all as key to meeting commitments made to the Millennium Development Goals by 2015, but also see that all of them demand greater urgency and priority due to their impact on the survival and quality of life of the large majority of people in the region.

A focus for action

'*Health must therefore constitute a central pillar of any coherent vision of African development...*'

The African regional health report 2006, WHO-Afro Region, 2006, Brazzaville

One challenge identified to concerted action for health equity in the region is building the shared message and organisation of the wider collective alliance of public interests for health that exist within the region. There is opportunity for this, given the political and policy level initiative in organisations like the African Union, SADC, Regional Health Ministers for East, Central and Southern Africa as well as the many technical, civil society, professional, research, parliamentary and academic forums. There are many examples of local alliances around issues, whether treatment access, malaria control, adolescent or workers' health.

This analysis seeks to contribute to that alliance.

Debates and conflicting views ...

As in all regions, we are aware that we are not a homogenous community, even among those involved in health. There are many areas raised in the analysis which are subjects of continued debate within and beyond the region.

There is debate about the strategic options for engaging in the global economy, including the role of new global powers such as China in Africa.

There are debates about how to deal with resource outflows. For example, there is debate about how to balance the rights of health workers to migrate and the benefits of remittance and other returns from migration, with the measures to deal with as yet unquantified losses to communities and health systems from migration, including losses to adequate care.

There are differing views about the role of the diverse for-profit health sector in east and southern African countries, with its range from large corporates managing hospitals to small local shops and individual health workers. There are strong competing positions on whether and how to support, control or co-ordinate this sector across these diverse forms.

Differing approaches are advanced on how to close the gap between rich and poor, whether targeting poor communities is sufficient or whether more comprehensive approaches to universal systems that close the gradients between rich and poor are more effective and or feasible. Debates continue about the relative virtues of applying resources to focused vertical programmes versus wider investments in more comprehensive services.

There is a diversity of views about what kind of state is best able to manage these challenges, with differences in position around the level of centralised authority or participatory functioning of the state.

We welcome these debates. The positions we have taken on them in the analysis derive from shared values and the evidence we have found.

The analysis has not explored all aspects central to our health and health systems. For example, the roles of indigenous knowledge, traditional health systems and local biodiversity are central to health in east and southern Africa, and while referred to in Sections 2 and 3, merit their own focus for their contribution to health equity. We would, however, argue that the broader challenges we describe of the global systems for intellectual property rights, the significant outflow of resources and the weak investment in the community level of health systems equally affect these areas of health.

We have also encountered gaps in evidence and knowledge that would be important to address in consolidating and developing shared messages and policy.

As in all regions, we are aware that we are not a homogenous community, even among those involved in health. There are many areas raised in the analysis which are subjects of continued debate within and beyond the region.

Knowledge gaps ...

Inequalities in health are commonly monitored along parameters of income, education and residence. Surprisingly, apart from the evidence on AIDS, there is little national evidence on gender differentials in health and there is a gap in evidence to support understanding of how inequalities in health and access to health care reflect differentials in gender, in wealth, in access to assets, such as land, and in the returns to employment.

Our information on health services is largely focused on measures of supply and availability. The barriers and facilitators of access to and uptake of health care in communities are derived through local ad hoc surveys and there is a gap in analysis of household surveys, such as the demographic and health surveys, routine health sector performance surveys or sentinel site surveillance. These would help us to better understand these barriers and facilitators across different communities nationally, and to assess how they are being affected by policy interventions.

While we are aware through various policy reports of the outflow of resources for health, as we discuss in Sections 2 and 5, our information systems poorly capture these flows. For example, in Section 5 we point out the greater ability of data systems in wealthy countries to capture the numbers of health workers who have migrated from east and southern African countries compared to records within the region. The flows of private finances out of and remittances into east and southern African countries are often informal and poorly monitored. The income in the largely informal sector of employment is difficult to track and include in systems for risk pooling and mandatory insurance. The time spent by health workers across public and private activities can be equally difficult to track. The labour contribution of the significant number of voluntary workers, community health workers, households, women and children to caring activities is poorly captured in national health accounts and seriously underestimated (and unrewarded). Policy design is not a simple task in the context of these unmapped flows, and means that evidence for policy needs to extend beyond quantitative evidence to include also qualitative and testimonial evidence.

A surprising gap is the weakness in systematically documenting positive experiences in east and southern Africa, with their context, design and impact. We found this in relation to evidence on primary health care, for example. While there is some communication of good practice, we need to improve documentation of positive experience. For example, we would benefit from experiences across areas such as improving access to antiretroviral treatment, retaining health workers, eliminating user fees, establishing financing strategies for universal coverage, enhancing food sovereignty, social empowerment and other key elements of equitable health systems. This would be important in building policy on an affirmative platform of regional knowledge and experience of what works.

Key areas for future equity oriented research in health?

- National level assessment of inequalities in health and access to health care along differentials in gender, wealth, access to assets and returns to employment.

- Analysis of national data sets and national surveys on the barriers and facilitators that communities face in accessing and using health care, and how they are being affected by policy interventions.

- Routine monitoring and specific surveys of the relative in and out flow of natural and financial resources and human resources for health to and from east and southern African countries.

- Improved assessment of the policy and system implications of the informal sector in health, for example, how to organise insurance and risk pools where there is high informal employment, how to recognise and reward informal health sector work in communities and households or how to manage a growing informal private sector market in health services.

- Documenting the many positive experiences in east and southern Africa, including their context, design and impact, specifically in implementing primary health care, improving access to antiretroviral treatment, retaining health workers, eliminating user fees, establishing financing strategies for universal coverage, enhancing food sovereignty, social empowerment and other key elements of equitable health systems.

Our own commitment to action ...

While this analysis organises knowledge and perspective, it also draws from, and aims to contribute to the use of this knowledge for practice. EQUINET was born out of the 1997 Kasane meeting and the SADC health sector commitment to equity in health. Institutions from within east and southern Africa, from government, civil society, research, parliament and other spheres have carried out, supported, mentored and disseminated research and policy analysis, held forums for skills development, analysis, dialogue, learning and engagement, and strengthened networks and alliances towards achieving health equity. These activities jointly have contributed to the affirmative vision of the health systems that we would want to build to deliver on the equity goals reported in this analysis. The bibliography to the analysis is testimony to an extensive network of actors working on equity in health that we have collectively interacted with, engaged, involved, shared with and learned from within the region.

The conclusions we draw are as much a challenge and an opportunity for us in EQUINET, as for any institutional network in the region. As a network of institutions, we will continue to support dialogue, analysis and debate to strengthen the exchange of knowledge and learning within the region.

Through this work we have identified a shared commitment to addressing differences in health status that are unnecessary, avoidable and unfair, and to promoting interventions that seek to allocate resources preferentially to those with the worst health status. From different disciplines and areas of work we seek to understand and motivate the redistribution of social and economic resources for equity oriented interventions, and to understand and inform the power and ability people (and social groups) have to make choices over health inputs and their capacity to use these choices towards health.

We will continue to contribute as organisations within the region towards this goal. The conclusions we draw are as much a challenge and an opportunity for us in EQUINET, as for any institutional network in the region. As a network of institutions, we will continue to support dialogue, analysis and debate to strengthen the exchange of knowledge and learning within the region. This analysis is disseminated to elicit feedback and we will listen to and share that feedback. There are important sites of learning within the region, and gains to be made in widening the communication on these. We will continue, with others, to carry out and support research and gather evidence to close knowledge gaps, including the knowledge that comes from the experience of disadvantaged communities, and from programmes that strengthen equity. We will share and communicate evidence, learning and knowledge, as one of the key resources for health. We will network and interact to support the transfer of skills, experience, knowledge and capacities to strengthen institutional practice to deliver on equity goals. As a network of institutions, we will engage to move knowledge into practice and into policy. We will monitor and review progress towards shared goals.

Will we have any impact on Mr Banda's life? In practice, this narrated experience draws from a report by one of the institutions in the network working to overcome barriers in access to health care in communities. The struggle continues. The experience presented in this analysis of gains and reversals in addressing equity in health suggest that struggles for equity and social justice demand robust engagement with powerful global forces, effective implementation of affirmative national policies and systems, and, perhaps most importantly, the strengthened capabilities and power of people like Mr Banda and his community to collectively claim and use the resources for health.

REFERENCES

African Union (2007) *Third Session of the African Union Conference of Ministers of Health, Johannesburg, South Africa, 9-13 April 2007*, CAMH/MIN/5(III), accessed 2 June 2007 at http://www.doh.gov.za/camh3/

Industrial Health Research Group (IHRG) (2006) 'Raising our voice, breaking our silence: Health workers' experiences and needs around occupational health services in Cape Town, South Africa', *EQUINET PRA project report*, EQUINET, Harare.

WHO Afro (2006) *The African regional health report 2006*, WHO-Afro Region, Brazzaville, accessed 2 June 2007 at http://www.afro.who.int/regionaldirector/african_regional_health_report2006.pdf

ABOUT EQUINET

The Regional Network on Equity in Health in east and southern Africa (EQUINET) (www.equinetafrica.org) is a network of professionals, civil society members, policy makers, state officials and others within the region who have come together as an equity catalyst, to promote and realise shared values of equity and social justice in health.

EQUINET networks people to overcome isolation, give voice and promote exchange and co-operation using bottom-up approaches built on shared values. We have come together in a spirit of self determination and collective self reliance working through existing government, civil society, research and other mechanisms and institutions in Southern and East Africa. Several thousand people have been involved in EQUINET training, research, policy dialogue and information activities over the past seven years. The network fosters forums for dialogue, learning, sharing of information and experience and critical analysis. We do this to build knowledge and perspectives, shape effective strategies, strengthen our voice nationally, regionally and globally and our strategic alliances to influence policy, politics and practice towards health equity and social justice. The network website provides information on the activities. EQUINET produces, with technical support from its secretariat, a monthly newsletter and a searchable web database with information and publications on equity in health in east and southern Africa.

EQUINET is governed by a steering committee involving institutions co-ordinating the network's work. Over the period of production of the analysis the steering committee has included:

Policy analysis:	Centre for Health Policy, South Africa;
Trade and Health:	Southern and Eastern African Trade Information and Negotiations Institute (SEATINI), Zimbabwe and Uganda;
Economic policy and Health:	Centre for Economic Justice, Municipal Services Project, South Africa;
Nutrition and food sovereignty:	Medical Research Council, South Africa;
Equity in responses to AIDS:	REACH Trust, Malawi;
District health systems:	Ifakara Health Research Development Centre, Tanzania;
Fair financing:	Health Economics Unit, University of Cape Town, South Africa;
Health workers:	Health Systems Trust, South Africa; University of Namibia, Namibia (in co-operation with the East, Central and Southern African Health Community);
Participation in health:	Training and Research Support Centre, Zimbabwe; CHESSORE, Zambia; Ifakara Health Research Development Centre, Tanzania;
Health rights:	University of Cape Town, University of Western Cape, South Africa;
Civil society alliances:	Community Working Group on Health, Zimbabwe; Southern African Trade Union Co-ordinating Council, Botswana; People's Health Movement, Tanzania;
Monitoring health equity:	University of Zimbabwe Medical School, Zimbabwe;
Parliamentary Alliances:	Association of Parliamentary Committees in east and southern Africa (SEAPACOH);
Country networking:	TANESA, Tanzania; Malawi Health Equity Network, Malawi.

EQUINET has also received significant support since 1998 in its information and website work from Fahamu, UK and South Africa.

The secretariat for the network is at Training and Research Support Centre (TARSC) (www.tarsc.org) . For further information on EQUINET please contact the secretariat:
TARSC, Box CY2720, Causeway, Harare, Zimbabwe Tel + 263 4 705108/708835 Fax + 263-4- 737220
Email: admin@equinetafrica.org Website: www.equinetafrica.org